# Labour economics

SURVEYS IN ECONOMICS
Series Editors: Robert Millward, Michael T. Sumner and George Zis

**Public Sector Economics**
**Macroeconomics**
**Labour economics**

*Forthcoming:*
**Economics of Empire**
**Industrial Economics**
**International Economics**
**Microeconomics**
**Monetary Economics**

DEREK CARLINE
CHRISTOPHER A. PISSARIDES
W. STANLEY SIEBERT
PETER J. SLOANE

# Labour economics

LONGMAN
London and New York

LONGMAN GROUP LIMITED
Longman House, Burnt Mill, Harlow
Essex CM20 2JE, England
*Associated companies throughout the world*

*Published in the United States of America
by Longman Inc., New York*

*First published 1985*

BRITISH LIBRARY CATALOGUING IN PUBLICATION DATA
Labour economics.—(Surveys in economics)
  1. Industrial relations—Great Britain
  I. Carline, Derek      II. Series
  331'.0941      HD8391
  ISBN 0-582-29564-5

LIBRARY OF CONGRESS CATALOGING IN PUBLICATION DATA
Main entry under title:
Labour economics.
  (Surveys in economics)
  Bibliography: p.
  Includes index.
  1. Labor economics—Addresses, essays, lectures.
  I. Carline, Derek, 1935-    . II. Series.
  HD4901.L14 1984      331      83-26837
  ISBN 0-582-29564-5

Printed in Singapore by
The Print House (Pte) Ltd

# Contents

# Editors' preface

The aim of this series is to survey the primary literature on selected economic topics at a level designed for intermediate and advanced undergraduate students. Few textbooks contain an adequate perspective on the development of their subject, and still fewer portray the focus of current research; but it has become progressively more difficult to supplement textbooks by selecting journal articles which provide a satisfactory comprehensive, coherent and self-contained treatment of a topic, at a length and level of technique within the capacity of a student. The widening gap between the pedagogic and the professional literature stems partly from the increasing volume of the latter, the consequent pressure to abbreviate manuscripts, and the dissemination of research in a growing number of more specialised journals. It also reflects the increasing technical sophistication of the subject in all spheres of application, and particularly the integration of theoretical and empirical analysis which characterises much recent research, in marked contrast to the teaching of economics and econometrics in separate compartments of most undergraduate courses.

The surveys have been written for those who are studying or have completed intermediate courses in economic theory and quantitative methods. They aim to guide the reader through the professional literature, paying particular attention to the introduction of empirical work and to synthesising relevant contributions from different areas of specialisation. The major issues are explained and attention is directed towards the most useful sources for further study. By providing a comprehensive overview of its subject, each survey enables users to pursue particular aspects of the topic in greater depth through the medium of primary sources, within a frame of reference which enables the significance of those individual contributions to be assessed in their broader context.

The subjects of the surveys have been selected for their economic importance and for the extent and inaccessibility of the literature in journals and monographs devoted to them. Each is complete and self-contained, and can be read without reference to the surveys of related topics which appear in the same volume. The volumes themselves are not intended to replace textbooks by providing comprehensive coverage of their area, but to supplement textbooks by conveying the current flavour of the state of the art.

The series as a whole has been designed for second- and third-year undergraduate students at universities and polytechnics, but individual surveys will also appeal to postgraduate students and to practising economists in government, nationalised industries and the private sector who wish to update their knowledge of the subject. Economics has developed rapidly in the last two decades, and even active members of the profession have experienced difficulty in keeping pace with progress outside their own field of specialisation. It is hoped that the series will prove useful to this wider readership of continuing students as well as those beginning their education in economics.

Robert Millward
Michael T. Sumner
George Zis

# CHAPTER ONE

# Introduction

Michael T. Sumner and George Zis

> The theory of the determination of wages in a free market is simply a special case of the general theory of value. Wages are the price of labour; and thus, in the absence of control, they are determined, like all prices, by supply and demand. The need for a special theory of wages only arises because both the supply of labour, and the demand for it, and the way in which demand and supply interact on the labour market, have certain peculiar properties, which make it impossible to apply to labour the ordinary theory of commodity value without some further consideration (Hicks 1932:1)

It is these peculiarities which justify the status of labour economics as a distinct specialism; but in the period since the publication of Hicks's book signalled its emergence, economists' perceptions of labour's characteristics have changed fundamentally.

The major development has diminished a former emphasis on the uniqueness of labour and has established common ground with other areas of specialisation. With the benefit of hindsight this process of integration appears to have been retarded by the most traditional form of generalisation. As Hicks (1932:4) noted, 'it has been the usual practice of economists to concentrate their attention on those features of exchange which are common to all markets'; but in a society which prohibits slavery the exchange of labour in a market is confined to transactions in the flow dimension of labour services. Hicks acknowledged that many of these transactions would be repeated in successive periods if there are economies of 'regularity'; but despite this early recognition of learning by doing, the pervasive influence of intertemporal choices on the labour market was obscured by the restricted scope of its operations. Yet the representative worker supplies labour services over a period which exceeds the average life of machinery, and the quality of those services depends not only on learning by doing and on-the-job training, but also on formal education and training before and after entry into the labour force. The length of the period itself will depend on decisions relating to further or higher education, but it will also be influenced by the less obvious factor of health care. The location in which labour services are offered involves a further dimension of choice. The unifying characteristic of these decisions is that they all entail a comparison between current costs, in the form of direct expenditures or forgone earnings, and future benefits, in the form of a higher, more consistent or less uncertain income stream. They are, in other words, all aspects of human capital theory which relate directly to the supply of labour. Other applications, to marriage, family planning, divorce and, in an amusing caricature (Blinder 1974) to dental hygiene, are of less immediate concern to labour economists, but they do illustrate the breadth of the theory and the diversity of the specialisms with which labour economics shares important analytical features.

The development of human capital theory prompted Johnson (1960: 562) to suggest 'that the time has now come to sever the link with the classical attempt to identify categories of income with distinctly different kinds of productive factors; and that a more useful approach would be to lump all factors together as items of capital equipment, created by past investment and rendering current services to production'. The functional distribution of income has not vanished from the realm of economists' discourse, but it has certainly featured less prominently in recent years as attention has shifted to the personal income distribution. The explanation of earnings differentials has centred on the contribution of investments in education and training; the emphasis on this branch of human capital theory is fully reflected in Siebert's survey.

The rich analogy between human beings and physical capital has destroyed 'the classical notion of labour as a unique original factor of production', but Johnson's disparaging reference to 'the liberal anthropocentricity of social science' (p. 561) is a considerable overreaction. An individual's personal characteristics, as well as educational attainments and work experience, are a legitimate concern of potential employers, even if their sole objective is the maximisation of profit; and the former qualities are of much more concern than the latter to potential colleagues. The intricate web of social relationships which centres on the work-place becomes a matter of economic interest when it exerts a discernible influence on employment or wages through discrimination on the basis of such economically irrelevant characteristics as race, sex, marital status or colour.

Sloane's working definition of discrimination as 'unequal treatment in terms and conditions of employment for groups of equally productive workers' makes its residual character immediately apparent. The scope for discrimination then depends on the basis adopted for comparing productivity levels. Differences in human capital may stem from 'pre-entry' discrimination which limits the access to educational opportunities of particular groups. The human capital view of education as a direct means of enhancing productivity leaves considerably smaller scope for post-entry discrimination than the screening hypothesis, that employers use paper qualifications as an imperfect sorting mechanism to select workers who are innately more able, better motivated or more receptive to on-the-job training than their fellows; in the 'credentialist' limiting case of screening, the qualifications indicate nothing about actual or potential productivity. Screening is itself a form of statistical or erroneous discrimination, on which other more familiar types may be superimposed. These examples illustrate the 'different perceptions' of discrimination which Sloane identifies in the existing literature, and also suggest that further progress in this area awaits the resolution of differences elsewhere.

Unfortunately, while their policy implications are radically different, to distinguish between the screening and human capital views of education on the basis of the available evidence is far from straightforward. Siebert's description of this issue as one of the most contentious in the field is wholly appropriate.

The literature on job search is less extensive than on the other topics covered in this volume, but its complexity amply justifies survey treatment. Pissarides traces its origins back to the 1930s, but these early analyses were largely forgotten until human capital theory established a new frame of reference. Job search, like education, is viewed as an investment activity motivated by the prospect of higher future wages. Unlike most other branches of human capital theory, however, the literature on job search has been concerned primarily with theoretical questions, initially suggested by macroeconomics. The focus shifted towards the labour market *per se* and to empirical issues only when the early hopes that search theory would resolve some long-standing macroeconomic puzzles were frustrated.

Whatever other charges may be levelled against them, few students of trade unions can be accused of excessive concern with the theoretical foundations of their subject. The attempts made to model union behaviour as an exercise in constrained optimisation have typically drawn an analogy between the union and a monopolistic firm, but they have enjoyed very limited success in identifying either the union's maximand or the constraints on its pursuit of the postulated goal. Even if this framework had proved more generally acceptable as a representation of union behaviour, it is far from clear that it could have served the generally avowed purpose of explaining wage inflation. Monopoly power, whether formally modelled or merely invoked in a more casual fashion, would influence the level of wages, implying a union effect on relative wages and possibly other dimensions of the income distribution, but not their rate of change.

Trade unions remain one of the most conspicuous 'peculiar properties' of the supply side of the labour market, and continued dissatisfaction with theoretical analyses of their role has not inhibited attempts to determine their contribution to wages empirically. The voluminous literature surveyed by Carline yields few clear conclusions, however. He documents the qualitative consensus that unions change the structure of relative wages, but finds less uniformity in the estimated magnitude of the union differential. There is not even qualitative consensus regarding the impact of trade unions on wage inflation.

Labour economics has changed in both scope and content since the publication of Hicks's book, but some of its earliest features still remain prominent. The reader who is duly impressed by the extensive ramifications of human capital theory or the rigour of search models will also find, in the survey of trade unions and wages, echoes of Shove's complaint (1933:469) that 'the employers' power of resistance and the unions' belief about it are somehow left out of the picture' painted by Hicks, and of his insistence that 'it is not possible to separate *the real process* from *its monetary reactions* when we are dealing with all-round changes in wage-rates' (p. 472). The persistence of these classic problems affords as much opportunity for further development as the opening of new areas of enquiry.

# References

**Blinder, A. S.** (1974) The economics of brushing teeth, *Journal of Political Economy*, **82**, 887–91.

**Hicks, J. R.** (1932) *The Theory of Wages,* Macmillan: London.

**Johnson, H. G.** (1960) The political economy of opulence, *Canadian Journal of Economics and Political Science*, **26**, 552–64.

**Shove, G. F.** (1933) Review of the Theory of Wages, *Economic Journal*, **43**, 460–72.

# CHAPTER TWO

# Developments in the economics of human capital

W. Stanley Siebert

## 1. Introduction

The aim of this survey is to give an exposition of the modern theory of human capital, and to survey the relevant empirical results. In this way it is hoped to convey an appreciation of the importance of this theory of earnings, and of its limitations.

The idea of education and training as determinants of earnings goes back to Adam Smith (1776: Ch. 10), but it is only in the last 20 years that this idea has been systematically developed and tested. During these years it has become apparent that a fundamental theory of earnings differences based on returns to different levels of skills (human capital) can be built up. This theory contributes to a better understanding of the earnings distribution. It also enables a clearer analysis of the effects of family background — including 'class' effects — and ability on earnings. This is mainly because the approach naturally segments earnings determination into the process of acquisition of skills, and the returns to skills once acquired. Individuals from low-income families seem to be disadvantaged mainly in the skills they acquire rather than in the returns to those skills. The same might be true of minority groups such as coloured workers — see Chapter 3 of this book. This direct modelling of the process of skill acquisition gives more precision to the theory of 'intergenerational transfer of inequality'.

Human capital theory also extends naturally to analysis of the issues raised by government subsidisation of education. There has been a large increase in education during this century. In the USA, for example, according to Denison (1962:73), the average labour-force member in 1960 received 2.5 times as many schooldays as in 1910. Part of this increase will have been due to direct government subsidisation of education. This in turn raises questions as to the correct amount of subsidy, which involves computing a 'social rate of return to education', the composition of the subsidy (has higher education received too much emphasis?) and its distributional implications (subsidising education mainly helps children of the better off).

The plan is as follows. The first sections are concerned with the theory of human capital. First the basic Mincer/Becker model is outlined together with its main practical implications for the earnings distribution (Mincer 1958, 1962, 1974;

Becker 1962, 1964). Then some problems concerned with ability and family background factors, and the difficulty of specifying a human capital 'unit' are raised. The theoretical discussion then proceeds to consider on-the-job training in detail using as its basis the Ben-Porath (1967) model of optimal human capital accumulation. This is the simplest possible model of the life cycle of earnings and investment, and is the basis for modern theoretical developments (Haley 1973; Polachek 1975; Wallace and Ihnen 1975; Blinder and Weiss 1976; Heckman 1976).

The second part of the survey considers empirical results. Particular attention is paid to the problem of estimating the effect of ability on measurements of rates of return to education. There is also a section on the importance of family background as a determinant of schooling investments. The paper concludes with a review of policy issues and a discussion of the 'screening' and credentialism arguments.

## 2.   Theory of human capital
### THE BASIC HUMAN CAPITAL MODEL

The basic human capital idea is that those who have been trained more, either at school or on the job, have incurred a forgone earnings cost. Their productivity will also have increased which enables them to be paid more, assuming that earnings equal marginal product.[1] The amount that productivity and earnings must increase will be determined by the forgone earnings costs of training. Since this cost is regarded as an investment, the extra payment should be just enough to secure the same return on the investment as on a comparably risky physical capital investment. This same idea is extended to other uses of work time which lower current earnings, such as migration or job search, but most research has been done on the training aspect. The theory is therefore one of individual earnings differences in a competitive labour market.

There are many factors other than training which determine an individual's pay, so the emphasis on training has to be justified. Smith in his famous discussion mentions the non-pecuniary aspect of an individual's occupation, such as whether it is intrinsically agreeable, or risky, as a determinant of long-run equilibrium pay, in addition to costs of training. He also stresses the fact that competition can be prevented as when entry to an occupation is restricted, or regional mobility is restricted. Two further major determinants can also be brought forward: ability differences among individuals, and differences in their home environment including the family funds available for their schooling. All these factors are important and will be discussed below.

Nevertheless the human capital element will receive most stress, and this can be justified in various ways. At the least, human capital theory can be seen to be a powerful organising tool when describing real world earnings differences – a baseline, as it were, from which to judge distortions of the earnings structure. The analogy here is with the theory of perfect competition which is an indispensable abstraction in the field of industrial economics. Even sceptics such as

Thurow (1970), Phelps Brown (1975, 1977: Ch. 7) and Blaug (1976, 1980) would probably admit this much. Human capital theory has also been fruitful in generating testable hypotheses. For example, it has the implication that rates of return on human and physical capital will be broadly comparable. The theory also bears on a major government activity, the funding of education and training. Thus even if human capital differences were not a primary determinant of earnings differences in capitalist economies (though in fact it seems they are), here is an area in which policy can have an impact. The model is therefore useful even though, as will become apparent, it requires some strong assumptions.

Let us begin by modelling the factors which a wealth-maximising individual would take into account when deciding on an extra year at school or university. This is 'general' training in that schooling raises productivity in all jobs so the student pays the cost of the training; problems raised by 'specific' training are considered later. The main cost, $C$, of the extra year is earnings forgone. Other costs such as books and fees are usually assumed to be covered by vacation earnings. The present value of the return, $R$, from the extra year is

$$R = \sum_{t=1}^{N} k_t (1 + i)^{-t} \qquad [1]$$

where    $k_t$ = expected earnings increment in the $t^{th}$ working year resulting from the extra schooling;

$i$ = rate of discount;

$N$ = length of working life after leaving school.

If $i$ is taken as the 'market' rate of interest then the individual should invest if $R > C$. We defer discussion of the appropriate 'market' rate of interest for the individual in question. Alternatively an internal rate of return, $r$, can be computed where $r$ is that rate of discount which equates $R$ with $C$, that is

$$C = \sum_t k_t (1 + r)^{-t} \qquad [2]$$

The individual should then invest if $r > i$. Assuming diminishing returns to educational investment, the individual will end up with the marginal investment earning $r \simeq i$.

If the earnings increment is assumed to be a constant, $k$, for each time period, then [2] simplifies and the main determinants of the schooling decision are more easily shown. We then have[2]

$$C = \frac{k}{r} (1 - (1 + r)^{-N}) \qquad [3]$$

For large $N$ [3] becomes even simpler, $C \simeq k/r$. It can be seen that a larger investment, $C$, is called for the larger is $k$ (the annual increment in earnings), and the smaller is the required rate of return $i$ (remember $r \simeq i$). Moreover, $C$ will be larger the larger is $N$. This demonstrates quite simply a fundamental proposition of the human capital model, that investment in human capital becomes less worth while as one ages. Equation [3] shows that if $N = 0$ then a human investment would only be contemplated if it were free. This means that working time devoted to education towards the end of life cannot be viewed as an investment, but is rather the result of enjoying studying.

The relevance of human capital theory to the earnings structure can now be shown in a simplified way. Let us take two grades of labour only: unskilled labour entering the labour force at age 16, and skilled labour entering with a degree at age 22. Assume that unskilled labour earns for example £5,000 p.a. on average over the life span, and ignore variations in earnings with age. This £5,000 can be thought of as a 'subsistence' wage given exogenously, perhaps by minimum wage legislation. It does not have a particular human capital rationale, though no doubt a society with more capital embodied in the workforce and thus higher labour productivity will have a higher subsistence wage, *cet. par.* But given the unskilled worker's wage, it is possible to determine how much college labour must earn.

Using the approximation of equation [3] and assuming $N$ is large, the internal rate of return to a degree can be written $r = k/C$. We also have the equilibrium condition that $r \simeq i$ where $i$ is the 'market' rate of interest. Suppose that $i = 10$ per cent. Then

$$r = 0.1 = k/(6 \times 5,000)$$

so that

$$k = £3,000 \text{ p.a.}$$

Therefore, given that the unskilled man earns £5,000, the college-trained worker must earn £8,000 on average over his life if he is to come forward to be trained, assuming no consumption benefits of education. It can be seen that, in order for both grades of labour to be equally well off with an interest rate of 10 per cent, the unskilled man's wage must be only 60 per cent of the skilled wage. The model therefore justifies quite large earnings differentials and this might be why it has provoked so much criticism from well-intentioned egalitarians (see for example Bowles and Gintis 1975). We are working with the simplest model here, but even with more realistic models this basic implication of wide competitive earnings differentials remains.

The consequences for the earnings distribution of changes in the demand for skilled relative to unskilled labour, and of education subsidies can also be simply demonstrated. The relevant supply and demand diagrams are given in Fig. 2.1, with the market for skilled labour shown in panel (a), unskilled in panel (b). Looking first at the question of an increase in the demand for skilled relative to unskilled labour, this is represented by shifts in the demand curves. In the case of skilled workers there will probably be a short-run increase in their pay, but in the long run according to simplified human capital reasoning their pay will be unaffected. The reasoning here is that in the short run it is difficult to increase the supply of skilled men — hence the upward slope of the short-run supply curve *SRS* in panel 1. For a while therefore, skilled men will be paid more than £8,000, so earning an above-equilibrium return on their human capital. This is supposed to induce more people to attend university, so eventually increasing the supply of

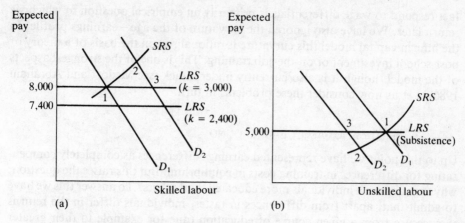

FIG. 2.1    Determinants of the earnings structure

skilled labour. (The simplifying assumption is that there are no ability or rationing constraints on university entrance.) In the long run we can take it as a first approximation that the equilibrium condition holds at its original level $r = 0.1$, so that the original differential is restored and the long-run supply curve is horizontal.

A similar analysis applies to the unskilled labour market in panel (b). Here there is a leftward shift in the demand curve and a transitory fall in predicted pay occurs (point 2). A complication arises if unskilled men are not permitted to earn less than £5,000, for then the *SRS* curve below point 1 becomes irrelevant. Unskilled unemployment will then occur. However, this increased probability of unemployment will reduce unskilled *expected* pay. The consequence will therefore be the same as if nominal wages were unconstrained, that is there will be a tendency for unskilled labour to move into the skilled labour market.

The impact of government subsidies for education on the earnings structure should be a compression of earnings differentials. Suppose, for example, that the government maintains non-fee-paying state colleges. In this case the forgone earnings cost of attending college would be lower by the amount of vacation earnings which up to now we have assumed to offset fees. Let the value of the subsidy be £1,000 so that the cost of college attendance is reduced to £4,000 a year. To obtain a 10 per cent rate of return the earnings differential $k$ would have to fall to $k = 0.1 \times 24,000 = £2,400$ a year. This is shown in Fig. 2.1 by a new long-run supply curve $LRS(k = 2,400)$, indicating a reduced skilled pay differential. It can be seen from this analysis that the human capital model relates differences in earnings by skill basically to the costs of producing that skill, ignoring for the moment the non-pecuniary aspects of the jobs. It is at bottom a supply-side theory with the demand side influencing earnings differentials only in the short run as shown in Fig. 2.1.

In this basic model we have not yet incorporated ability or family background factors. These certainly muddy the waters. There is also the objection that making training decisions according to the present value of expected returns requires too much information on the part of students. Whether students do in fact respond to wage differentials is primarily an empirical question to which we return later. We have also ignored the curvature of the age – earnings profile. In the human capital model this curvature is rationalised on the basis of a theory of post-school investment or on-the-job training. This is one of the strongest aspects of the model though it is also currently under attack (see Medoff and Abraham 1980). Let us now consider these problems in turn.

## ABILITY AND FAMILY BACKGROUND

Up to this point we have represented earnings differences as completely compensating for differences in training costs in equilibrium. But this raises the question: why then are some individuals more educated than others? To answer this we have to admit that, apart from differences in tastes, individuals differ in the returns they secure from a given course of education (due for example to their greater ability), and in the funds available to finance the courses. Those with greater ability or cheaper funds will accumulate more education. Each individual will behave as if he were performing a calculation such as that shown in equation [2], but the result for each individual will be different. In particular the more able could receive rents to ability.[3] Also those born poor, because they cannot borrow due to the imperfections of the human capital market discussed later, will receive less education and have lower incomes than those born rich. Both these factors mean that, in terms of Fig. 2.1, the long-run supply curve for skilled labour slopes upwards. To the extent that these factors are important, particularly the background factor, we move away from the competitive model towards the dualist model described by J.S. Mill (1878).[4]

To anticipate our later empirical discussion, allowing for ability serves to reduce the rate of return to schooling by at most 50 per cent (Taubman 1975, 1977). Background, while apparently important in determining access to schooling, does not have a major effect on earnings after school (see Table 2.8). Moreover, simple human capital models allowing only for school and post-school investments are informative in explaining earnings variation. Also rates of return to education adjusted for ability (Griliches 1977; Hausman and Taylor 1981) are estimated to be in the range 5–10 per cent, which implies that earnings differentials do indeed compensate for education costs at this rate of interest. Thus ability and family background can be fairly well incorporated in the model.

Analysis of the individual can best be pursued by applying a supply and demand framework to the market for education as in Becker (1975: 94ff.). On the demand for education side we can draw up a schedule of internal rates of return associated with different amounts of schooling. This schedule can be thought of as varying among individuals. In particular more 'able' individuals should have a demand curve displaced to the right of that for less able. For a given supply of funds schedule they will invest more in education and receive higher earnings. In a sense, however, these higher earnings will not be due to education, but to ability. If ability is not allowed for, the return to education will be overestimated. In a more general analysis, however, we might conceive of some individuals as possessing 'mechanical ability' which individuals with 'academic ability' do not possess

(Rosen and Willis 1978). Those who finish formal education early do so in part because of this mechanical ability, so their earnings overstate the income forgone by those who remain in college. Neglect of this consideration would therefore tend to bias the estimated return to education downwards, and tend to counteract the above-mentioned upward bias, but this is probably rather a minor point.

Consideration of the ability question takes us to one of the fundamental problems of human capital analysis. *There is no precise way of measuring units of human capital.* All we can say for sure is that every type of human capital takes time to acquire (thereby requiring income and leisure sacrifices), and must therefore increase pay and so bring a return. But neither the forgone earnings nor the returns provide an independent measure of the amount of human capital accumulated, that is, of the increase in the individual's potential worth on the market. This is because of the ability problem. Individuals will experience different productivity increases from the same course. This is why we are always faced with the question: what does education 'do'?

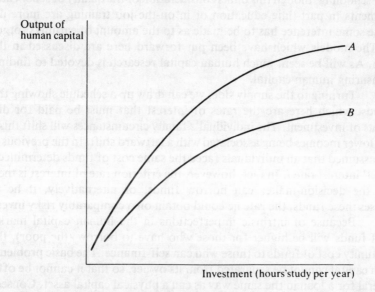

FIG. 2.2   The human capital production function

This problem is shown best if we consider a human capital 'production function'. This is shown in Fig. 2.2 and will be used extensively in the next section. On the horizontal axis there is a measure of investment per unit time, and on the vertical there is a notional measure of capital 'output'. For any individual we assume diminishing returns to investment. This is the reason why the individual's human investment demand curve, derived from the slope of the production function, is assumed to have a negative slope. Diminishing returns can be justified by an appeal to the fixed capacity of the human brain. Ability can be thought of as controlling the height of the function, for example, curve A relates to an individual who is able to benefit more from the course than individual B. A given size of investment will bring a greater return to $A$ than $B$, that is, $A$ will have accumulated more 'units' of capital than $B$. But it can be seen that we should not use investment costs (by definition the same) to measure these units. Ideally the returns would be an appropriate measure, but returns can differ for reasons other than differing amounts of human capital. Also we often wish to use the returns to work out the rate of return to a given amount of human capital, not as a measure of the amount of human capital itself.[5] In practice, however, human capital has to be measured in terms of estimates of average earnings forgone in making the investment. Individual differences in ability to benefit from particular investments are then allowed for in part by holding a measure of ability such as IQ constant, or by comparing twins (see below), or by using panel data.

Additional difficulties arise in measuring human capital. There are many types of capital — schooling of different qualities, training courses formal and informal, knowledge about health and job alternatives. Full-time schooling investments are the easiest to measure in terms of average earnings forgone per year of schooling, though this omits consideration of the quality of school attended. Investments in part-time education or in on-the-job training are more difficult because some inference has to be made as to the amount of earnings forgone per year. The models which have been put forward here are discussed in the next section. As will be seen, much human capital research is devoted to finding ways of measuring human capital.

Turning to the supply side, we can draw up a schedule showing the costs of funds, which here are the rates of interest that must be paid for differing amounts of investment. The individual's family circumstances will shift this supply curve, lower incomes being associated with a leftward shift. In the previous section it was assumed that all individuals faced the same cost of funds determined by the 'market' interest rate $i$. In fact, however, the criterion rate of interest is the rate at which the decision-maker can borrow funds, or alternatively, if he already possesses these funds, the rate he could obtain on a comparably risky investment.

Because of intrinsic imperfections in the human capital market, the cost of funds will be higher for those who have to borrow (the poor), than the opportunity cost of funds to those who can self-finance. The basic problem is that human capital cannot be separated from its owner, so that it cannot be offered as collateral for a loan in the same way as can a physical capital asset. Consequently lending for human capital purposes is riskier for banks than is the case with physical capital. Compounding the problem for lending institutions is the fact that much human investment has to be made at a young age, just when the individual's prospects are most difficult to assess. Therefore there is the strong possibility that the poor will have little opportunity to invest in human capital on the same terms as the rich.

There are several other reasons why funds for education are likely to be more expensive for children from poor families. Poor families might demand lower child 'quality', assuming child quality is a normal good, implying fewer funds for the child's education. Poorer families might also be less efficient in the production of child quality, perhaps due to ignorance, again with the corollary that education funds are not forthcoming (Edwards 1975). There is also the point that educational investments are indivisible – one cannot purchase half a degree. To a poor family, making such an investment is akin to putting all their eggs in one basket. A given education investment is more risky for a poor than a rich family therefore, and the equilibrium rate of return should be higher.[6]

Putting the supply and demand schedules together, there will be a distribution of equilibrium rates of return to education, and a distribution of education investments. If ability and favourable family circumstances are positively correlated, as is likely, there will be a wide dispersion in amounts invested, but not such a large dispersion in rates of return.[7] Where there is widespread government subsidisation of education however, it might be more plausible to think of a reasonably elastic supply curve applicable to all. All individuals then have a similar rate of return to education, and differentials in education spring only from differences in the demand for education, due for example to differences in ability. This characterisation can be tested, for it implies that family circumstances should not have much impact on education decisions.

## ON-THE-JOB INVESTMENTS

The theory of human capital accumulation also offers a productivity-based explanation of why the old earn more, on the whole, than the young. The logic of this explanation makes it one of the most satisfying aspects of the model. Nevertheless this explanation has proved controversial among those who believe that wages increase with age mainly for institutional reasons such as incremental pay scales or seniority provisions (Medoff and Abraham 1980). Human capital theory gives these administrative arrangements a productivity rationale.

The typical male post-school age – annual-earnings profile is concave from below, with a maximum reached in the mid-forties. The age – hourly-earnings profile peak is reached later, however, at about age 60 (Ghez and Becker 1975: Ch. 3). The earlier peak in annual earnings is explained by the fact that annual hours worked by males fall off well before the peak in hourly earnings. This could be because 'capacity' wages peak before observed wages (see below). The basic problem is to explain this increase in earnings, and subsequent apparent decrease over the life cycle. The Ben-Porath (1967) model of optimal capital accumulation is the best way of analysing this, but first it is worth giving a heuristic explanation.

The model is really one of time allocation: the individual is pictured as allocating time between work and training so as to maximise the present value of his lifetime income. A more general model is where leisure is a third activity to which time can be allocated, and utility rather than income is maximised (Heckman 1976). However, this does not yield very different conclusions from the simpler model, so we will stick with that.[8] The earnings profile is then built up as follows. Early in life all potential earnings are forgone in favour of the production of human capital. This is the formal schooling period, when returns to accumulation of capital are so high due to the long horizon, that it pays all individuals to specialise completely in producing human capital. Call this 'phase I' (see Wallace and Ihnen 1975). Compulsory schooling laws might induce people to specialise for longer than they wish, however, and we will consider some evidence that this is in fact so.

After leaving school the individual is supposed to stop investing all his potential earnings, but will continue to invest a certain fraction thereby reducing current earnings. Call this 'phase II'. The way in which this investment is thought to occur is that the individual takes a lower-paying job in exchange for its learning opportunities and later 'career path'. Costless learning is ruled out. This current sacrifice is made because it raises earnings in later life. As retirement approaches, however, this type of activity becomes less worthwhile. A smaller and smaller fraction of earnings capacity is invested and the individual's stock of capital grows at a slower and slower rate. In turn this is reflected in a slower rate of growth of earnings capacity, and also in observed earnings which differ from capacity earnings by the ever-decreasing amount devoted to human capital accumulation. Eventually investment will no longer offset depreciation, and the stock of human capital – and with it earnings capacity – will begin to shrink. For a few years longer, observed earnings will continue to increase as the reduction in earnings forgone to accumulate human capital offsets the shrinkage of earnings capacity. But eventually observed pay too declines.

It is instructive to consider the theoretical basis of the above explanation of the age – earnings profile, though at a first reading the reader can skip over the next few paragraphs straight to equation [12] and the discussion of Fig. 2.4. First define 'capacity earnings' $Y_t$,

$$Y_t = R K_t$$

where    $K_t$ = individual's stock of human capital in year $t$;
         $R$ = market value of the services of a 'unit' of $K$, i.e. the imputed rental of capital services.[9]

Disposable earnings $E_t$ are defined as

$$E_t = Y_t - I_t \qquad [4]$$

where    $I_t$ = value of human capital investment.

For simplicity, $I_t$ is supposed to consist only of forgone earnings, i.e. it excludes purchased inputs such as books and fees, thus

$$I_t = R s_t K_t \qquad [5]$$

where    $s_t$ = fraction of the capital stock used to produce further capital, or the proportion of time the individual devotes to human capital production in the $t^{th}$ period. $s_t = 1$ in 'phase I', $0 < s_t < 1$ in 'phase II', $s_t = 0$ in retirement.

Therefore disposable earnings vary with $s$

$$E_t = R K_t (1 - s_t). \qquad [6]$$

$K_t$ also depends on $s$. This is because we posit a human capital production function, which relates human capital output $Q_t$ to $s_t$,

$$Q_t = \beta(s_t K_t)^b,$$

[7]

and the rate of increase of the capital stock $\dot{K}_t$ depends on $Q_t$,

$$\dot{K}_t = Q_t - \delta K_t$$

[8]

i.e. the increase in capital stock equals gross investment minus depreciation. The parameter $\beta$ in [7] governs the height of the function in Fig. 2.2, that is it measures 'ability', and $b$ governs the curvature of the function. In this model $s_t$ is the individual's choice variable or control variable because all the elements of disposable earnings in [6], apart from initial human capital $K_0$, depend on $s_t$. $K_0$ is given exogenously and can be assumed to be determined by genetic factors and mother's care (Leibowitz 1974, 1977).

The problem for the individual is to allocate his time between market work and training, that is choose a time path for $s_t$ so as to maximise the present value of his lifetime disposable earnings subject to his ability to produce human capital. The expression for discounted lifetime disposable earnings $W$ is

$$W = \int_0^T (RK_t(1 - s_t))e^{-rt}dt,$$

[9]

where    $T$ = end of working life.

$W$ is to be maximised subject to [8] and a 'transversality' condition which states that at the end of life the return from further capital accumulation is zero (see below). The solution can be approached intuitively by accepting that maximisation of [9] requires that, for every period, the marginal cost of producing capital equals the marginal return from capital.

The situation is shown in Fig. 2.3. Total costs of producing capital as a function of capital output are shown by the $I$ curve, derived from Fig. 2.2. For simplicity we assume that the $I$ curve is the same from year to year. The benefits from capital accumulation do change however: for a young man the benefits schedule is $PV$(young), a straight line from the origin with slope $\psi_y$. $\psi_y$ is the price per unit of capital a young man would be prepared to pay. As the individual ages the $PV$ line falls, for example to $PV$(old).[10] The individual chooses $s$ and therefore $Q$ so as to maximise the difference between costs, $I$, and benefits, $PV$. With $PV$(young) the individual is best off if he chooses $s = 1$ (the schooling period). But as the $PV$ curve declines he moves back towards the origin, passing the point at which capital accumulation just offsets depreciation and the capital stock is static, and eventually reaching the point at which $s = 0$ and the stock is declining at rate $\delta$.

More precisely, the investment costs schedule is, from [5] and [7]

$$I_t = R(Q_t/\beta)^{1/b}.$$

The $MC_t$ schedule, $\partial I_t/\partial Q_t$ is therefore

$$MC_t = \frac{R}{b\beta} \frac{(Q_t)}{\beta}^{(1-b)/b}.$$

[10]

On the benefits side we derive an expression for the marginal value of capital $\psi$, by

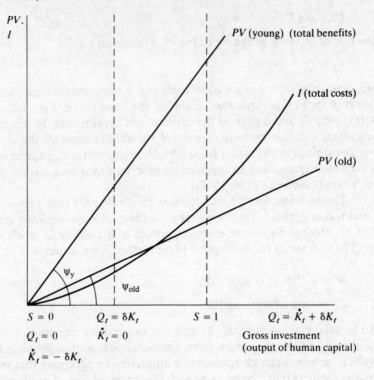

FIG. 2.3    Determination of optimum human capital production

applying Pontryagin's maximum principle explained in Appendix 1. It is shown in Appendix 1 that

$$\psi_t = \frac{R}{\delta + r} (1 - \exp(-(\delta + r)(T - t))).$$    [11]

For those who want to bypass Pontryagin, it can be seen that [11] is merely the continuous-time analogue (incorporating depreciation) of the expression in note 10. As $t$ approaches $T$, $\psi_t$ declines and eventually reaches zero as already shown in Fig. 2.3.

To derive the optimum path for human capital production, $Q_t$, in the post-school period ('phase II') we equate $\psi_t$ with $MC_t$. (During phase I, $\psi_t > MC_t$, as can be seen from Fig. 2.3.) Thus from [10] and [11],

$$\frac{R}{\delta + r} (1 - \exp(-(\delta + r)(T - t))) = \frac{R}{b\beta} \left(\frac{Q_t}{\beta}\right)^{1/(b-1)}.$$

Therefore the time path is

$$Q_t = \beta \frac{b\beta}{\delta + r} (1 - \exp(-(\delta + r)(T - t)))^{b/(1-b)}.$$    [12]

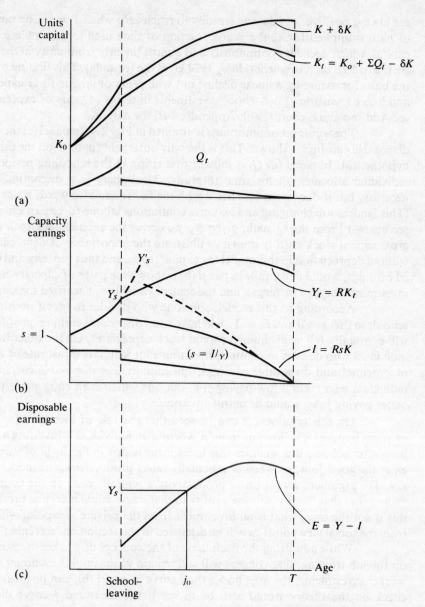

FIG. 2.4    Time paths of gross human capital investment, capital stock, and capacity and observed earnings

This equation is important because it gives us a hold on the post-school investment concept. It can be seen that $b < 1$ is a necessary assumption – if $b = 1$, $Q_t$ becomes indeterminate.[11] Equation [12] shows that $Q_t$ depends negatively on the interest rate, $r$, and the depreciation rate, $\delta$, and positively on ability, $\beta$, returns to scale, $b$, and the period to the end of life, $T - t$. Gross additions to human capital are always positive, but decline steadily to reach zero when $T = t$. The same type of path is implied for $s_t$, the yearly fraction of time used to accumulate human capital, which declines continuously and almost linearly from unity in the school period to zero on retirement (Haley 1973 gives the formula). This finding provides the basis for assuming a linear decline in $s$ with years of labour-force experience, and hence measuring post-school investments in terms of years of experience – see Addison and Siebert (1979: Appendix 4-B) for details.

The whole set of time paths is graphed in Fig. 2.4. In panel (c) the path of disposable earnings is shown. This is the only observable path – all the others are hypothetical. In panel (a) $Q_t$ is shown, first rising in the schooling period as the individual allocates all his time to study. Then there is a discontinuity, not necessary but it does seem consistent with the facts, and afterwards a steady fall. (This ignores job changing and assumes continuous labour-force participation – see below.) From the $Q_t$ path, given $K_0$, we derive the capital stock path $K_t$. The gross capital stock path is shown to illustrate the importance of depreciation – without depreciation in this model the capital stock, and thus capacity and observed earnings, would never fall. In panel (b) is shown the paths of capacity earnings, investment (forgone earnings), and the control variable $s_t$, linearised for simplicity.

According to this model, someone who decides to invest nothing after school, so that $s = 0$ and $E_t = Y_t$, will have a flat disposable earnings profile which will eventually fall as his human capital stock depreciates. On the other hand, an individual who decides to continue investing a lot will have a fast rate of increase of potential and disposable earnings, but initially low disposable earnings. An individual who takes a low-paying job, but one which is an entry point to later, better-paying jobs, would be in this situation.[12]

On this argument it can be seen that the rate of increase of observed earnings in panel (c) allows us to infer whether an individual is investing a lot or a little after school. But whether this investment is just in the form of queuing to enter the good jobs, or whether it actually raises productivity, the model cannot say. The argument that it raises productivity essentially rests on the competitive assumption that firms maximise profits so that wages equal marginal products. If this is not the case, what is an investment from the private viewpoint will not be from the social viewpoint, as will be discussed in the section on 'screening' below.

While admitting the usefulness of the concept of worker investments in on-the-job training, that concept will still remain vague until the amount of these worker investments, the area under the $I$ curve in panel (b), can be measured. A check on the theory would also be to see if the measured $I$ curve did trend downwards towards zero at retirement (in fact it seems to reach zero before that). A further check is provided by the model's implication that those who leave school later have higher capacity earnings on entry into the labour market, so their post-school investments will be higher, but decrease faster – see the dotted $I$ curve in panel (b). Mincer (1974) has provided the following method of measuring training investments. Capacity earnings are the return on net capital,

$$Y_t = r K_{t-1}. \qquad [13]$$

Capital is formed of original capital $\bar{K}$, and yearly investments $I_t$. These all have to be depreciated appropriately to derive net capital. In the entry year we have

$$Y_0 = r\bar{K}.$$

In year 1

$$Y_1 = rK_0 = r(\bar{K}(1-\delta) + I_0),$$

and year 2

$$Y_2 = rK_1 = r(\bar{K}(1-\delta)^2 + I_0(1-\delta) + I_1)$$

or

$$Y_2 = (1-\delta)Y_1 + rI_1.$$

In general

$$Y_t = (1-\delta)Y_{t-1} + rI_{t-1}$$

or

$$Y_t = r\bar{K}(1-\delta)^t + r\sum_{i=0}^{t-1} I_i(1-\delta)^{t-1-i}$$

$$= Y_0(1-\delta)^t + r\sum_{0}^{t-1} I_i(1-\delta)^{t-1-i}. \qquad [14]$$

Equation [14] gives capacity earnings in terms of original earnings capacity and the stream of depreciated investments. The equation can be rewritten in terms of post-school investments only,

$$Y_j = Y_s(1-\delta)^j + r\sum_{i=0}^{j-1} I_i(1-\delta)^{j-1-i}$$

where  $Y_s$ = earnings capacity after $s$ years of schooling;
       $Y_j$ = earnings capacity $j$ years after leaving school.

Disposable earnings from [4] are capacity earnings minus current investments

$$E_j = Y_s(1-\delta)^j + r\sum_{0}^{j-1} I_i(1-\delta)^{j-1-i} - I_j. \qquad [15]$$

It is possible to use [15] to measure $Y_s$, earnings capacity on leaving school, and then given $r$ and the path of actual earnings, the amount of post-school investments. As can be seen from Fig. 2.4, $E$ grows and eventually equals $Y_s(1-\delta)^j$ at time $j_0$. Mincer has called $j_0$ the 'overtaking year'. During the overtaking year, $j_0$, we have from [15],

$$E_{j_0} = Y_s(1-\delta)^{j_0} + r\sum_{i=0}^{j_0-1} I_i(1-\delta)^{j_0-1-i} - I_{j_0}.$$

It is simpler to ignore depreciation at this point, since $j_0$ will not be a large number, so there will not have been much depreciation. Then in year $j_0$, $E_{j_0} = Y_s$ so

$$r\sum_{0}^{j_0-1} I_i = I_{j_0}.$$

If $I_i \simeq I$ a constant during the years up to $j_0$ then $r\sum_{0}^{j_0-1} = rj_0I_i$ and $j_0 \simeq 1/r$.

TABLE 2.1   Earnings streams by schooling level and age, US white males, 1959

| | Annual earnings ($) | |
| --- | --- | --- |
| Age | 9−11 years' schooling (age of entry = 18) | 12 years' schooling (age of entry = 20) |
| 14 | 0 | 0 |
| 18 | 1,306 | 0 |
| 22 | 2,519 | 2,930 |
| 27 | 3,924 | 4,461 |
| 37 | 5,398 | 6,052 |
| 47 | 5,478 | 6,281 |
| 57 | 5,242 | 6,023 |
| 67 | 3,079 | 3,897 |

Source: Hanoch (1967).

Thus if $r = 0.1$, then the overtaking year is approximately the tenth year of work experience. It will be larger than 10 to the extent that $\delta > 0$, but the fact that the sequence $I_t$ is not constant but declines with time will pull it back towards 10. For example, from the data used by Hanoch (1967), presented in Table 2.1, the earnings capacity of a man with 12 years' schooling would be approximately $4,800 (earnings 10 years after entry). His earnings on leaving school would be about $2,200 (extrapolating back from age 22), implying his initial amount of post-school investment was $2,800, about 50 per cent of earnings capacity. Mincer (1974: 51ff.) also argues that in the overtaking year earnings should reflect the influence of schooling investments alone, without the 'noise' introduced by individuals' different post-school investment profiles. This has the implication that taking, say, the 10-year-experience group only and regressing earnings on schooling, schooling should account for a greater proportion of this group's earnings variance than for all experience groups combined.

Using these formulae, Mincer (1974: 73−4) has also proposed a simple method for estimating the amount of post-school investments for a given schooling group. Once earnings capacity is at its maximum, $Y_p$, investment equals depreciation, i.e. $I_{p-1} = \delta K_{p-1}$ so $Y_p = Y_{p-1}$. The sum of past positive net investments is derived from

$$Y_p = Y_s (1-\delta)^p + r \sum_{i=0}^{p-1} I_i (1-\delta)^{p-1-i}$$

so that

$$\frac{Y_p - Y_s (1-\delta)^p}{r} = \sum_{i=0}^{p-1} I_i (1-\delta)^{p-1-i}. \qquad [16]$$

Approximating $Y_p$ by peak actual earnings, $E_p$, formula [16] can be seen to give a reasonably simple method of estimating worker-financed net post-school investments. Mincer (1962) has also made some famous direct estimates of worker on-the-job training investments, using equation [14]. We will consider these estimates later. Note that all the above refers to worker financed investments – employer-financed investments in workers can also be reflected in earnings profiles. This matter is discussed in the next section on 'specific' training.

To end this section on on-the-job investments we raised the question of whether the return to these investments is the same as that to schooling. This has been a maintained hypothesis in the above derivations. However, it would be reassuring to be able to test this hypothesis and there is in fact a simple way of doing so (see Psacharopoulos and Layard 1979). From equation [3], assuming $N$ is large, the return, $r_1$, to the first year of education can be written

$$r_1 = (Y_1 - Y_0)/Y_0$$

remembering that costs $I_0 = Y_0$ ($Y_0$ being the flat profile of earnings without training, $Y_1$ earnings with one year of training). Rewriting in terms of the time allocation choice fraction $s_t = I_t/Y_t$

$$Y_1 = Y_0 (1 + r_0 s_0).$$

In the second year

$$
\begin{aligned}
Y_2 &= Y_1 (1 + r_1 s_1) \\
&= Y_0 (1 + r_0 s_0) (1 + r_1 s_1),
\end{aligned}
$$

and in general

$$Y_t = Y_0 \prod_{j=0}^{t-1} (1 + r_j s_j)$$

$$= Y_0 \exp \left( \sum_{j=0}^{t-1} r_j s_j \right) \qquad [17]$$

using the approximation, $e^{rs} \simeq (1 + rs)$.

To specify the sequence of $s_t$ we use the Ben-Porath results, i.e. that $s_t = 1$ where $t$ ranges over the $S$ years of schooling and

$$s_t = a - bt \qquad [18]$$

where $t$ ranges over the working period.
Thus in logarithmic terms [17] becomes after substituting in [18]

$$\ln Y_t = \ln Y_0 + r_s S + r_p \sum_{j=0}^{t-1} (a - bj)$$

where we distinguish between the rate of return to schooling, $r_s$, and training, $r_p$. Taking the sum in brackets and using the relation $E_t = Y_t (1 - s_t) \simeq Y_t \exp(-s_t)$ to obtain an expression for observed earnings.[13]

$$\ln E_t = \ln Y_0 + r_s S + r_p (at - \frac{bt}{2}(t-1)) - a + bt$$

$$= \ln Y_0 - a + r_s S + (r_p a + b + \frac{b}{2} r_p)t - \frac{r_p}{2} bt^2. \qquad [19]$$

The coefficients in [19] are estimated simply by regressing $E$ on $S$, $t$ (years of experience) and $t^2$.

It is possible to obtain a rough estimate of $r_p$ straight from [19], given some assumptions about [18]. For example, let us assume for [18] that $a \simeq 50$ per cent (using the 'overtaking year' reasoning explained above) and that $s_t \simeq 0$ when $t = 40$, so therefore $b = -0.013$. A usual value for the coefficient on $t$ is (see below)

$$0.1 = r_p a + b + \frac{b}{2} r_p \qquad [20]$$

giving $r_p \simeq 0.23$, which is considerably higher than the usual returns estimated for schooling. However, it could be argued that the specification of the basic Mincer earnings function in [19] is too restrictive. For example, it is quite possible that people with more schooling have a higher post-school rate of return $r_p$. This would be the case if ability were correlated with education, so that the more educated learned more quickly on the job. In such a case the estimate of $r_p$ in [19] would be incorrect. This possibility is illustrated in Fig. 2.5 for two schooling groups.

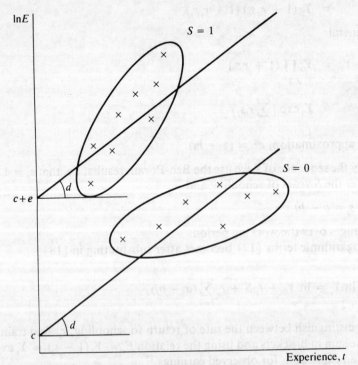

FIG. 2.5   Bias in estimating the returns to experience

Estimating

$$\ln Y = c + dt + eS, \qquad S = 0 \text{ or } 1$$

forces the regression line to have the same slope, $d$, for both groups, consequently getting both slopes wrong, and overestimating the return to schooling, $e$.

The appropriate course of action here is to specify an interaction term, $tS$, thus

$$\ln Y = c' + d't + e'S + ftS$$

which allows both slope and constant terms to differ for the two groups. Psacharopoulos and Layard (1979) have added a full set of interaction terms, $tS$, $t^2S$, $tS^2$, $t^2S^2$. To anticipate our later discussion, the results do indicate that $r_p$ increases with schooling, though $r_p$ is still implausibly high. This could be because the model takes no account of specific human capital investments, to which we turn next. It is worth noting that the authors find the rate of return to schooling is just about unchanged in their extended model, which shows that the simpler model is robust in this respect at least.

## GENERAL AND SPECIFIC INVESTMENTS

Up to this point we have kept the firm in the background, simply assuming that the worker is paid the value of his marginal product which in turn depends on worker human capital investments. We have also assumed that conditions within the firm are not a determinant of these investments. But once we come to analyse investments that raise an individual's productivity not generally but in a *specific* firm, it turns out that wages will differ systematically from marginal products. Conditions within the firm, such as the continuity or discontinuity of jobs within the firm, will also affect the worker's time pattern of investments. The longer a worker expects his tenure with a firm to be, the more he will be prepared to invest in specific training in that firm (Bartel and Borjas 1978). This means that even quite old workers will invest if they have recently changed jobs, so worker investments, and the rate of increase of pay, will not decline monotonically with age as we have previously argued. The notion of specific human capital is also useful when analysing other aspects of employment such as the incidence of overtime payments (Ehrenberg 1971; Kuratani 1972; Hashimoto 1979), employment variation (Oi 1962; Parsons 1972) and pension plans and mandatory retirement (Lazear 1979), as well as topics in the area of occupational choice (Polachek 1981) and sex disadvantage (e.g. Mincer and Polachek 1974; Siebert and Sloane 1981). First we will consider the basic ideas, then more recent developments.

The definition of a specific capital investment is an investment which raises the worker's marginal product only in one firm. An example would be training in a production process which only the given firm has. Since the skills are valueless to a worker outside the firm, the question arises as to who will pay for the training. As we will see, the answer is that both the employer and employee will have to come to an agreement to *share* the costs and benefits of the training. This raises difficulties, because some sharing formula has to be agreed, and some continuity of employment is necessary. Specific investments therefore pose more problems than general ones where only the individual in question need make the training decision, and a continuous employment relationship is not necessary.

The diagram illustrating the main points about specific investments is presented in Fig. 2.6. The contrasting diagram, for general investment, is Fig. 2.7. The explanation of Fig. 2.6 is as follows. Suppose that the employee's alternative marginal product, $MP_A$, and hence alternative wage without the specific investment, is given by line $W_A$. By definition the alternative wage, $W_A$, will be unaffected by programmes specific to the firm. However, a programme of specific training will change the course of marginal product *within* the firm. While the worker is being trained his marginal product, $MP$, will presumably be low, but later it will be higher than it would have been. A linearised path for $MP$ satisfying these conditions is given in Fig. 2.6. The firm might also incur direct training costs, such as instructors' pay, and a dotted $I$ segment is added for completeness. Finally a wage path for the employee within the firm has been drawn as $W$. What determines the slope and position of this wage path?

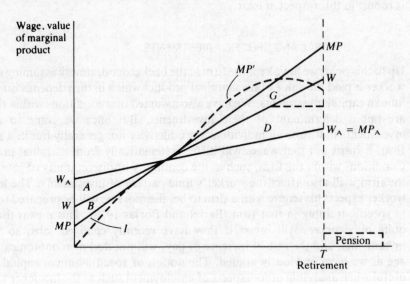

FIG. 2.6  Wages, alternative wages and marginal product in the specific training case

Suppose that the wage path coincided with the worker's alternative wage. This would mean the employer bore all the costs and collected all the returns from the investment. That is, the employer would pay out the triangle to the left of the cross-over point (areas $A + B + I$) and collect the triangle to the right (areas $G + D$). Note that the triangles to the right must be larger than those of the left to satisfy the rule that the present value of future returns, $R$, equal investment costs, $E$,

$$\sum_{t=0}^{T} R_t (1+r)^{-(t+1)} = \sum_{t=0}^{T} E_t (1+r)^{-(t+1)}. \tag{21}$$

However, if the employer adopted this course of action, the employee would have no enhanced incentive to stay with the firm. This risk of the employee leaving means it would be less profitable for the employer to make large investments and, in the limit, no specific training might be worth while. The $MP$, $W$ and $W_A$ paths would then be the same. The $W$ and $MP$ paths are therefore dependent and it pays the two sides to come to an agreement on the sharing out of costs and returns to specific training. *A suitable agreement will make for a steeper* MP *curve and profits for both sides.* The steeper $MP$ curve could result not only from the direct productivity-enhancing effects of training, but also from greater workforce motivation and stability if the workers have shared in specific investments (Lazear 1979). An additional reason for sharing specific training costs between worker and employer is that it will encourage workers to self-select. This is because if workers fail to meet the employer's productivity requirements and are fired, they will lose their investment (White 1980).

To clarify the analysis it is worth giving the main algebraic relationships.[14] Assuming investment takes place only in the first period, [21] becomes

$$H = \sum_{t=1}^{T} (MP_t - MP_{A_t})(1 + r)^{-t} = MP_{A0} - MP_0 + I = C \qquad [22]$$

where $MP_0$ and $MP_{A0}$ are first-period marginal products in the firm and in alternative firms. Equation [22] states that $H$, the discounted value of areas $G$ and $D$ in Fig. 2.6, equals $C$, the value of area $A + B + I$, where $r$ is the internal rate of return (and in equilibrium $r \simeq i$, the market interest rate as before). Let $a$ be the employer's share of discounted returns and therefore costs. For the employer in equilibrium,

$$aH = W_0 - MP_0 + I = ac \qquad [23]$$

Equation [23] shows that (setting $I = 0$) if the employer is to make a positive gain, that is, if $aH > 0$, then $W_0 > MP_0$ as Becker states (1975: 19). Also substituting [23] in [22]

$$C = MP_{A0} + a C - W_0$$

so that

$$W_0 = MP_{A0} - (1 - a)C.$$

This shows that the worker's wage while training will be less than his alternative wage by an amount equal to his share of the costs and returns. If employees get no share in the returns ($a = 1$), then wages in the firm equal alternative wages.

The determination of the employer's share, $a$, is a matter of bargaining (Kuratani 1972; Hashimoto 1979). It will depend on factors other than the specificity of the training, so it would be misleading to regard $a$ as an index of specificity (Becker 1975: 31), though it is true that in the extreme, if $a = 0$, any training is likely to be general since it will all have to be worker financed. In bargaining about the amount of investment and shares in this investment the two parties have first to agree about the likely paths of $MP$ and $W_A$. If the costs of reaching an agreement are high because these paths are uncertain this will hinder specific capital accumulation. The parties will set $a$ in accordance with the likelihood of quits and dismissals or lay-offs in the firm, with the aim of securing maximum stability — since continuity of employment is necessary if the maximum potential returns on the investment are to be realised. A high $a$ will reduce the likelihood of dismissals or lay-offs, but increase the probability of quits, *cet. par.* This line of reasoning suggests that there should be a negative correlation between a firm's quit rate (lay-off rate) and measures of the workers' share (firm's share) in specific human capital, and this does seem to be the case (Parsons 1972). Also, individuals who make successful agreements, that is 'match' their job, will have more specific capital — hence longer tenure with the firm and steeper wage profiles (Mincer and Jovanovic 1978).

The specific human capital concept might also explain the mandatory retirement and pension clauses in employment contracts. If a long employment relationship is envisaged it helps planning to know the termination date. This is not so obvious from Fig. 2.6, where all the paths are linear and maintain a steady relationship to each other. But this linearity is not necessary, so long as the paths preserve the basic property of equality of investment costs with discounted returns stated in equation [21]. A more realistic curve would probably be $MP'$, with productivity tailing off in old age. If wages continue to increase, for example because of an incremental pay scheme, the date of retirement becomes important from the employer's point of view. Another case would be where the employees limit the increase in their pay in later life (shown as the dashed horizontal line) in favour of a pension on retirement. The date of retirement would then be an important element in cost — benefit calculations on the employee side.

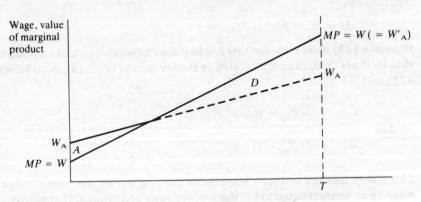

FIG. 2.7   Wages, alternative wages and marginal product with general training

The 'alternative' wage means a different thing in the theory of general capital from the theory of specific capital, and this can give rise to confusion. Fig. 2.7 gives a general human capital diagram for comparison with Fig. 2.6. The confusion arises because general training *changes* the alternative wage, but the pre-training alternative wage is still the relevant wage for planning whether or not to invest. The pre-training alternative wage path is shown as $W_A$ in Fig. 2.7, and the course of the trainee's marginal product (which equals his wage) is shown as $MP$. The present values of areas $A$ and $D$ must, for equilibrium, be equal at time $t = 0$ as usual. After the cross-over point, the trained man's alternative wage, $W'_A$, increases with his marginal product, but $W_A$ is still relevant for reckoning the returns on his investment. Formula [22] above, for the gains from *specific* training, does *not* therefore apply to *general* training: since $MP = MP_A$ after general training is completed, $H$ would always be zero in [22].

For earnings functions, the main implication of extending the human capital model to include specific investments is that a worker's service with a company (his tenure) also becomes a determinant of earnings. This is because we expect those with long tenure to have made a good job 'match', other things being equal. This good match will be reflected in the production of specific human capital and, to the extent that the worker has shared in the costs of this human capital production, in a higher wage. This dependence of human capital production on tenure is shown by generalising Ben-Porath's (1967) expression for the marginal value of capital, $\psi_t$, in equation [11] to include specific human capital. As Bartel and Borjas (1978) have shown, $\psi_t$ becomes[15]

$$\psi'_t = \frac{R}{\delta + r} (1 - \gamma a - (1 - \gamma) \exp(-(\delta + r)(T - t))$$

$$- \gamma(1 - a)\exp(-(\delta + r)(T_t^* - j)) \qquad [24]$$

where　$\gamma$ = proportion of the individual's capital which is specific;
　　　　$a$ = employer's share in the cost of producing specific capital;
　　　　$j$ = length of tenure in the firm;
　　　　$T_t^*$ = expected total tenure in the firm, so $T_t^* - j$ is expected remaining tenure.

If all capital is general $\gamma = 0$, and [24] reverts to [11]. Otherwise it can be seen that $\psi'_t$ and thus the production of human capital will be greater the greater is expected tenure, given $\gamma$ and $a$. This gives rise to the interesting result that as an individual comes to the end of a job his human capital production must taper off since $T_t^* - j$ approaches zero, but on entering a new job his human capital production will jump upwards again since $T_t^* - j = T_t^*$. Individuals entering a new job must increase their investments, so the typical individual's investment path will have a saw-tooth pattern, not be smooth as was previously hypothesised. Investment will still eventually decline however, because job changing becomes less frequent with age, and also $T_t^* - j$ falls with age.

Omitting to consider specific capital investments can bias estimates of the return to general training, though the picture will be different for young and old workers (Mincer and Jovanovic 1978). For older workers the situation can be represented in Fig. 2.8. Here the group with the longer job tenure (the stayers) has been separated from the group with shorter tenure (the movers). If the stayers accumulate more capital than the movers, as described above, then they will receive higher pay for given levels of experience. Ignoring this and fitting line $AA$ will give an overestimate of returns to experience for both groups. For younger workers, however, the bias could be reversed. This is because it is probably the

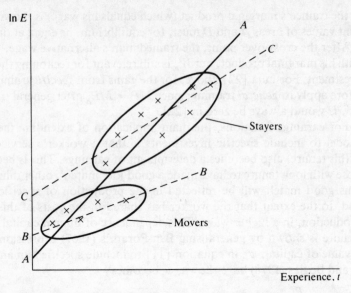

FIG. 2.8   Tenure effects on estimates of returns to experience

more able young workers who change jobs most (job shopping). This ability effect could obscure the effect of frequent job changing on specific capital production. Nevertheless the implication is that for all worker groups, the number of job moves, and job tenure, should be taken into account as well as labour-force experience when analysing earnings.

## 3.   Empirical results

The plan of this section is first to present some estimates of, and problems connected with, rates of return to schooling, then to turn to post-school investments, and finally to consider determinants of schooling. The main results refer to the USA because a lack of data has hampered British research in this area. For example, there is no income or earnings question in the decennial census. However, the situation has improved over the last few years as data tapes from the General Household Survey (Office of Population Censuses and Surveys, 1973), an annual survey initiated in 1971 of the incomes and personal characteristics of a sample of about 35,000 individuals, have become available to researchers through the SSRC Survey Archive.

### RATES OF RETURN TO SCHOOLING

Rates of return to schooling are generally computed from equations such as [19] above. Schooling is entered either as a continuous variable measured in 'years', or as a separate dummy for each course. This latter specification does not force the returns to all years of education to be the same. The coefficient on the course

TABLE 2.2    Private rates of return to education, USA 1969, and England and Wales, 1967 and 1972

| | USA, 1969 | | | |
| | Male | | Female | |
| Incremental schooling level | White (%) | Black (%) | White (%) | Black (%) |
|---|---|---|---|---|
| High school (12 years compared with 8 years' schooling) | 14 | 20 | 15 | 19 |
| College (16 years compared with 12 years' schooling) | 16 | 14 | 15 | 19 |

| | England and Wales, 1967 and 1972 | | |
| | 1967 | | 1972 |
| Incremental schooling level | Male (%) | Female (%) | Male (%) |
|---|---|---|---|
| High school plus university (18 years compared with 10 years' schooling) | 15.0 | 20.5 | — |
| 'A' level only (14 years compared with 'O' level (= 12 years)) | 10.0 | — | 11.7  (9.2)† |
| University degree (18 years compared with 14 years) | 22.5 | — | 9.6  (7.7) |

† Figures in parentheses are based on differences in weekly earnings among schooling groups. All other figures in the table relate to annual earnings.
Sources: USA: Carnoy and Marenbach (1975); England and Wales: 1967 — Ziderman (1973); 1972 — Psacharopoulos and Layard (1979).

dummy measures approximately[16] the percentage increase in earnings from having completed the course, hopefully holding all other relevant factors — such as experience, tenure, ability — constant. Indeed in the effort to make other things equal some researchers have included dozens of variables, in addition to schooling and experience, on the right-hand side of [19]. For example, Taubman (1975: Table 7) has computed a regression with over fifty right-hand side variables, including variables representing health and tastes. However, we will consider simpler formulations.

Some British and American estimates of private returns to schooling are shown in Table 2.2. The figures have the meaning explained in the previous section. Thus for white American males, 14 per cent is an estimate of the real internal rate of return to the earnings forgone in completing high school rather than going to work after only 8 years' schooling, other things equal.[17] While a number of difficulties arise in interpreting rates of return to schooling such as those shown in Table 2.2, it should be said that they are of a plausible order of magnitude (see also Becker 1975: 166). The rate of return to schooling is expected to be similar to that on equally risky physical capital and to the market interest rate. The rates shown in the table are on the high side when judged against this standard, but it should be remembered that they are subject to various biases, such as inappropriate ability correction, to be discussed later. *The point remains that the numbers are reasonable, and this corroborates the model.* Had the figures been much above or much below 10 per cent, this subject would not have received the attention it has.

Let us now turn to the difficulties. Perhaps the foremost problem is one of making an allowance for ability. Second, there is the question of the impact of the non-pecuniary benefits and disbenefits of jobs which up to this point have been ignored, but which would bias estimates of rates of return to education. Third, there is the problem of measuring schooling. School years completed is a crude measure, given the variation in schooling quality as shown by expenditures per pupil, for example. Fourth, there is the problem of dispersion in rates of return to schooling. We want to know how large this is relative to the average, and also the determinants of dispersion, such as restriction of competition due to occupational licensing. Fifth, there is the question of what variables to include in the earnings function, since this has an impact on estimates of the returns to education (compare columns (a) and (b) in the last row of Table 2.2). Finally, there is the problem of the relevance of the private returns given in Table 2.2 to the policy question of government subsidisation of education. This is the question of the 'social' rate of return to education, which, however, we will hold over to the last section which considers these and other policy issues.

### Ability

First consider results on measuring the impact of ability. As explained above, we would expect a correlation between schooling achieved and ability. Empirical results on this correlation will be discussed later and it does in fact appear to be strong (Hause 1972: 131; Becker 1975: 158; Link and Ratledge 1975: 85; Taubman 1975: 17). However, until Taubman's (1976b) study of identical twins, which allowed a more reliable control for ability than had hitherto been possible, it did not seem that allowance for ability much reduced the rate of return to education. This conclusion was reached by including measures of ability such as IQ test score in the earnings regression. The coefficient would fall, but not by much, for example from about 9 to 7 per cent[18] (Jencks *et al.* 1979; see also Griliches and Mason 1972; Hause 1972; Leibowitz 1974; Raymond and Sesnowitz 1975; Sewell and Hauser 1975; Griliches 1977). Therefore, the implication was that most of the measured returns to schooling could not be ascribed to ability, though ability certainly had a significant impact, and the more able seemed to secure a somewhat higher rate of return to education (see below on dispersion of returns to education, and also Welland 1980).

However, it is difficult to measure ability. We can never be sure we have included all aspects (the same is true of family background). All that analysis of the type described in the above paragraph can do is give us a minimum estimate of the effects of ability. But adding further ability measures could increase this effect.

A possible way around this difficulty is to consider comparisons between identical twins. These have the same genes and also the same family environment, and presumably therefore the same 'ability'. All the difference in earnings between a given pair of identical twins must be due only to differences in the way their parents treated them at home, differences in their schooling, and differences in their labour-market experience since leaving home. Taubman (1976b) has performed such an analysis of 1,000 pairs of identical twins aged 45–55 in 1973. There are problems associated with the study, but first consider some basic results which are presented in Tables 2.3 and 2.4. For comparison, results from a national survey of income, conducted by the University of Michigan, and a sample of 346 pairs of brothers from Kalamazoo[19] are also given. The brothers sample will be useful later in considering the effect of family background, since comparisons between brothers – like twins – allow the background effect to be kept constant. Looking at the first row of Table 2.3, it can be seen that the simple correlation between the logarithm of earnings and years' schooling is about the same size for the national sample as for the brothers and twins samples. This is reassuring because it implies that the brothers and twins are reasonably representative of the general population.

TABLE 2.3   Individual and cross-sibling correlations

|  |  | 1970/71 Panel Study of Income Dynamics | Kalamazoo brothers | Identical twins |
|---|---|---|---|---|
| Individuals: | $r_{\ln Y, S}$ | 0.443 | 0.409 | 0.442 |
| Cross-sibling: | $r_{S_1 S_2}$ |  | 0.549 | 0.764 |
|  | $r_{\ln Y_1 S_2}$ |  | 0.269 | 0.406 |
|  | $r_{\ln Y_1 \ln Y_2}$ |  | 0.220 | 0.545 |

Note: $r_{\ln Y, S}$ is the simple correlation coefficient between ln annual earnings and years of schooling for all the individuals in the given sample; $r_{S_1 S_2}$ is the correlation between one brother's schooling and the other brother's; $r_{\ln Y_1 S_2}$ is the correlation between one brother's earnings and his brother's schooling; $r_{\ln Y_1 \ln Y_2}$ is the correlation between brothers' earnings.

Sources: Jencks et al. (1979), Appendix Tables A2.4, A2.9 and A3.4; Taubman (1976).

The bottom three rows of Table 2.3 give the correlations between pairs of brothers. For example, for identical twins the correlation between one brother's schooling and his twin's schooling is 0.764. We might have expected a correlation closer to unity, given that this is a sample of identical twins and they make their schooling decisions while still at home. That the correlation is only 0.764 shows the importance of differences in twins' tastes and parental treatment. The correlation for brothers is even lower, 0.549, which reflects the fact that brothers differ not only in tastes and treatment within the home but also in ability. As for the cross-sibling correlation between log earnings and schooling, we see that this is 0.269 for brothers and 0.406 for twins. These correlations are lower than those for individuals shown in the first row since the cross-sibling correlations hold more constant. The final row shows the correlation for log earnings between pairs of brothers. The correlation is only 0.545 for identical twins, reflecting the fact that they were about 50 years of age when these earnings data were collected, and so had had a long time to 'grow apart' — different job matches and specific capital investment.

The correlations in Table 2.3 can be used to make some interesting inferences about differences between twins relative to differences in the population as a whole. This throws further light on the relation between ability and income. It can be shown that if the distribution of log earnings differences, $\Delta \ln Y$, is normal, which is reasonable since log earnings are approximately normally distributed, then the average absolute[20] log earnings difference is (Johnson and Kotz 1970: 81–3)

$$E(\,|\,\Delta \ln Y\,|\,) = \sigma(\Delta \ln Y)\sqrt{2/\pi} \qquad [25]$$

where $\sigma(\Delta \ln Y)$ is the standard deviation of the distribution of $\Delta \ln Y$. It can also be shown (see Appendix 2) that

$$\sigma^2(\Delta \ln Y) = 2\sigma^2(\ln Y) - 2\sigma(\ln Y_1, \ln Y_2) \qquad [26]$$

where $\sigma^2(\ln Y)$ is the variance of individuals' log earnings;

$\sigma(\ln Y_1, \ln Y_2)$ is the covariance of brothers' log earnings.
Substituting [26] into [25],

$$E(\,|\,\Delta \ln Y\,|\,) = \frac{2}{\sqrt{\pi}}\sigma(\ln Y)(1 - r_{\ln Y_1, \ln Y_2})^{1/2} \qquad [27]$$

for brothers since

$$r_{\ln Y_1, \ln Y_2} = \sigma(\ln Y_1, \ln Y_2)/\sigma^2(\ln Y).$$

To obtain an estimate of the average difference in log earnings for twins we substitute actual values into [27]. The estimate is very sensitive to the value of $\sigma(\ln Y)$. The most appropriate value seems to be the standard deviation of log earnings for the twins in the sample taken as individuals, i.e. $\sigma(\ln Y) = 0.55$. This holds any peculiarities in the twins sample constant. It also holds age roughly constant. For the US non-farm population as a whole, $\sigma(\ln Y)$ varies between 0.71 and 0.88 (Jencks et al. 1979). Equation [27] then becomes

$$E(\,|\,\Delta \ln Y\,|\,) = \frac{2}{\sqrt{3.142}}\,0.55(1 - 0.545)^{1/2} = 0.418.$$

Thus on average

$$\Delta \ln Y = \ln Y_1 - \ln Y_2$$
$$= \ln(Y_1/Y_2) = 0.418 \text{ for twins.}$$

This means that $Y_1/Y_2 = e^{0.418} = 1.519$ or that $(Y_1 - Y_2)/Y_2 = 0.519$, that is, the average differences in twins' incomes is about 52 per cent of average income. That this difference is so large is partly because of the low correlation between twins' earnings which we have already noted — this follows from the formula expressed in [27].

Turning to the average difference between unrelated individuals' earnings, formula [27] becomes simply

$$E(\,|\,\Delta \ln Y\,|\,) = \frac{2}{\sqrt{\pi}}\,\sigma(\ln Y).$$

This is because the correlation between randomly selected individuals' earnings $r_{\ln Y_1, \ln Y_2}$ is zero. Substituting $\sigma(\ln Y) = 0.55$ into this formula gives

$$E(\,|\,\Delta \ln Y\,|\,) = \frac{2}{\sqrt{3.142}} \times 0.55 = 0.620.$$

This means that $Y_1/Y_2 = 1.86$, or that the average difference in individuals' earnings is 86 per cent of average earnings (age constant). This difference is larger than for twins, as we would expect, since unrelated individuals differ in both family background and ability.

To judge the effect of genetic ability on earnings using this technique, it is instructive to compare identical twins with brothers. The former have the same genetic ability and background, the latter the same background and probably some similarity in genetic ability. Taubman gives results for a sample of non-identical twin brothers: the correlation between their log earnings is 0.30. This means that, using formula [27], the average difference between non-identical twins' earnings as a per cent of average earnings is 68 per cent. This is higher than for identical twins and presumably reflects the ability factor. Family background on the other hand seems about as important − income differences between non-identical twins are not nearly as large as among random individuals − but we will have more to say about this later.

Table 2.4 gives the material necessary for analysing the impact of ability on the rate of return to education. The upper panel gives results of regressing log earnings on schooling and background variables including a conventional measure of ability such as IQ test score. In all cases inclusion of these other variables lowers the coefficient on the schooling variable a little. The Kalamazoo and Taubman studies both have low schooling coefficients. But this could be due to the failure to control for experience − those with more schooling necessarily have less experience, and this lowers the apparent return to schooling. Taubman's controlling for age will not pick this up, since twins have the same age but can have different experience and tenure. Moreover, some factors relevant to ability might still be uncontrolled. Therefore, the bottom panel presents results from regressing *differences* in log earnings among pairs of brothers on differences in their schooling. All factors relevant to family background and ability must be constant in the within-identical twins regression, while the within-brothers regression holds family background constant. It can be seen that the coefficient on schooling in the identical twins case is only 0.027, a large drop from the uncontrolled coefficient of 0.079. The coefficient for brothers is also low. If 2.7 per cent is indeed the true rate of return to schooling, this seems very low, too low for an investment interpretation of schooling.

TABLE 2.4    Individual and cross-sibling earnings functions

| | Coefficient on years' schooling | $\bar{R}$ | Other variables in regression |
|---|---|---|---|
| **Individuals:** | | | |
| Panel Study of Incomes | 0.093† | 0.179 | Experience, exp² |
| Dynamics | 0.065† | 0.284 | Experience, measured background, test score |
| Kalamazoo brothers | 0.057† | 0.151 | None |
| | 0.049† | 0.171 | Measured background IQ score |
| Identical twins | 0.079† | 0.201 | Age |
| | 0.069† | 0.264 | Age, measured background |
| **Cross-siblings:** | | | |
| Kalamazoo brothers | 0.031† | 0.297 | IQ score difference |
| Identical twins | 0.027† | 0.012 | None |

† Denotes significance at the 5 per cent level.
Source: As for Table 2.3. The measured background variables include measures of factors such as father's education, mother's education, family income, religion, number of children in family.

There seem to be three main arguments against accepting that the true rate of return to schooling is as low as 2.7 per cent. The first is that many factors other than differences in schooling determine differences in identical twins' earnings. That this is the case is shown in Table 2.4 by the low $\bar{R}^2 = 0.012$ in the cross-sibling regression for twins, and also by the low correlation between twins' earnings. These factors will have manifested themselves particularly in the 20 or 30 years from the time the twins left home to the time their earnings were sampled. Some factors such as motivation will be positively correlated with schooling, imparting a positive bias to the schooling coefficient; others such as experience in the labour force will be negatively correlated with schooling, giving a negative bias. This means we cannot be sure on balance what the resultant bias will be. Nevertheless it must be admitted that an $\bar{R}^2$ of only 1 per cent does not give Taubman's result a strong basis.

The second point, recognised by Taubman (1976b, 1977), is that the effect of errors in measuring schooling will be greater in the cross-sibling than the individual regression. This will definitely bias the coefficient on schooling in the cross-sibling regression downwards. For twin cross-sibling regressions the relation between the true coefficient on schooling, $\beta^*$, and the measured coefficient, $\beta$, can be shown to be (see Appendix 2)

$$\beta = \beta^* \left( 1 - \frac{\text{var}(v)/\text{var}(s)}{1 - r_{s_1 s_2}} \right) \qquad [28]$$

where $s = s^* + v$, $s^*$ being true schooling and $v$ being random measurement error;
$r_{s_1 s_2}$ = correlation of twins' schooling;
var = variance.

For individuals, [28] becomes $\beta = \beta^* (1 - \text{var } (v)/\text{var } (s))$, since $r_{s_1 s_2} = 0$ for individuals. As measurement error rises, so var $(v)$ rises. We do not know what the measurement error is, but if var $(v)$ is 10 per cent of var $(s)$ then [28] becomes

$$\beta = \beta^* (1 - 0.1/(1 - 0.76)) = 0.58 \, \beta^*.$$

In other words, for twins the measured $\beta$ is only 58 per cent of true $\beta^*$, but for individuals measured $\beta$ is 90 per cent of true $\beta^*$. Thus for $\beta = 0.027$, $\beta^*$ would be 0.047, bringing the true rate of return close to 5 per cent.[21]

Thirdly, there is the point that the above analysis is couched in pecuniary terms. But pecuniary costs will overstate true investment costs if, as is likely, education has consumption aspects. Some people enjoy being in college and learning for its own sake. Also pecuniary returns are likely to understate true returns for the more educated. This is because the better educated tend to get jobs which bring not only money but also 'status'. Both these factors will push the measured rate of return below the true rate. All in all therefore, we would accept that *allowing for ability does reduce the average rate of return on education; but it still lies in the 5–10 per cent range.* The main role of ability is in determining the acquisition of education (see below), not in influencing the rate of return to education once it has been acquired. However, it can still be said that the rate of return to education is on the low side when compared with returns on physical capital; that is, there is over-investment in education. The most likely reason for this is that education has consumption aspects, but it could also be due in part to the fact that some of the return to schooling lies in its revealing ability. This is discussed in the section on 'screening' below.

## Non-pecuniary aspects of jobs

We can put the point above about the effect of non-pecuniary job elements on returns to education more rigorously. Moreover, while we have not yet really considered the non-pecuniary aspect of jobs, to the man in the street this factor appears above all to controvert human capital theory. He asks (with J. S. Mill) why it is that the dirtiest jobs are also paid the least? Our reply is that this simple negative correlation should turn into a positive partial correlation, when human capital variables such as schooling and experience are held constant. In other words, comparing two individuals with the same education and experience, the one with the dirtier job should receive higher pay. In fact the evidence does back this up (Taubman 1975; Lucas 1977a; Duncan and Stafford 1980; Hartog 1980; though Brown 1980a is ambiguous).

Consider first the bias on the schooling coefficient from taking money income rather than 'full' income, $F$, as the dependent variable. Full income is money income plus psychic income. Psychic income is negative if the job has on balance conditions which are regarded as nasty by the marginal worker and we measure nastiness on an increasing scale. Thus

$$F = w - N$$

where $N = 0$ is the value of a pleasant job, and the greater $N$ the worse the job.

The individual's choice problem is illustrated in Fig. 2.9, with the individual choosing between goods (pay) and bads (poor job conditions). For the individual with schooling, $S_0$, an opportunity line is drawn in as

$$w = F(S_0) + cZ$$

where $c$ = shadow price of the bads, $Z(cZ = N)$.

$c$ would be determined jointly by the firms' supply of, and workers' demand for, various working conditions (Lucas 1977a). A tangency at point 1 is illustrated. Also illustrated is a tangency at 2 for the individual with more schooling, $S_1$. If this individual uses his greater earnings capacity to buy nicer working conditions, it can be seen that simply looking at pay alone will understate the improvement in earnings capacity.

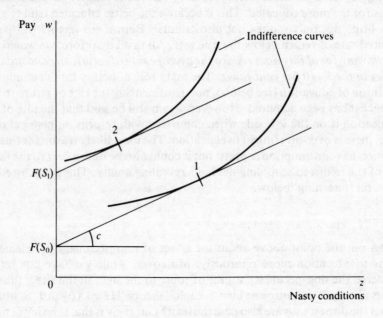

FIG. 2.9   Worker choice between pay and job conditions

The above result can be demonstrated using the omitted variable formula which is also useful below in analysing possible biases in the equalising pay differentials model. The simplest human capital model is

$$\ln w = a + bS. \tag{29}$$

However, we should have full pay on the left-hand side

$$\ln (w - cZ) = a + bS. \tag{30}$$

In terms of $\ln w$, [30] becomes

$$\ln (w - cZ) = \ln w (1 - Zc/w) \simeq \ln w - Zc/w = a + bS.$$

Rearranging,

$$\ln w = a' + b'S + c'Z \tag{31}$$

where $c' = c/w$ and primes have been added to $a$ and $b$ to indicate that they could be different from $a$ and $b$ in [29].

In fact the omitted variable formula gives the possible bias in estimating [29] rather than [31] (Yule and Kendall 1950: 300) as

$$b = b' + c'b_{S,Z} \tag{32}$$

where $b_{S,Z}$ = the coefficient from a simple regression of $S$ on $Z$.

Equation [32] implies that $b < b'$, if $c' > 0$, as it will be if the equalising differences theory holds, and $b_{S,Z} < 0$ (as illustrated in Fig. 2.9). In practice $c'$ appears to be positive (see below) and the correlation between $S$ and $Z$ negative, so the measured rate of return to schooling is lower than the true rate.[22] In Lucas's sample of male whites (data relate to 1966–67), this understatement was of the order of 15–30 per cent of the measured rate of return (Lucas 1977a) which is considerable.

The result that average returns to schooling are underestimated if no allowance is made for working conditions depends on there being compensatory payments for these working conditions, that is, equalising differentials or $c' > 0$. There is a growing body of evidence that such differentials exist, not only as regards physical working conditions but with respect to fringe benefits as well. For example, companies which have better pension schemes appear to pay lower wages (Schiller and Weiss 1980), and this is also true of local government departments (Ehrenberg 1980). Indeed there is even evidence that some of the union–non-union differential in wages is in fact a compensatory payment for a machine-set work pace. Duncan and Stafford (1980) have found that when variables for flexibility and speed of work are introduced in an earnings equation for blue-collar males (1975–77 data) the union–non-union differential falls from 24 to 6 per cent. Moreover there is also a clear-cut relationship in the expected positive direction between income instability in a job and the job's pay, cet. par. (Weiss 1972; Mantell 1974).[23]

Brown's recent results (Brown 1980a) for very young men, aged 14–24 with an average of 4 years' work experience, are exceptional.[24] The only working conditions variable which is significant is repetitive working conditions, which carries a *negative* payment, contrary to expectation. In estimating the shadow price of nasty conditions, $c$ above, it is essential to keep other things equal. This can be illustrated using equations [29] – [32] above if we let $S$ represent poor conditions, and $Z$ schooling for the moment. If $Z$ is omitted when the attempt is made to compute the compensating payment for $S$, the coefficient on $S$ will be underestimated, given that there is a positive return to schooling and that the correlation between $S$ and $Z$ is negative. Since we can rarely include all determinants of productivity, for example motivation, the suggestion is that the compensating payment for poor working conditions will tend to be underestimated – so long as there is a negative correlation between motivation and poor conditions. This argument probably does not apply to Brown's results since he has six years of observations per individual which allows him to include a separate intercept term for each individual in the sample, and this term hopefully picks up individual differences in factors such as motivation. But the argument does apply to the results mentioned in the preceding paragraph and in fact strengthens them. Brown's poor results could be due to the extreme youth of his sample. Therefore we can conclude that there is good evidence of compensating differentials, and failure to allow for them biases downward the estimated return to education.

### Education quality

Up to this point education has been measured in years with the implication that each year is homogeneous, apart from ability effects already discussed. In fact this is not the case, and individuals pay anxious attention to the quality of school or university they attend. There are also strong political movements to equalise educational provision for the various population groups in the UK (for example the programme to do away with grammar schools) and in the USA (the 'bussing' programme). Empirical results show that this emphasis is well placed – education quality is well correlated with earnings. To some extent there might be a trade-off between years of education and the quality of the years. However, ignoring the quality variable leads to an upward bias in measurement of the average rate of return to a 'year' of education. This is because those with more years also tend to have high-quality years (Johnson and Stafford 1973; Ribich and Murphy 1975; Taubman 1975). Using the omitted variable formula [32] above, and letting $Z$ represent schooling quality for the moment, it can be seen that a positive coefficient on $Z$ and a positive correlation between $S$ and $Z$ will give an upward bias to the coefficient on $S$ if $Z$ is omitted.

Looking at the magnitude of the quality effect, if quality is measured as average expenditures per pupil in the individual's school or district, it seems that a 1 per cent increase in state education expenditures increases earnings of US white males by between 0.1 and 0.2 per cent, *cet. par.* (Rizzuto and Wachtel 1980). This represents a good investment for the state, apparently: a higher rate of return is earned by increasing education quality than by increasing the period which individuals stay in educational institutions. However, it does not help in judging whether the individual equalises the return on the marginal pound spent on quality and quantity, for this depends on the fees of the higher-quality schools. Johnson and Stafford (1973), making the assumption that students incur no extra costs for higher-quality schools, calculate a private return to schooling quality of around 10 per cent for white males, which seems low. A result which is easier to interpret from the individual's point of view is Layard's for British males, using 1971 General Household Survey data. He found that individuals who had been to a 'selective entry secondary school' earned 11 per cent more than those who had not, *cet. par.* (Layard 1977). Since there is rationing by ability and waiting lists to get into these schools, the implication is that this 11 per cent is good value for money, and that individuals (like the state) cannot equalise the returns to educational quantity and quality. The tendency for individuals to make up in quantity of schooling what they cannot obtain in quality will weaken the positive correlation between quantity and quality of schooling. Omitting schooling quality from the earnings regression in fact appears to have very little effect on the estimated return to schooling, probably for this reason, and perhaps also because of errors in measuring quality.

It is interesting to consider what the school 'quality' variables mean. The variable might be measuring the additional skills that a good school or university imparts. This interpretation is backed up by the finding that direct measures of school quality, such as teacher–pupil ratio, average teacher salary, capital outlays per pupil, are all positively related to an individual's earnings (Rizzuto and Wachtel 1980). On the other hand, schooling quality could be a proxy for ability, with the better schools attracting the more able. However, ability and quality do not seem to be well correlated (Ribich and Murphy 1975; Taubman 1975). An alternative explanation could be that higher-quality schools lead to the making of more useful contacts in later life. The argument gains strength from the correlation between school quality and family wealth (Taubman 1975), and between quality and an index of the socio-economic status of the individual's peers at school (Ribich and Murphy 1975). The quality variable in fact probably serves a dual role, indexing both better skills and better information (contacts) on how to match the skills to jobs.

### Dispersion in rates of return

Up to this point we have taken the rate of return as an average concept. In fact however, as discussed earlier, individuals' demands for educational investments and their supplies of funds to meet these investments will differ. This will give rise to different equilibrium rates of return to educational investments, and to a dispersion of rates of return round the average. If this dispersion is very wide, then the 'average' rate of return could be a misleading concept. A further factor causing dispersion is occupational licensing restriction. It has been shown that certain licensed professions, such as medicine and law, give rates of return to their members' education which are higher than average (Friedman and Kuznets 1945; Siebert 1977; Mennemayer 1978). The implication is that these licensing laws disrupt competition. Analysis of the dispersion of rates of return to education is therefore a means of evaluating the human capital assumption of competitive labour markets.

Looking at dispersion of rates of return in general, Mincer has estimated an upper limit for the standard deviation of $r$ of about 5 percentage points (1974: 56). This gives a coefficient of variation of $r$ (standard deviation divided by mean) of about a half. Interestingly, Hirsch has recently estimated a similar standard deviation of $r$ of about 3 percentage points, using within-state earnings regressions (Hirsch 1978). Becker, however, estimates a much higher figure. Using the simplified formula for the rate of return in [3] above, $r = k/C$, var$(r)$ is (see Goodman 1960)

$$\mathrm{var}(r) = \bar{k}^2 \, \mathrm{var}\left(\frac{1}{C}\right) + \left(\frac{1}{\bar{C}}\right)^2 \mathrm{var}(k) + \mathrm{var}\left(\frac{1}{C}\right)\mathrm{var}(k). \qquad [33]$$

Equation [33] shows that var $(r)$ increases with both the variation in costs and the variation in returns. Becker (1975: 185–9) estimates the coefficient of variation of *k* for college graduates in 1949 to be in the region of 2, with the variation in costs somewhat less than this, and a resulting coefficient of variation of *r* of between 1.0 and 2.0. If the coefficient of variation were 1.5 and *r* were normally distributed with $\bar{r}$ = 10 per cent, then one-quarter of the population would receive an *r* above 20 per cent, and one-quarter less than zero.[25]

The dispersion of returns to human capital therefore seems high, but in evaluating this it should be remembered that the dispersion of returns to *physical* capital is also high. This is shown in Table 2.5. In both the UK and the USA the standard deviation of profit rates is of a similar order of magnitude to mean profit rates. There are also signs that small companies are more variable in the profit rates they achieve.

TABLE 2.5　Estimates and mean and standard deviation of rates of return for small companies, UK and USA

| | UK | | | | USA | |
| | Pre-tax profit rate, quoted companies, manufacturing and distribution | | | | Post-tax profit rate, 99 industries, manufacturing | |
| | (a) | | (b) | | | |
| | Small | All | Small | All | Small | All |
|---|---|---|---|---|---|---|
| $\pi$ | 18.6% | 14.1 | 17.9 | 18.3 | — | 9.1 |
| $\sigma(\pi)$ | 9.2 | 6.8 | 12.8 | 10.6 | 17.0 | — |

Note: UK (US) figures for 'small' companies relate to companies with assets under £250,000 ($50,000 to $100,000). The UK figures relate to companies existing over 1954–63 (a) or 1948–54 (b). The US figure relates to 1950 and includes corporations taking losses.
Sources: UK: (a) Samuels and Smythe (1968), (b) Whittington (1971); USA: Stigler (1963).

Some dispersion of profit rates is to be expected even with perfect markets, being a consequence of the fact that adjustments to shocks take time to work themselves out. Differences in the riskiness of enterprises will also be associated with differences in profit rates (see Stigler 1963). Increasing this basic dispersion will be the impact of market imperfections – monopolistic firms, barriers to entry, non-profit maximising behaviour, lack of knowledge. As already noted, these imperfections are likely to have a special weight in the human capital market, so one would expect the dispersion of returns to be higher here. Nevertheless it cannot be said on the basis of available data that the dispersion of returns to human capital is so much greater than that to physical capital as to call into question the application of capital theory concepts to humans.

It is also interesting to consider variability in the rate of return over the business cycle. This will depend on the unemployment experience of the more relative to less educated, and on changes in skill margins for those remaining in employment. How hourly skill margins will change over the cycle is problematic (Perlman 1958). However, the unskilled certainly experience relatively more unemployment when times are bad, so *annual* earnings differentials will widen in business contraction. This probably accounts for the American finding that rates of return to education widen slightly when unemployment rises (Kneisner *et al.* 1978; King 1980). It is interesting to note, however, that there is no similar British tendency. Male rates of return to a university first degree, and to 'A' level, show no trend during the 1970s despite the marked rise in unemployment over this period (Adamson and Reid 1980).

As a final point on the rate of return to education, let us briefly consider possible long-run *particular* deviations of educational returns from average. Unions' and professional associations' main *raison d'être* is to improve pay and conditions for their members, and it would be surprising to find they do not. As a corollary excluded groups would have their pay lowered, as is argued in the 'crowding' theories applied to women and black workers (see Ch. 3 of this book). There is evidence of a positive union−non-union differential for workers of apparently the same skill − though some of this will be a compensating differential (see above). Similarly members of professions such as doctors, lawyers, pharmacists earn more than equally educated workers not in professions (Siebert 1977; Mennemeyer 1978; Muzondo and Pazderka 1979). Again, part of this is likely to be a compensating differential for the extra 'trust' (Adam Smith's term) required of the professional worker, and their longer hours.

However it is necessary to tread carefully here, because it is possible that in the long run unions and professional associations secure no rate of return advantage to their average member, but simply raise the price of unionised/ professionalised services. In other words, there is a loss to the consumer with no corresponding gain to association members, so it would be Pareto optimal to dismantle or at least reduce the powers of these associations over a period of time, with compensation for members who would suffer a capital loss when their pay fell. This is because the difficulties which are placed in the way of new entrants to a licensed occupation (stiffer exams, queuing, licence fees) will tend to dissipate the very rents which this restriction of entry causes. The process is similar to the way in which the monopoly rents of, say, a prime central trading site become capitalised, so that the purchaser of the site earns only a competitive return. The advantage accrues only to the first in the field. If there is nepotism in deciding who is to enter the occupation, as with the 'brothers and sons' lists for entry into printing, *then new entrants can capture the monopoly returns*, otherwise they will find it difficult. The excessive returns which we measure for the professions are therefore probably largely a result of our failing to take into account the extra ability, effort and patience of the members − assuming away nepotism. These extra efforts raise the price and the quality of the service, but to the extent that the consumer prefers lower price and quality they are wasted from the consumer viewpoint as well. The excessive measured returns are therefore an indication of the misallocation of resources from licensing restrictions which have limited or zero benefits for both producer and consumer. It is interesting to consider why restrictions of so little worth remain, but this is presumably because of the costs consumers and producers face in transacting a 'buy out' scheme. In practice nepotism will also be a factor maintaining the restrictions.

ON-THE-JOB INVESTMENTS

We now move on to consider investments made after the full-time education period
has ended. These investments are both general and specific, and can be related to
time in the labour force and time in the current job as discussed above. A question
which has generated much interest is how well the concepts of schooling and on-
the-job investments perform in accounting for observed variations in earnings
among individuals. If the fit ($R^2$) is good, the implication is that omitted variables,
such as family background, do not exercise much influence on returns to human
investments (even though these variables may be important in determining the
distribution of these investments), that is, the market is in a sense impartial. The
political importance of this question has probably led to some exaggeration of the
power of simple human capital models to explain earnings differences. Other
subjects which arise under the post-school investment heading are: the returns to
these investments relative to returns on schooling, their pattern over the life cycle
(do those with more schooling have higher post-school investments, which decrease
faster?), the 'sharing' of specific investment costs between worker and employer,
and the impact of specific investments on labour productivity.

Table 2.6 presents a set of earnings functions including experience,
schooling and tenure (service in the current job) for the USA, and a function
without tenure for England and Wales. No male earnings functions using data for

TABLE 2.6   Earnings functions including education, experience and tenure

| Constant | USA (1959) | England and Wales (1972) | 'Over-taking' group USA (1959) | USA (1975) | | |
|---|---|---|---|---|---|---|
| | | | | 16–24 | Over 50 | |
| Constant | 6.20 | 5.20 | 6.36 | −0.0311 | −0.0025 | 1.085 |
| S | 0.107 | 0.097 | 0.162 | 0.085 | 0.080 | 0.065 |
| | (72.3) | (32.3) | (16.4) | (18.4) | (16.4) | (9.2) |
| e | 0.081 | 0.091 | | | 0.066 | 0.049 |
| | (75.5) | (45.5) | | | (7.9) | (5.2) |
| e² | −0.0012 | −0.0015 | | | −0.002 | −0.002 |
| | (55.8) | (37.5) | | | (3.4) | (2.1) |
| j | | | | | 0.062 | 0.012 |
| | (6.3) | (1.8) | | | | |
| j² | | | | | −0.005 | −0.0001 |
| | | | | | (4.8) | (0.6) |
| R² (R² including ln W) | 0.285 (0.525) | 0.316 | 0.306 (0.575) | 0.190 | 0.226 | 0.224 |
| var (ln Y) | 0.668 | 0.436 | 0.469 | | | |

Note: | t | values appear in parentheses, the dependent variable is ln annual earnings;
  S    refers to years of schooling;
  e    refers to years of experience;
  j    refers to years of tenure;
  W    is weeks worked per year;
  Y    is annual earnings.
Sources: Mincer (1974), Mincer and Jovanovic (1978), Psacharopoulos and Layard
(1979).

a nationwide British sample appear to include tenure, though there exist some studies for firms (e.g. Siebert and Sloane 1981). Let us begin with the first two equations whch ignore the specific investments issue. The coefficients have the interpretation indicated above in equation [19]. On this interpretation the average rate of return to a year of schooling is about 10 per cent in both the UK and the USA. However, the average rate of return to a year of labour-market experience is apparently about 20 per cent, if we accept a linear decline in the amount of time devoted to human capital accumulation as is suggested by the Ben-Porath model. This is implausibly high (Psacharopoulos and Layard 1979 obtain even higher figures), but remember that these two equations are misspecified in that they omit tenure.

Remaining with the simple specification for the moment, we see that the explanatory power of schooling and experience is about 30 per cent in both countries. A higher result could be achieved by including weeks worked — see the bracketed $R^2 = 0.525$ figure for the USA — but this is not appropriate since weeks worked is endogenous. If 30 per cent seems 'low' for the human capital model, thereby implying a large amount of play for factors such as luck, nepotism and discrimination, it should be remembered that we are dealing with the very simplest model which, in particular, omits ability and non-pecuniary differences in individuals' jobs. It is more sensible to judge the contribution of human capital factors to earnings by looking at the size, sign and significance of coefficients than by looking at the $R^2$ value which is very sensitive to the number of right-hand-side variables included. For example, the extended earnings function of Taubman (1975) has $R^2 = 0.42$, and Brown (1980a) has $R^2$ ranging from 0.64 to 0.84.

It is of interest to find out what the explanatory power of schooling alone is in the earnings function. One approach is to consider the 'overtaking' group, that is the group whose years of experience are such (around 10) that their earnings are what they would have been had no post-school investments been undertaken — see the equations following [16] above. A regression for this group is presented in the third column of Table 2.6. (It is not possible to calculate schooling explanatory power simply by regressing earnings for the whole population on schooling, because schooling and experience are negatively correlated — such an exercise gives an $R^2$ of only about 5%.) Looking at the overtaking group we see that in the USA schooling alone is quite powerful, explaining about 31 per cent of the variance of earnings of the overtaking group. The equivalent British result for plausible overtaking years is only about half of this, however (Psacharopoulos and Layard 1979), which is puzzling. But at least in both countries the residual variance is smallest in the overtaking experience group, which lends credence to the overtaking year idea — since differences in post-school investments are not contributing to earnings variation in the overtaking year, the residual variance should be lower then (see Brown 1980b). In any case it can be seen that the explanatory power of years of schooling alone is quite large in both countries, and this shows why so much attention has been paid to this variable.

Let us next consider the effects of introducing a tenure variable to allow for specific capital investments. Regressions for old workers and young workers are presented in the last three columns of Table 2.6. Young workers are considered separately because they are at the job-shopping stage of their careers and generally have short tenure. It can be seen that earnings increase by about 6 per cent per year of tenure for young workers, and 1 per cent for old. To convert these coefficients to rates of return we must know the costs involved, and the discount period. The costs will be small, to the extent that the worker is sharing with the employer, implying a plausible rate of return even from the small coefficients. The higher coefficient for young workers can be rationalised in terms of their shorter expected discount period − because of their higher probability of moving − which implies higher required returns for given costs. Unfortunately no estimates have yet been made of the general time path of worker-specific investments by age, though some work has been done on young workers in particular training situations (see below). As a final point, note how introducing the tenure term reduces the coefficient on experience for young workers from 0.066 to 0.049, which is in the direction expected.

As for the size of post-school investments, these can be estimated using the procedures developed by Mincer (1974) in equation [16] above. Since these procedures ignore tenure, the post-school investment estimate should be thought of only as indicating the average worker's situation. That is, it ignores the extra earnings that result from a suitable worker−employer specific capital cost-sharing agreement, which makes for steeper marginal product and wage curves and thus profits for both parties, and the lower earnings in the absence of such an agreement. Mincer (1974: Table 4.2) has calculated that, as of 1959 the person who moved on to 12 years of schooling from 8 years invested about $3,000 extra in schooling, and later in life accumulated about $12,000 extra of post-school investments. The individual who undertook a further 4 years of schooling invested $24,000 and accumulated $23,000 in post-school investments. Note how school and post-school investments rise together. This has been illustrated above in Fig. 2.4, and is explained in the Ben-Porath (1967) model by the reasoning that those who leave school later have higher capacity earnings on entry to the market, so their post-school investments will begin at a higher value (see also Haley 1973). Their investments should also decline faster with age than those with less schooling, since everyone's investment schedule must tend to zero on retirement. Mincer's (1962) calculations of age profiles of investment given schooling category also bear this out. However, it should be noted that Mincer's measured investment profiles reach zero at about age 45, that is some 20 years before retirement. Since his profiles apparently related to *net* investments (Johnson 1970: 555), they might be compatible with gross investment reaching zero towards age 60 as required by the Ben-Porath model. Still, 45 is uncomfortably early, and calls into question Ben-Porath's 'neutrality' assumption − that the marginal cost schedule for producing human capital (see equation [10] above) does not depend on the individual's age. If the $MC$ schedule moves leftwards with age, perhaps because $\beta$ ('ability') declines, gross investments will taper off earlier in life as is consistent with the facts.

An alternative explanation for the higher measured post-school investments of the more educated is that these individuals make more profitable, in the specific capital investment opportunities sense, job matches. On this argument much of the investment, at least for the educated, would be specific in nature −

and this view receives some support in the literature. Oi (1962), for example, believes that a higher wage rate is an *index* of higher human capital specificity, *cet. par.* (see also Parsons 1972). This is because the high-wage jobs have more hiring, screening and training costs — a greater degree of 'fixity' (Oi 1962: 545). Educated individuals could obtain the more stable jobs because they have better knowledge, or are trained to take the longer view. Alternatively they might be better able to *afford* to take the longer view, to the extent that wealth and education are correlated. The particular reason we stress depends upon our view of what education 'does'.

Up to this point we have relied on indirect measures of training investments. That is, we have had to infer the size of human investments from earnings patterns which the investments are supposed to explain. It would be reassuring if some more direct measures were available. There have been several recent attempts at such direct measures which it is interesting to consider (Woodward and Anderson 1975; Horowitz and Sherman 1980; Medoff and Abraham 1980; Ryan 1980). All these studies have as their basis an attempt to measure a worker's productivity directly. It is then possible to answer the question of whether schooling and experience do make for higher productivity, as opposed simply to higher wages, *cet. par.* We can also see whether in the specific training context the productivity of a trainee is lower than his wage, which is in turn lower than his alternative wage as implied by human capital theory (see Fig. 2.6 above).

On the question of whether education and experience make for higher productivity, the indications are that the answer is yes, but Medoff and Abraham (1980) enter a dissenting note. Looking at the positive evidence first, the Horowitz and Sherman study measured labour productivity by the number of hours specific pieces of naval equipment such as boilers and guns were out of service ('downtime'). Downtime was related to the pay, the education and the experience of the crew members allocated to maintain the equipment, and these variables performed well. In particular we should note that a team with more highly paid members maintained equipment to a higher standard (less downtime), *cet. par.*, showing unequivocally the link between blue-collar pay and productivity in the US Navy. This type of result is rather similar to that which has been found in studies of agriculture, another field in which the productivity measurement problem can be tackled directly. Agricultural output has been found to be closely related to farm-worker education, *cet. par.* (Griliches 1964; Welch 1970; Huffman 1981). Medoff and Abraham, on the other hand, find a strange result when analysing performance of managerial and professional workers in two large companies. Their measure of performance is the worker's performance rating within his grade as made by his superior. They find that education, experience and the performance measure are all significant in explaining pay given grade, but that *the education and experience coefficients and significance remain the same whether performance is included or not*. The implication is that education and experience are not picking up performance given grade.

The main difficulty with this study, accepting for the sake of argument that the performance evaluations are meaningful, is that individuals of low performance in a grade are likely to have lower returns to experience than individuals of high performance. By not allowing for this in their regression the authors will obtain an incorrect estimate of the coefficient on experience. This point can be illustrated using Fig. 2.5. Interpret the lower cloud of observations as being the low performers, and the upper cloud the high performers. Not adjusting for performance will give a regression line sloping upwards through the middle of these clouds. Adjusting for performance *incorrectly* by forcing the regression line to have the same slope, $d$, for both groups, will get both slopes wrong. The way Fig. 2.5 has been drawn the unadjusted slope is about the same as the wrongly adjusted slope, $d$, which accords with the Medoff and Abraham finding. What they should include is an interaction term, allowing the return to experience to be higher for the more able than the less able group. Therefore it must be concluded that this study is worth while, but more work is needed before we need revise the human capital assumption that pay is related to productivity, but not necessarily a one-to-one relation − see Fig. 2.6.

On the question of direct estimates of the costs and benefits of specific training courses, and the sharing of costs and benefits by employer and worker, results are less clear-cut. Ryan (1980) and Woodward and Anderson (1975) have calculated the productivity of shipyard apprentices relative to journeymen. By also taking into account the pay of apprentices (and instructor's pay), these authors are therefore able to work out the shipyard's training investment (areas $B$ and $I$ in Fig. 2.6 above). In the US case (Ryan) this came to about $6,000 in 1975, or about 60 per cent of a journeyman's annual wage. In the British case the invest- ment was about zero, because in some years of his training the apprentice was paid sufficiently less than the calculated value of his marginal product to compensate for the company's expenses. Apprenticeship in the British case seems to have been more akin to general training (Fig. 2.7), as one would expect. The US shipyard case had another peculiar feature: trainees, far from sharing in their training costs, appeared to be paid *more* than their best alternative wage. The trainees had no in- centive to stay once trained, therefore, and in fact generally left. 'We're training for the whole region' one manager is even quoted as saying (Ryan 1980: 344). So the company lost on its investment, and also paid its trainees more than it needed. This US study acts as a sort of negative confirmation of human capital principles, by showing what happens if poor management ignores these principles. Before we blame management however, it would be interesting to know who is enforcing high rates of pay for trainees and therefore making their training unprofitable. It could well be unions (see Rottenberg 1961) in the effort to restrict entry, but unfor- tunately Ryan does not go into this.

Before leaving the subject of earnings functions it is worth considering the question of the impact of family background on earnings. We have already seen from Table 2.6 that this could be quite large, since human capital variables, admittedly a greatly simplified selection, explain only about one-third of the varia- tion in individuals' earnings. In assessing the evidence it should be remembered that it is necessary to hold ability constant (Becker 1975: 118). This is because background can pick up ability effects if we are already controlling for schooling. For example, a person from a poor family is likely to have greater ability than a person from a rich family with the same schooling. This lack of control for ability makes the finding of significant family effects by Layard (1977) and Bowles (1972)[26] difficult to interpret.

Some idea of the independent effect of family background on earnings can be gained from the data in Table 2.3. Using formula [27] above, we have calculated that the average difference in pairs of randomly selected unrelated individuals' earnings (at about age 50) is 86 per cent of average earnings. The average difference in identical twins' earnings, that is, holding all family background and ability effects constant (but allowing schooling to vary), is 52 per cent of average earnings. The average difference in brothers' earnings (background alone constant) is 68 per cent of average earnings. Similarity of background, however it is transmitted, thus moves individuals' earnings differences about 16 (= 86 − 68) points closer. Similarity of ability has about the same effect, causing a 16 point shift (= 68 − 52). But most of the difference, 52 points out of 86, can be explained neither in terms of ability nor of background *but is a result of what happens to the individual after he leaves home.* This can also be seen by looking at the correlation between identical twins' earnings which is 0. 545, implying that at least 45 per cent of the variation in log earnings *cannot* be explained by common background or ability. Differences in income after leaving home must be the result of differences in schooling, luck or tastes, presumably leading to differences in specific job investments (job matches) and also to differences in non-pecuniary job attributes.

The contribution of schooling to income differences seems low on the basis of Taubman's results, because schooling only appears to explain 1.2 per cent of identical twins' earnings differences − see Table 2.4. That this $R^2$ is so low can be explained partly in terms of the small difference in twins' schooling, 1.6 years − see Table 2.7. It is also likely to be due in part to misspecification of the earnings function, since Taubman does not include experience, or tenure, or motivational factors, for example family responsibilities.[27] Nowhere does Taubman discuss his low schooling $R^2$ result, though it and his finding of high ability and background effects (which seem to him to be mainly genetic, though in this we need not follow him; see Goldberger 1979) are the basis for his pessimistic conclusion regarding the importance of family effects in the transmission of inequality (1976b: 869). Looking at brothers, schooling alone explains between 7 per cent (Taubman 1976a, dizygotic twins) and 25 per cent (Kalamazoo brothers) of earnings variation. Even if we halve these percentages to allow for unmeasured ability effects we still obtain a schooling impact far higher than 1.2 per cent. It is probably reasonable to take 10 per cent as an upper measure of the returns to the purely productivity-enhancing effect of schooling, that is, net of schooling's aspect as a channel for ability and nepotism or discrimination. (We have a pure schooling effect only in the case of identical twins.) Therefore in the case of twins, schooling is responsible for an income differential of about 16 per cent (1.6 × 0.10), and more in the case of other individuals who have bigger school differences. The twins' pay difference adjusted for school is thus about 36 per cent (= 52 − 16).

The above discussion suggests that two unrelated males with the same home environment and education will have by age 50 a large earnings difference, equal to 36 per cent of average earnings. Home effects can be split up into ability, mainly genetic presumably, and family background − including factors such as investments in children, and also nepotism. Included in home effects would be those factors influencing the acquisition of formal schooling (see below), to which we allocate a weight of 10 per cent p.a. per year of schooling in explaining later earnings variation. Under the non-home effects heading come post-school investments in general and specific training, career motivational effects (possibly marriage and children), and non-pecuniary job attributes. The twins and brothers studies have shown us that these non-home effects are more important than previously thought, just as they have indicated that formal schooling is less important.

## DETERMINANTS OF SCHOOLING

If we give to formal schooling only a somewhat small effect, independent of background and ability, on earnings it might well be asked why so much fuss has been made about schooling by academics, government and parents. Several observations should be made at this point. First, even though schooling does not have the most important effect, it can still be analysed within the investment rate of return framework as in equation [3] above. After allowing for measurement biases, the rate of return to schooling appears still to be in the 5–10 per cent range (see above). This is rather lower than the return required by capital theory. However, second, from the private point of view the effects of schooling *include* those effects which work through ability and family background. If acquiring schooling is a way of showing ability and making good connections, this is relevant from the individual's viewpoint. It might be 'unfair', or too expensive, but that is a social question. This will be discussed in more detail in the next section.

Third, it is true that formal schooling has been overemphasised. This might be because it is more visible and more easily measureable than other forms of human investments. Perhaps it is also because *the extent to which earnings are under an individual's control, apart from schooling, ability and background, has simply not been realised*. Who would have thought that identical twins, with reasonably similar schooling, would have an average earnings difference at age 45–50 that was 52 per cent of average earnings? This shows that the emphasis in human capital research in the last few years on the post-school investment period, and on specific human capital, is well placed.

There has been a lot of research into the determinants of schooling (for references see Harnquist 1978; Gordon and Williams 1979; Halsey *et al.* 1980). In the UK this research has been conducted mainly by sociologists who have certainly demonstrated a strong link between family background ('class') and educational achievement, but have not been so interested in the ability factor − or even in earnings (neither Becker nor Mincer are mentioned in Halsey *et al.* 1980). In the USA, perhaps because better data are available, a more methodical approach has been adopted (see Duncan and Featherman 1973; Leibowitz 1974; Parsons 1975; Taubman 1975; Jencks *et al.* 1979). We will first discuss some of these results, and then try to come to an overall judgement as to the contribution of schooling to earnings differences.

A useful way of analysing the ability−background−schooling−earnings nexus is to postulate a recursive model. In such a model, ability is determined first, when the individual is a child, then schooling, then earnings. Determinants of ability would be genetic factors, and the amount and quality of time inputs to children, which are expected to be related to parents' education and family income (Leibowitz 1974; Sewell and Hauser 1975). The education of the mother is expected to have most influence on IQ in this theory because it is the mother rather than the father who spends most time with the child. Leibowitz in fact finds this, but Sewell and Hauser (1975: 80) and Taubman (1975: 173) find both to be important.[28] Another implication is that children who are first born, or born into smaller families will have higher IQs, *cet. par.*, because they receive a larger share of the mother's attention. This is usually strongly borne out (see e.g. Taubman 1975).

In the recursive model, education is determined after IQ. In accordance with the supply and demand analysis already discussed, schooling achieved should depend on the costs and benefits of schooling, which are in part dependent on IQ and family background.[29] Other factors determining these costs and returns will be prevailing rates of interest, opportunities for part-time work (see Parsons 1975), prevailing returns to schooling (including whether these returns rise or fall with additional levels of schooling — see Tannen 1978), school fees, and tastes. The tastes factor, on the part of both the individual and his family, seems potentially quite important since even twins differ in schooling, presumably due in part to taste differences.

One way of testing the theory above is to see if individuals really make the sorts of calculation implied by the theory. On the basis of surveys of students' intentions (Freeman 1971; Gordon and Williams 1979), it seems that individuals are aware of forgone earnings, do make reasonably accurate predictions of post-training incomes and do move to those courses of study which have the highest expected monetary returns relative to costs net of scholarships. For example, Freeman shows that the change in the number of engineers graduating in any year has a significant, positive correlation with the starting salaries of certificated engineers two or three years earlier (1971: 108). This is as expected by human capital theory. It is true that calculations are imperfect and it is therefore likely to take some time for disequilibria to be cleared, but this is to be expected (see also Leffler and Lindsay 1977 for a test of how student doctors' expectations are formed). In any case we are concerned mainly with the long run.

An alternative approach is to see if the variables in the schooling function satisfy reasonable prior expectations. (Only one schooling function exists for the UK — Psacharopoulos 1977.) In fact empirical schooling functions generally behave quite well. Tannen (1978), for example, is able to explain no less than 60 per cent of the variation across states in college enrolment rates using human capital variables. It is interesting to note that he found the variable with the strongest effect to be parental schooling (this seems true of all countries — see Anderson 1979; Psacharopoulos and Soumelis 1979) — closely followed however by state interest rates, which had a negative correlation with enrolment rates. It is this marked family background effect (see also Campbell and Siegel 1967), which has caused concern about 'intergenerational transmission of inequality'. In fact individuals tend to have widely varying levels of schooling particularly in the USA — see Table 2.7. If we believe that returns to schooling are of the order of 5–10 per cent per year, then schooling becomes a sizeable contributor to earnings variation, and concern about intergenerational transmission of inequality has a good basis.

TABLE 2.7   Schooling distributions in the USA and UK

|  | Mean (yrs) | $\sigma_S$ (yrs) | $r_{S_1 S_2}$ | $E(\|\Delta S\|)$ (yrs approx) |
|---|---|---|---|---|
| UK: |  |  |  |  |
| Males | 10.5 | 2.2 |  | 2.5 |
| Oxford study brothers |  |  | 0.548 | 1.6 |
| US: |  |  |  |  |
| White non-farm males | 10.9 | 3.5 |  | 3.9 |
| Panel Study of |  |  |  |  |
| Income Dynamics |  | 3.3 |  | 3.7 |
| Kalamazoo brothers |  | 2.7 | 0.549 | 2.1 |
| Twins; DZ |  | 3.6 | 0.540 | 2.4 |
| MZ |  | 3.0 | 0.764 | 1.6 |

Note: The last column is calculated from formula [27] in the text; DZ(MZ) refers to dizygotic (monozygotic).
Sources: Mincer (1974 :60), Taubman (1976b), Jencks et al. (1979 :App. A2.1) Psacharopoulos and Layard (1979), Halsey (1980 et al. :156).

Data which assist in assessing the impact of background, ability and tastes on schooling are presented in Table 2.7. The mean level of education is around 11 years in both countries, but with much smaller variation in the UK than in the USA. This is shown in the second column. The third column gives the cross-sibling schooling correlations. The fourth column gives the approximate average difference in years of schooling for the various samples. The average difference figures are approximate because the assumption of normality underlying formula [27] is violated in the case of schooling distributions, which have a truncated lower tail, but are useful for description.

## 4. Social issues

We have not yet considered the question of social rates of return to education. Social returns will differ from private returns to the extent that the social costs and the social benefits of education differ from private costs and benefits. The judgement implicit in the considerable state subsidisation of education certainly appears to be that education has beneficial externalities, for example in the form of reduced earnings dispersion, and increased receptivity to technical change with faster growth of national income (Denison 1962: Tables 32 and 33). But we must also consider the argument that state subsidisation of education reflects the work of pressure groups. Recently, the view has also been growing that eduation might have negative externalities. It is thought that education might often be used as a 'credential' to ration the better jobs (Berg 1971; Taubman and Wales 1974), in which case it would waste resources and reduce growth. Alternatively, there is the view that education does more to convey information about its recipient's innate productivity than to raise that productivity (Arrow 1973; Spence 1973; Riley 1979; Albrecht 1981). In this case it is possible that under some circumstances the public return to education will be driven below the private return. Finally, increasing concern has been raised about the equity aspects of state subsidisation of education. This is because the correlation between education and family wealth means that it is the children of the better off who tend to be subsidised (Hansen and Weisbrod 1969; Schultz 1972; Peltzman 1973; Conlisk 1977; Crewe and Young 1977). Below we will consider some screening models and results, then go on to the problems of education subsidies.

### SCREENING PROBLEMS

'Screening' is one of the most contentious issues in the area of education. This is because it is difficult to *prove* what schooling (the debate has centred mainly on this aspect of human capital) 'does'. Indeed, as we have seen, it is even difficult to define the units in which human capital is measured, and much of human capital analysis is a *tour de force* of inferring the unobservable from the observed. Schooling can raise productivity, *and* act as a 'signal' for pre-existing abilities *and* act as a means for the already better off to get the best jobs, that is, as left-wing critics put it, for 'legitimising the intergenerational transfer of inequality' (Bowles and Gintis 1975). 'Screening' often appears to be used to refer to both the last two headings. However, it is better to distinguish these headings, for under the second – where schooling acts as a signal – wages still equal marginal product in equilibrium as Riley (1979) notes. This is because competitive employers will use educational attainments as a screen only to the extent that these in fact do on average help them find the more productive employees. However, under the third heading, wages do not equal marginal product. Schooling as a means of transmitting privilege (educational discrimination) is really part of a theory of non-competing groups. We shall use the term 'credentialism' for this type of theory and reserve 'screening' for the signalling view. Table 2.8 below provides an assessment of the relative impact of these three forces from the private point of view. The next step is to see their impact on the social return to education, and we shall take the three headings in turn.

From the fourth column of Table 2.7 we see that identical twins had about 1.6 years' difference in schooling. This presumably reflects differences in tastes, since we are holding everything else constant. With a 10 per cent pure rate of return to education this schooling difference corresponds roughly to a 16 per cent earnings difference between identical twins,[30] that is about one-third of the 52 per cent difference observed. Comparing identical twins with brothers, that is, not controlling ability, increases the schooling difference by about 0.6 years. Comparing brothers with the population as a whole increases the difference by around 1.5 years, and one year in the UK. This is presumably the contribution of variations in family environment. Therefore about half the 3.9-year US difference in schooling is attributable to influences working through the environment at home (somewhat less in the UK), with the remainder attributable as much to differences in tastes as to ability. This importance of background implies that differences in education spring mainly from differences in access to funds – the same supply curve of funds is not applicable to all.

TABLE 2.8   Determinants of Earnings Differences, US and UK

| Factor | Approx. average earnings difference as % of average earnings | Calculation |
|---|---|---|
| Identical twins' earnings | | |
| 1. Difference, total of which: | 52 | Formula [27] using correlation for twins' incomes, $r_{Y_1Y_2} = 0.545$ |
| 2. Schooling contribution | 16 | 1.6 years' school difference at 10% p.a. |
| 3. Residual due to different post-school investments and non-pecuniary job aspects | 36 | $52 - 16 = 36$ |
| Population earnings | | |
| 4. Difference, total (at age 50) of which: | 86 (78) | Formula [27] using $\sigma(\ln Y) = 0.55$ |
| 5. Schooling contribution | 39 (25) | 3.9 years' school difference at 10% p.a. |
| 6. Contribution due to different post-school investments and non-pecuniary job aspects | 36 (36) | From row 3 above |
| 7. Residual due to other home effects (ability, nepotism/ discrimination − channelled in part by schooling) | 11 (17) | $86 - 39 - 36 = 11$ |

Sources: Tables 2.3 and 2.7, UK estimates in parentheses.

To calculate the full effect of the family on acquisition of schooling, we should probably add together the ability and the home environment effects. This is because ability is likely to be determined mainly by home influences. Hence family circumstances probably account for about two-thirds of differences in individuals' education in the USA, and probably somewhat less in the UK. In the UK stricter and more uniform state policies with respect to minimum schooling acquisition are presumably the factor reducing the impact of family circumstances on schooling.

The complete account of the breakdown of the average earnings difference is given in Table 2.8. The average pair of identical twins have an earnings difference which is 52 per cent of average earnings. This can be broken down into a

16-point pure schooling contribution and a 36-point remainder. It is this remainder which is the main result of the identical twins study, for it shows the importance of *completely meritocratic* factors. Individuals, whatever the diplomas they hold or the accents they have, simply struggling by themselves and following their own inclinations end up with an earnings difference which is about 36 per cent of average earnings. This represents almost half the total population (aged 50) earnings difference of 86 per cent (78% in the UK).

The lower panel gives the picture for the population as a whole: 36 points of difference are ascribed to the individualistic factors derived from the identical twins study; 39 points are ascribed to the productivity-raising effects of schooling. This leaves 11 points as the *average* contribution of 'other home effects' such as ability differences and nepotism or discrimination. If we ascribe half of this 11-point remainder to ability which is benign, this leaves 5 points (about 6% of the total) to reprehensible factors of nepotism and discrimination. This is the occupational licensing factor together with the sociologists' 'class' effect, but we now have an estimate of its size.

The above calculations are predicated on a pure schooling contribution of 10 per cent p.a. per year of school, which might be an overestimate. Suppose therefore that we take Taubman's low figure, likely to be biased downwards as I have already stated, of 3 per cent. This reduces the schooling contribution in the identical twins case to 5 points and raises the individualistic residual to 47 points. For the population as a whole, the pure schooling contribution is reduced to only 12 points and other home effects rises to 46 points. If we allocate half of this ability as before, much of it recognised via education and therefore an indirect benefit of education, then 14 points becomes the contribution of reprehensible factors (16% of the total). On this extreme assumption therefore, non-competitive elements assume more importance, but even so we should not allocate them a weight of more than a sixth in the overall picture.

We have already considered some positive evidence as to the effect of education on directly measured productivity for blue-collar workers (Horowitz and Sherman 1980), and in agriculture (Welch 1970; Huffman 1981). A clear effect has not been demonstrated yet in the case of white-collar workers (Medoff and Abraham 1980), but there are problems with that study. It has been surmised that one of the main ways in which education raises productivity is by enabling individuals to 'discern the new opportunities' brought about by technical change (Schultz 1972). Education, therefore, not only has a role in increasing worker productivity given the production function, the 'worker effect' in Welch's (1970) terminology, but in improving that function via better management and incorporation of new techniques. This pushes the production frontier outwards — Welch's 'allocative' effect. A result backing up this allocative effect idea is that college graduates earn relatively more on farms in states in which there is more research expenditure per farm, and therefore more opportunities to push the frontier outwards (Welch 1970).

Further important evidence on the possible productivity effect of education is contained in Denison (1962). Over the period 1929–57 US real GNP per person employed grew at 1.60 per cent p.a. The largest contributor to this growth he estimated to be the improved quality of the labour force (0.67% p.a.), measuring quality by increased education, the education categories being weighted by their 1950 income differentials (1962: Table 33) reduced by 40 per cent. Denison subtracted 40 per cent from the differentials to allow for 'ability' effects on earnings which were independent of education (1962: 69). This might be too much if, as in some screening theories, education is a necessary part of the 'sorting' of workers into jobs so that ability can be utilised − see below. If education is not thought to have a productivity effect it is in fact difficult to know to what to ascribe the large increases in real income over this century. More evidence of a productivity effect is contained in the Taubman twin study already considered (see Table 2.4), which gives a lower bound to the productivity effect of 3 per cent p.a. per year of schooling, again netting out the ability effect. If earnings differentials by educational category do largely reflect productivity differentials, then private rates of return are a good reflection of social rates. Basically all that need be done to derive the social rate is add to the private costs of education the public subsidies and calculate returns on a pre-tax rather than post-tax basis. This would reduce the US rates of return shown in Table 2.2 by 2 or 3 points (see Raymond and Sesnowitz 1975), but the UK returns probably by a greater amount because of the higher UK state costs (Adamson and Reid 1980).

Let us now turn to the idea of education as a screen for pre-existing abilities. Screening can be seen to be useful to society once it is admitted that there are benefits to *sorting* the more able people into the more demanding jobs. This does not deny that there can still be 'too much screening', in the sense that education courses are too long in relation to the precision with which they identify ability (their efficacy in sorting). What is required is an optimum level of screening given its marginal benefits and costs, and perhaps a more efficient certification system. It is basically towards these conclusions that the famous Arrow (1973) model directs us. Spence obtains his alarming results − private benefits to education signals, but no social benefits − because there is no room in his model for the benefits of 'allocating the right people to the right jobs' to appear, as he eventually admits (1973: 364).

Sorting can be shown potentially to benefit society, though some worker groups might lose if compensation cannot be transacted − see below. This is graphically seen if we take the view recently put forward by Akerlof, of a job as a 'dam site' (Akerlof 1981). A dam which is too small for a given site wastes the site. In the same way efficient employers will insist on a given hiring standard for a job so as to extract the most from the job, even though lower-standard employees could do the job reasonably well. This sorting of workers will raise profits and national income, but will also widen the dispersion of income. Since national income has risen it should be possible in principle for the gainers from screening to compensate the losers, so no one is worse off even though income dispersion has increased.

The social benefits side of screening can be illustrated using the Arrow (1973) model, illustrative data for which are contained in Table 2.9. Two groups of individuals are assumed, one of which can supply more efficiency units of Type 2 labour than the other. For simplicity both are assumed capable of supplying the

TABLE 2.9   Illustrative data for screening model

| Individual: | | Labour | |
|---|---|---|---|
| | | Type 2 | Type 1 |
| | Group A | 3 efficiency units per person | 1 efficiency unit per person |
| | Group B | 1 efficiency unit per person | 1 efficiency unit per person |

same amount of Type 1 labour. One unit of $T1$ and one unit of $T2$ labour are assumed to be required per unit of output, so that for maximum output ($Q$) the supply of $T1$ labour must equal that of $T2$. It can then be shown that output is lower if there is random allocation of $A$ and $B$ workers to $T1$ and $T2$ jobs than if there is sorting. Suppose there is random allocation. The efficiency condition is $T2 = T1$, where $T2$ and $T1$ are the total supplies of the two types of labour. The supply of $T2$ with random allocation is

$$T2 = T_2 \cdot \bar{z}$$

where $T_2$ = numbers doing $T2$ labour;
   $\bar{z}$ = average number of $T2$ efficiency units per person.

$$\bar{z} = \frac{T_2^A}{T_2} \cdot z^A + \frac{T_2^B}{T_2} \cdot z^B,$$

where $T_2^A$, $T_2^B$ = numbers of group $A$ and $B$ persons doing Type 2 labour;
   $z^A$ and $z^B$ = efficiency units supplied by $A$ and $B$.
The supply of $T1$ is simply $T1 = T_1$ ($T_1$ being the numbers in the category) since we assume one efficiency unit per person. Therefore,

$$N_1 = \frac{T_1}{L} = \frac{T_2}{L} \bar{z} = (1 - N_1)\bar{z} = \bar{z}/(1 + \bar{z})$$

where $L$ is total labour force;
   $N_1$ is the fraction doing $T1$ work.
If we assume $L = 100$ equally divided between $A$ and $B$, then $N_1 = 0.66$ (using the productivity data of Table 2.9) and $T1 = Q = 66$.

Now assume there is sorting. With only $A$ making up the $T2$ labour force we have

$$T2 = 50 \times 3 = 150$$
$$T1 = 50$$

This is not efficient, so $R$ members of $A$ will have to be allocated to $T1$; $R$ is determined from the $T2 = T1$ equality condition so that

$$(A - R) \times 3 = B + R$$

and $R = 25$. In this case $N_1 = 0.75$ and $T1 = T2 = Q = 75$, $Q$ being bigger than before. A different case could be illustrated if there were fewer $A$ workers in the economy, so that $B$ workers had to be reallocated to $T2$ work. But this would not change the basic point − that $Q$ rises if there is sorting.

Let us look now at the costs side of sorting. In the screening model the higher[31] education system is thought to play a major role in finding out who the group $A$ and group $B$ type individuals are, that is, in screening individuals for quality. Firms will also have their own screening systems. In the Arrow (1973) model, the education certificate system appears to have two aspects, with each of which we can associate a cost. Colleges set an entrance standard, $y_0$, and students then have to undergo a certain length of course, $c$, before being pronounced fit to graduate. The social cost, ignored by Arrow, of setting a high entrance standard is presumably that this would 'waste ability', that is, increase the probability of Type II error (the probability of incorrectly accepting the null hypothesis that there is no difference between the applicant and the average member of the population). There are likely to be strong egalitarian pressures not to set too high $y_0$, given the association between parental circumstances and school achievement, for this would discriminate against the poor. 'Mass education' requires a low $y_0$. The costs associated with the length of course are the forgone earnings of students, as usual. The system will also have other costs associated with its plant and staff.

In the screening approach the benefits of the education system are that it identifies pre-existing characteristics more or less precisely. Note that it is this *precision*, the expected quality of the graduate, which is important. Both benefits and costs will be determined by $c$ and $y_0$ and other characteristics such as staff−student ratios which are taken as given. This is illustrated in Fig. 2.10. The top panel shows an assumed trade-off between $c$ and $y_0$ for given expected graduate quality. Lower $c$ and $y_0$ presumably reduce expected quality. A more efficient system for other reasons will cause the isoquants to move towards the origin. An easier entrance policy ($\bar{y}_0$) means that longer courses are required to achieve the same precision of certification, *cet. par.* Or if course lengths remain unaltered as $y_0$ is reduced, as might roughly characterise the historical pattern, the system just delivers less precision. This is illustrated in the lower panel as a shift in the (present value of) social benefits curve downwards. If we take a long-run cost curve as illustrated (a function of the costs of Type II errors, $x$, forgone earnings, $w$, and other factors, $z$), the combination ($\bar{c}, \bar{y}_0$) is not optimal. Looked at solely as a screen, in this situation education is costing society more in terms of students' forgone earnings and other certification costs than society is gaining in benefits. However, adding on the productivity-raising effects of education would make the picture more favourable.

The above analysis is only meant to be illustrative of the problems involved. It would be useful to model the interaction of the educational and employer screening systems − better public screening is likely to mean lower hiring costs for employers. Better screening will also confer benefits by reducing mistakes in hiring and so encourage specific capital formation. However, the analysis does bring out the point that precision in sorting is a good with benefits and costs like any other, and we might be paying too much for the precision

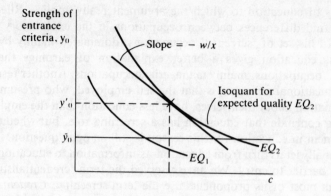

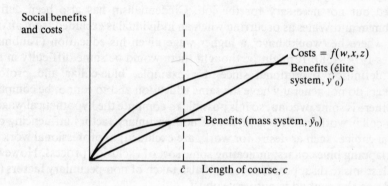

FIG. 2.10   Benefits and costs of a screening system

generated by the educational system. It also raises the issue of whether ability revealed by the educational system should be taken into account as a social benefit. We can assume that the ability would have been revealed less certainly without educational certification, and accept the point that revealing ability is socially beneficial because it helps sorting to raise output. Then the answer must be that some of the private returns on ability should also be regarded from the social point of view as a return to the educational system.

Research on educational screening is still at an early stage. It has been concerned more with whether such screening exists at all than with the more interesting efficiency questions considered above. Albrecht's (1981) study of blue-collar worker hiring did not find evidence of educational screening. Education had the same positive effect on a worker's probability of being hired whether the company concerned could be presumed to have non-educational information about him or not. The index of other information was whether the worker had been recommended by a current company employee. If there was educational screening, education should have been given less weight when hiring such recommended employees. However, it might be argued that blue-collar workers do not have the higher levels of education to which the argument really applies. Riley's (1979) study does find differences between occupations in the explanatory power of education. In his set of 'screened' occupations, dominated mainly by teaching occupations, education gives a better explanation of earnings than in the 'unscreened' occupations, mainly managerial occupations. Another result consistent with educational screening is that the self-employed, who presumably have more information about themselves, have less education than the employed, *cet. par*. We can conclude that education has a screening role, but whether there is over-investment in education for this reason is still an open question.

Finally let us turn from education-as-information to education as a non-competitive barrier to entry. We have reserved the term 'credentialism' for this view, though most of its proponents use the term screening. *Credentialism can simply be thought of as discrimination based on education*, that is education is required but not necessary for the job. Credentialism has also been defined by Taubman and Wales as occurring when an individual is excluded from an occupation where he 'would have' a higher wage given his education (Taubman and Wales 1974: 158). It might be thought there would be some difficulty in making this definition operational since, for example, blue-collar and professional workers do not generally have the same education and so cannot be compared. In fact there is some overlap, so it is possible to compute the hypothetical wage of the blue-collar workers. This is higher (if non-pecuniary factors influencing occupational choice, such as desire for work, are excluded) in professional work for the overlapping blue collars, indicating some sort of exclusion process. However, this result seems to disappear if account is also taken of non-pecuniary factors (Haspel 1978), so the method is not very robust.

In any case, we know from the results discussed above in connection both with occupational licensing, and with the breakdown of the average earnings difference into individualistic, education, ability and nepotism or discrimination effects (Table 2.8), that credentialism exists. It is more likely to be a credentialism based class and family than on education, however. Remember that an education barrier is not enough of itself to ensure than entrants to a licensed occupation capture its rents, for competition for entry will bid away the rents. The barrier has essentially to be a non-competitive one, such as nepotism, or perhaps a 'taste' for people with the 'right' accent and school background. Note that indulgence of these tastes requires that the employing agency be non-profit maximising (see Layard and Psacharopoulos 1974) — the upper regions of the civil service for example. At any rate if we give to these nepotistic and class elements a weight of a fifth in determining earnings differences, it should be remembered that these elements are only channelled in part by education. Therefore we should subtract less than a fifth from the private rate of return to education to account for any unproductive (i.e. class or education discrimination) effects of education.[32] Consequently we may conclude that neither screening nor credentialism is likely to cause the social rate of return to education to be much lower than the private. There will also be beneficial democratic effects from education, pulling the public return above the private. For example, there is a correlation between education and participation in democratic processes such as voting (see Butler and Stokes 1974).

## EDUCATION SUBSIDIES

We will consider only government intervention in formal education here, leaving aside the question of intervention in the field of industrial training (the British Industrial Training Act, and the US Manpower Development and Training Act – see e.g. Ziderman 1975). On both sides of the Atlantic the taxpayer pays a considerable proportion of the costs (40% in the UK, 25–30% in California of costs including forgone earnings) of college education. Both systems have the same curious gap at the higher secondary level, however, where the student is left to rely mainly on family funds. Consequently it appears to be mainly the children from better-off families who take up higher education subsidies, which raises the possibility that the current subsidy system is regressive.

Both efficiency and equity reasons are put forward for subsidisation of education. The efficiency argument depends on there being external benefits to education, which we have already discussed. There are likely to be some positive externalities to education, for example in promoting democracy. However, the main reason for subsidisation appears to be an equity one, the attempt being to even up the educational opportunities of children from different family backgrounds. Subsidisation is here justified in terms of the unavoidable imperfection of the human capital market, which arises because human capital cannot serve as collateral for a loan. The evidence is mixed, but points on balance to this equity objective to some extent having been met.

Looking at the pessimistic side first, Hansen and Weisbrod first showed that, in California, children from high-income families received subsidies that were higher in relation to their parents' schooling taxes than children from low-income families (1969: 75). This results from the strong correlation discussed above between achievement at school and favourable family circumstances, and will therefore hold in most countries, including the UK. It has been pointed out, however, that if a child's income is only weakly correlated with his parents' income, then the subsidy the child receives will be only weakly correlated with the *child's* later income, so education subsidies will not promote inequality (Conlisk 1977). This is something of a detail, because it requires that schooling and income not be correlated. Whatever the facts of the matter are, and schooling and income do appear quite well correlated, if schooling and income are not correlated, then subsidising schooling is just a waste of money. So schooling subsidies are either a waste, or regressive (Johnson 1978). In any case education subsidies might be quite wasteful, because it looks as though they mainly displace private expenditures which would have been made anyway (Peltzman 1973).

Looking at the optimistic side, over time there has been a considerable increase in the average level of schooling, and also a reduction in the white-collar–blue-collar differential (see Addison and Siebert 1979: 344 for details). Subsidisation of education must have been a factor in both these developments – see Fig. 2.1. It should be remembered, however, that a rise in the *level* of schooling, its dispersion and the level and dispersion of returns to schooling being unaltered, will raise the dispersion of earnings – see note 30.

There also appears to have been an increase in social mobility in the UK in the post-war period. For example, Glass's 1949 inquiry showed that 49 per cent of the individuals currently in professional and higher administrative occupational categories had fathers whose main occupation was in these categories, with none having unskilled manual fathers (1954: Ch. 8). However, the 1972 Oxford study gives corresponding percentages of 25 and 12 per cent (Goldthorpe 1980: Table 2.1). This striking difference is no doubt partly due only to differences in definitions, but it is also in part real (Goldthorpe 1980: 72). A factor here could be the increased subsidisation of education in the UK in the post-war period which has given greater *numbers* of working-class children educational opportunities – though their *proportion* in the increased undergraduate population appears to have remained stable (Crewe and Young 1977). It is true that over the post-war period there has been an expansion in white-collar relative to blue-collar jobs, which would of itself improve occupational opportunities for those with low-income backgrounds. But one of the factors underlying this expansion of white-collar jobs could have been the growth of the educated labour force. Therefore it is possible that policies to lower the private cost of education have been a basic cause of the increase in observed social mobility.

In conclusion, there is a good chance that the present educational subsidy system has had some egalitarian effects, though these have probably been weak. If education is to continue to be subsidised then the emphasis should perhaps be changed. Since it is the close link between family financial resources and educational investments which we are attempting to weaken, the subsidy system must be more selective. In addition, there should be subsidisation of children from poor families at the higher secondary levels, which are presently ignored.[33] It makes little sense from an equity viewpoint to subsidise the higher education levels when many poorer individuals will not be able to take advantage of this – having already left the education system. At the university level, subsidisation via a selective loan scheme could increase student motivation, and also perhaps reduce the costs of the system.

## Conclusions

The problem we have been attacking is, *how to account for earnings differences among individuals*, abstracting from sex and colour complications. It is helpful to think of earnings differences as being a consequence partly: (a) of differences in the characteristics which individuals acquire *before* they enter the labour market; and (b) of differences in their careers once in the market. Human capital theory, defined broadly as analysis of the acquisition of earnings-augmenting skills, bears on both categories. Under (a), the home phase, capital theory analyses why some individuals acquire much more education than others. The implication is that this results mainly from the non-transferable nature of the assets acquired during education, which prevents the emergence of a commercial market for human capital, so throwing the individual back on his family's resources.

Under (b), the market phase, human capital theory analyses the acquisition of further skills obtained on the job, and the rate of return to these investments and to education. The chief empirical question is whether education and on-the-job training, together with other competitive factors such as the non-pecuniary returns from different jobs, 'ability' and chance, are more important in determining earnings difference than are non-competitive factors. Under the non-competitive heading would come lack of information, social stratification (taking place sometimes via occupational licensing) and tastes for discrimination. Discrimination in this context can be characterised as firms' preference for educated employees (credentialism), and perhaps for upper-class employees. Above, the focus has been on the competitive approach, because this is the most systematic and because the evidence (summarised below) favours it on balance. Nevertheless we have not avoided analysing non-competitive elements such as discrimination. Indeed, these often become clearer once a rigorous, competitive, 'baseline' has been established.

To summarise, we have a simplified two-equation model of individual earnings determination.

(a) the home phase:

$$S = a + bF + \varepsilon_1 \qquad [34]$$

(b) the market phase:

$$Y = c + dS + eT + fF + \varepsilon_2 \qquad [35]$$

where $S$ = an index of education;
  $F$ = an index of family advantages;
  $T$ = a measure of on-the-job training;
  $Y$ = market earnings;

  $\varepsilon_1$ and $\varepsilon_2$ capture the effects of omitted variables such as ability and non-pecuniary job advantages.

For equation [34], the debate centres on explaining coefficient $b$, the strength of the relationship between $F$ and $S$. For equation [35], the debate centres on whether coefficient $f$ is different from zero. There are many other issues but these are the main ones. The human capital approach is a help in both debates.

One influential critic (Blaug 1976, 1980) has made the following criticisms of human capital theory. Firstly, that it makes implausibly strong assumptions as to the knowledge that students have of forgone earnings and future earnings differentials. Secondly, that lack of knowledge and stratification mean that labour markets are not perfect enough to equalise the returns on all types of education and training investments. He also believes that too much has been made of models of optimal investment such as Ben-Porath's − which simply imply a concave age−earnings profile and a concentration of investment in the younger age ranges. For evidence to support these criticisms he points to the apparent differences in the rates of return to schooling and to training, and to the apparently differing rates of return to different levels of schooling. He also points to the apparent importance of family background factors in determining earnings even given measured human capital. Finally, he stresses the difficulty of measuring what education *does*, so that it might simply be 'an occupational selection mechanism' (i.e. a credential) rather than a 'resource invested in improving the quality of the labour-force' (1980: 235).

Most of these criticisms have been analysed already in the body of this survey, but it is worth considering the conclusions we have reached, and their empirical bases. Looking at the evidence, the best assessment of the overall importance of the various factors determining earnings differences is presented in Table 2.8. There the net schooling contribution — holding constant ability and family background — is set at a maximum of 39 points out of 86 (86% being the expected earnings difference between any pair of (age 50) individuals in the population as a percentage of average earnings). On the basis of identical twins studies, 36 points are then attributed to 'individualistic' factors such as chance and different tastes. The residual 11 points are attributed to the combined effect of ability and nepotism or discrimination. Attributing half of this combined effect to ability alone — on the basis of comparison between brothers and twins — leaves a hard core of 5 points due to class or discrimination factors. This rises to 14 points if we assume only a 3 per cent net rate of return to schooling, but it still cannot be said to be a major influence.

The results from the recent twins studies therefore provide a powerful means of demonstrating that competitive determinants of earnings are relatively much more important in general than non-competitive determinants. (However, non-competitive elements will be important in particular occupations.) To put this in another way, the implication is that the force of $F$ in equation [35] above is small. The results of Table 2.8 are also the best way of answering the point that some occupations have a higher present value of lifetime earnings than others (Wilkinson 1966; Phelps Brown 1977). If differences in education were the only source of earnings differentials (the simplified human capital model — see Fig. 2.1), then all individuals should have the same present value of lifetime earnings when education costs are ascribed a return of, say, 10 per cent. However, the finding on occupations does not have a clear bearing even on this simplified prediction, because most individuals have to take several occupations during their working lives in order to realise the returns on education. In fact, as we have seen, individuals differ in much more than formal education. We can explain most of individual differences in earnings by adding differences in ability, tastes and the effects of 'chance', to differences in education.

Looking at Blaug's other criticisms, his arguments emphasising the dispersion of rates of return to human capital also question the generally competitive nature of the labour market. We should note, however, that some dispersion is compatible with competition, and there is in fact quite a wide dispersion of rates of return to *physical* capital (Table 2.5). It is true that the rate of return to years of labour-force experience seems higher than that to schooling (equation [20] above). But research here is still at an early stage. It seems that different specifications of the earnings function can cause marked changes in the estimates of returns to experience, so we cannot yet be conclusive on this point.

As for questioning the value of the Ben-Porath type of model, it is difficult to conceive of how we could analyse post-school investments without an explicit model. For example, the very estimate of the rate of return to experience in equation [20], referred to above, is based on the Ben-Porath model, specifically its implication of a decline in worker on-the-job training investments with age. The Ben-Porath model has also served as a springboard for further developments. On the theoretical front there is the finding that worker-training investments must move upwards whenever a new job is begun, the amount of the move being related to expected tenure on the job (Polachek 1975; Bartel and Borjas 1978). Those who make more successful job matches will have longer tenure and will therefore be able to share, with the employer, in the returns from larger specific capital investments. On the empirical front there have been encouraging results using tenure as an explanatory variable in the earnings functions, and also in measuring actual worker and firm investments in particular training situations. Moreover, it is worth remembering that identical twins have a large income difference — the difference, adjusted for education, is 36 per cent of average earnings. This indicates the scope for otherwise quite similar individuals to make different job matches and specific capital investments. However, note that part of this difference should also be allocated to the unmeasured *non-pecuniary* advantages and disadvantages of the different jobs which twins take. That these non-pecuniary factors have an effect on earnings in the direction expected long ago by Adam Smith is nicely shown in some of the findings surveyed. I have not made an overall estimate of the effect of non-pecuniary elements on earnings dispersion, but their force is suggested by the fact that not allowing for non-pecuniary effects causes a downward bias in the rate of return to schooling of an estimated 15–30 per cent (Lucas 1977a). The main criticisms of human capital analysis, at least as far as it is applied to the market phase of an individual's life, can therefore be answered.

However, if we are prepared to proceed on the assumption that most individuals face reasonably competitive conditions during the market phase of their existence (equation [35]), this does not mean we should be complacent. There is still no reason to disagree with Tobin's recent statement that 'wealth breeds wealth and poverty breeds poverty' (Tobin 1981). The mechanism whereby this occurs is to be found mainly in the home phase (equation [34]). We have found a strong family background effect on the acquisition of schooling. Holding ability constant, background differences account for about half the differences in individual's schooling, using the identical twins results (Table 2.7). Capital analysis explains this in terms of the fact that human capital cannot be collateral for a loan. Moreover the overall family background effect on education, since background influences ability, is probably somewhat stronger than this.

Our findings with regard to the weight of family background in determining education in the home phase (equation [34]) lead to the equity argument for public subsidisation of schooling — and perhaps on-the-job training. It can be seen that human capital theory really reinforces this argument. However, the theory directs our attention to the home phase rather than the market phase as the source of 'social stratification'. This knocks 'dual labour market' theories on the head, at least as far as white males are concerned. If we give to the productivity-raising effects of education a weight of about one-third in determining earnings differences, it therefore seems that policies to widen educational opportunities have potentially quite a powerful egalitarian effect.[34]

Finally there is the question of how divergent are the social and private returns to education. Above (in the screening discussion) we concluded that there was not much divergence, contrary to Blaug. Admittedly it is difficult to prove what higher education does. But there is a lot of indirect evidence that it increases productivity directly. There is also the point that education does play a part in revealing ability. This is necessary both from the individual and the social point of view. Formal education might have 'crowded out' employer screening procedures it is true, and research is needed into how cost-effective a screen schooling is. Nevertheless, screening − revealing ability that would otherwise not be revealed, or revealed less precisely − is one of the ways that education increases national income and this should not be forgotten. Screening should be carefully differentiated from biased employee selection rules, i.e. credentialism, which we have already concluded is in any case of minor importance on average.

# Appendix 1    Derivation of the optimum time path of an individual's demand price for human capital

Pontryagin's maximum principle (see Dorfman 1969) states that text equation [9] will be maximised subject to [8] when

$$\partial H/\partial s_t = 0 \qquad \partial H/\partial K_t = -\dot{\lambda}_t \qquad \partial H/\partial \lambda_t = 0,$$

where $H$ is a Hamiltonian,

$$H = RK_t(1 - s_t)e^{-rt} - \lambda_t(\dot{K}_t - Q_t - \delta K_t);$$

$\lambda_t$ is a multiplier which is to be interpreted as the discounted marginal value of capital (see below); and, $\dot{\lambda}_t = \partial \lambda_t/\partial t$.
Thus

$$\partial H/\partial s_t = -RK_t e^{-rt} + \lambda_t b Q_t/s_t = 0 \qquad\qquad [A1]$$

$$\partial H/\partial K_t = R(1 - s)e^{-rt} + \lambda_t(bQ_t/K_t - \delta) = -\dot{\lambda}_t \qquad [A2]$$

$$\partial H/\partial \lambda_t = (\dot{K}_t - Q_t - \delta K_t) = 0.$$

Define $\psi_t = \lambda_t e^{rt}$ so that $-\dot{\lambda}_t = -\dot{\psi}_t e^{-rt} + r\,\psi_t e^{-rt}$.

Substituting into [A2] we derive

$$\dot{\psi}_t = -R + \psi_t(\delta + r). \qquad\qquad\qquad [A3]$$

This is a differential equation of a standard form with a solution†

$$\psi_t = R/(\delta + r) + Ce^{(\delta + r)t}, \qquad\qquad\qquad [A4]$$

where $C$ is the constant of integration.

† The formula is $\dot{\psi} + P = Q$, where $P = -(\delta + r)$ and $Q = -R$. The formula for solution (see Yamane 1968) is

$$\psi = e^{-\int P\, dt}\int e^{\int P\, dt} Q\, dt + c\, e^{-\int P\, dt}.$$

Remember the transversality condition $\psi(T) = 0$, so

$$\psi_T = R/(\delta + r) + C \cdot \exp(\delta + r)T = 0.$$

Therefore

$$C = -\frac{R}{\delta + r} \exp(-(\delta + r)T).$$

Substituting into [A4] gives the text equation [11] for the time path of $\psi_t$,

$$\psi_t = \frac{R}{\delta + r}(1 - e^{-(\delta + r)(T - t)}).$$ [A5]

We have called $\psi_t$ the 'marginal benefit of capital', so $\lambda_t = \psi_t e^{-rt}$ means that $\lambda_t$ is the 'discounted marginal benefit of capital'. This can be understood as follows.† Consider a one unit increase in $K$ at time $t$. The present value of the earnings provided by this unit of capital, discounted to time zero, and adjusted for depreciation is,

$$\int_{u=t}^{T} Re^{-ru - \delta(u - t)}du = \frac{R}{r + \delta}e^{-rt}(1 - e^{-(\delta + r)(T - t)}) = \psi_t e^{-rt} = \lambda_t.$$

This shows that $\lambda_t$ is the discounted marginal value of capital.

### EXAMPLE‡

Suppose that we wish to maximise

$$W = \int_0^T (1 - s_t)K_t dt$$

subject to

$$Q_t = (s_t K_t)^b = \dot{K}_t.$$

Here we have ignored discounting and depreciation, and set $R = 1$ (by appropriate choice of the 'units' of human capital), and set $\beta = 1$.

The Hamiltonian is then

$$H = (1 - s_t)K_t - \lambda_t(\dot{K}_t - (s_t K_t)^b).$$

Pontryagin's conditions are then

$$\partial H/\partial s_t = K_t - \lambda_t bs_t^{b-1}K_t^b = 0$$ [A1′]

$$\partial H/\partial K_t = 1 - s_t + b\lambda_t s_t^b K_t^{b-1} = -\dot{\lambda}_t$$ [A2′]

$$\partial H/\partial \lambda_t = \dot{K}_t - Q_t = 0.$$

† I am grateful to Richard Barrett for this explanation.

‡ I am indebted to Sol Polachek for this example.

From [A1'] we have

$$\lambda_t = \frac{K_t}{bs_t^{b-1}K_t^b} \ .$$

Substituting this into [A2'] we have

$$-\dot{\lambda}_t = (1-s_t) + bs_t^b K_t^{b-1} \frac{K_t}{bs_t^{b-1}K_t^b}$$

$$= 1. \qquad\qquad\qquad\qquad\qquad\text{[A3']}$$

The solution to [A3'] is found in the same way as for [A3].
The solution is $\lambda_t = -t + C$, $C$ being the constant of integration.
By the transversality condition $\lambda_T = 0$,
therefore

$$\lambda_T = -T + C = 0 \qquad\qquad\qquad\qquad\text{[A4']}$$

and

$$C = T.$$

So the final solution is

$$\lambda_t = -t + T \qquad\qquad\qquad\qquad\qquad\text{[A5']}$$

which is a simplified version of [A5].
Solving for $s_t$ we substitute [A5'] into [A1'] to derive

$$s_t = (K_t/bK_t^b(T-t)^{1/(b-1)}. \qquad\qquad\qquad\text{[A6]}$$

$s_t$ has to be $< 1$ in phase II, and can be seen to decline to zero when $t = T$ (since $b < 1$).

We can use [A6] to work out how long the individual will stay at school. Let the year at which the individual leaves school (the end of phase I) be denoted by $t^*$. During phase I, $s_t = 1$. Therefore from [A6]

$$1 = K_{t^*}/bK_{t^*}^b(T-t^*),$$

$$t^* = T - \frac{1}{b}K_{t^*}^{1-b}.$$

By differentiating this function with respect to its various arguments we can work out the determinants of $t^*$. For example, it can be seen immediately that $\partial t^*/\partial T > 0$, meaning that a lengthening of the planning horizon (postponement of retirement) will lengthen time spent at school. Using this method in a more realistic model, Wallace and Ihnen show the effect of other determinants of $t^*$. For example, they find that the higher is $\beta$ ($\beta$ is set to unity in our simple example), the individual's ability to produce human capital, the higher will be $t^*$. Interestingly, they also find that the higher is $K_0$, the individual's initial human capital stock, the lower will be $t^*$ (1975: 148).

# Appendix 2   The effect of measurement error on the estimated rate of return to schooling

Suppose that we wish to measure $\alpha^*$ and $\beta^*$ from

$$Y^* = \alpha^* + \beta^* S^* \qquad\qquad\qquad\qquad\text{[A1]}$$

where $Y^*$ = true log earnings; $S^*$ = true schooling.

In fact we can only observe reported earnings $Y$ and reported schooling $S$, where $Y = Y^* + u$ with $u$ a random variable uncorrelated with $Y$; $S = S^* + v$ with $v$ a random variable uncorrelated with $S^*$ and with $u$.

Thus in fact we measure

$$Y = \alpha + \beta S + \varepsilon, \qquad \varepsilon = u - \beta^* v.$$

The formula for $\beta$ is †

$$\beta = \frac{\text{cov}(Y,S)}{\text{var}(S)}$$

$$= E(Y - E(Y))(S - E(S)))/\text{var}(S)$$
$$= \beta^* \text{var}(S^*) / \text{var}(S)$$
$$= \beta^* \text{var}(S - v) / \text{var}(S)$$
$$= \frac{\beta^* \text{var}(S) - \beta^* \text{var}(v)}{\text{var}(S)}$$

where var and cov denote variance and covariance respectively.

Therefore the biased coefficient, $\beta$, is smaller than the true coefficient depending on the variance of the error in measuring schooling relative to the variance of observed schooling

$$\beta = \beta^* - \beta^* \text{var}(v) / \text{var}(S). \qquad [A2]$$

Now suppose we use between-pair differences to estimate [A1] (the same $\alpha^*$ and $\beta^*$ will be estimated if [A1] is the correct model) and measure

$$\Delta Y = \alpha + \beta \Delta S + \varepsilon', \qquad \varepsilon' = \Delta u - \beta^* \Delta v.$$

Using the same reasoning as was used to derive [A2], the estimate for $\beta$ is

$$\beta = \beta^* + \beta^* \text{var}(\Delta v) / \text{var}(\Delta S). \qquad [A3]$$

The bias in $\beta$ now depends on var $(\Delta v)$ /var $(\Delta S)$.

There is reason to suspect that

$$\frac{\text{var}(\Delta v)}{\text{var}(\Delta S)} > \frac{\text{var}(v)}{\text{var}(S)}. \qquad [A4]$$

Remember that var $(\Delta v) = 2$ var $(v) - 2$ cov $(v_1 v_2)$, and similarly for var $(\Delta S)$ (see equation [26] in the text for another application). This result follows from the rule for variances and covariances:

var $(\Delta v) =$ var $(v_1 - v_2) =$ var $(v_1)$ + var $(v_2) - 2$ cov $(v_1, v_2)$
$\qquad\qquad\qquad = 2$ var $(v) - 2$ cov $(v_1, v_2)$, since var $(v_1) =$ var $(v_2)$.

Therefore

$$\frac{\text{var}(\Delta v)}{\text{var}(\Delta S)} = \frac{\text{var}(v) - \text{cov}(v_1,v_2)}{\text{var}(S) - \text{cov}(S_1,S_2)}.$$

But if brothers' errors in reporting education are uncorrelated, cov $(v_1 v_2) = 0$.

† See for example Common, (1976:306-7).

Therefore

$$\frac{\text{var } (\Delta v)}{\text{var } (\Delta S)} = \frac{\text{var } (v)}{\text{var } (S) - \text{cov } (S_1, S_2)}$$

and [A4] follows since cov $(S_1 S_2)$ is certainly not zero in the case of identical twins. Note var $(\Delta v)/\text{var } (\Delta S)$ can be computed as

$$\frac{\text{var } (\Delta v)}{\text{var } (\Delta S)} = \frac{\text{var } (v)/\text{var } (S)}{1 - r_{s_1 s_2}}$$

since $r_{s_1 s_2} = \text{cov } (S_1, S_2)/\text{var } (S)$.

## Notes

1. If earnings differ from marginal product widely throughout the economy human capital concepts become less useful (Thurow 1970: 18ff. stresses this). For example, if people were paid more simply because they had more education (credentialism), and not because education raised their productivity, education would be wasteful from the social viewpoint. However, it would still be 'capital' from the private viewpoint in that the costs of taking a course of education would still have to be related to the returns in some investment framework. Below we look in detail at the question of the weight to be put on the productivity-raising aspect of education, and the weight to be put on credentialism and nepotism. Our conclusion is that the latter are not widespread throughout the economy, though they are important in particular occupations.
2. This step involves using the formula for the sum of a geometric progression: sum (GP) $= A(1 - h^N)/(1 - h)$ where $A = k/(1 + r)$ is the first term, $h = 1/(1 + r)$ is the common ratio, $N$ = number of terms.
3. Actually it is not inevitable that the more able accumulate more education. This is because, while their returns from education will be higher than for the less able, their forgone earnings costs of education will be higher too, so the net outcome is uncertain. In practice, however, we do find that intelligence (measured in various ways) correlates well with years of education.
4. Mill compared the demarcation between the educated and uneducated to 'an hereditary distinction of castes'. 'The fact that a course of instruction is required of even a low degree of costliness, or that the labourer must be maintained for a considerable time from other sources, suffices everywhere to exclude the great body of labouring people from the possibility of any such competition (with the skilled)' (1878: 479–80).
5. In other words, the wage that a man commands could be taken as the best measure of his human capital. But if we assume this we canot independently evaluate human capital theory.
6. There is also the point that if the marginal utility of current income rises as income falls, the poor will have a higher rate of time preference than the rich. This will be a further reason for them to invest less in human capital (see Thurow 1980: 78).

7. Note also that since the interrelation of supply and demand determines rates of return by level of education, there is no reason to expect rates of return to decline on average with increasing education (contrary to Psacharopoulos 1972 and Phelps Brown 1975). Only if all individuals had the same demand curve for education, but faced different supply conditions, would this occur. See the section on dispersion of rates of return below.

8. If human capital has non-market benefits (education increases enjoyment of leisure), the incentive to accumulate is increased (Graham 1981).

9. Ignoring inflation, $R = P(i + \delta)$ where $P$ is the price of the capital good in question, say a school diploma, $i$ is the interest rate, $\delta$ is the rate of depreciation. If $i = 10$ per cent, $\delta = 5$ per cent, and $P = £10,000$ per school course, $R = £1,500$ per course p.a.

10. In the notation of equation [3] we have

$$C = \frac{k}{r}\left(1 - \frac{1}{(1 + r)^N}\right) \simeq k/r \text{ for } N = T-t \text{ large (young man)}$$
$$\simeq 0 \text{ for } N \text{ small (old man)}.$$

$k$ is the rental rate of capital. Suppose this is £1,500 per unit of capital, and $r$ is 15 per cent. Then a young man would pay approximately £10,000 per unit, but as he ages his demand price will fall to zero.

11. If $b = 1$, $I$ is a straight line so $s$ can only be 1 or 0 − the individual either spends all his time producing human capital, or none at all.

12. This is why Wilkinson (1966) and Phelps Brown (1977) are wrong to hold occupation constant when estimating returns to education. It is generally necessary to move from one occupation to another to obtain the pay-off to education − so holding occupation constant will cause an underestimate of returns.

13. This is a rough approximation. For a more correct derivation see Addison and Siebert (1979: Appendix 4).

14. Following Becker (1975: 27ff.) but hopefully with more clarity.

15. Equation [24] is derived by reasoning that the marginal value of human capital produced at time $t$ is the average of discounted returns from the general capital produced at $t$ for the rest of one's life $(T - t)$ and discounted returns from specific capital produced at $t$ for the rest of one's expected stay with the firm $(T_i^* - j)$. Ben-Porath's formula [11] includes only the first. In integral terms [11] is

$$\psi_t = R \int_0^{T-t} e^{-(\delta+r)v}dv.$$

Similarly $\psi_t'$ is

$$\psi_t' = (1 - \gamma)\psi_t + R\gamma(1 - a) \int_0^{T_i^*-j} e^{-(\delta+r)v}dv,$$

which when integrated out gives [24]. The weights in this average are the respective proportions of general $(1 - \gamma)$ and specific $(\gamma)$ capital production in time $t$. Note also that the worker only obtains a fraction $(1 - a)$ of the return on specific capital as previously explained.

16. Suppose we estimate $\ln Y = a + bD + X$ where $D = 1$ or 0, and $X$ represents other variables. Then the percentage effect of $D = 1$ is

$$R = e^X(e^a.e^b - e^a)/e^{X+a} = e^b - 1.$$

Thus $b = \ln (1 + R) \cong R$ if $R$ is small. If those in category $D$ earn 35 per cent more than those who are not, then $b \cong 0.3$.

17. The figure 14 per cent is produced by comparing the present value of lifetime earnings of a man with 12 years' schooling to one with 8 years, holding other relevant factors such as experience constant. A worked example of this type of calculation is given in Addison and Siebert (1979). An estimate of the rate of return is also obtained by looking at the coefficient on years of education, $s$, in equations such as [19]. See Table 2.6 for an empirical version of such equations.

18. This is an average coefficient for the four studies for which data are available in Appendix Table 6.5 of Jencks et al. (1979). Olneck's study is omitted since the earnings equation appears not to include experience, whose omission would bias the coefficient on schooling downwards.

19. These interesting data were collected with the help of the Kalamazoo school authorities who had administered an IQ test to the men when they were in the sixth grade. These men were followed up and income data and other information collected from them in 1973 when they were aged about 45 (see Olneck in Taubman 1977).

20. It is necessary to take absolute earnings differences (one-half of the distribution of $\Delta \ln Y$) since the average earnings difference is simply zero. I am grateful to A. Chesher for discussing formulae [25] – [27] with me.

21. We should note as well that the recent Hausman and Taylor (1981) study using panel data (from the Panel Survey of Income Dynamics, for the years 1968 and 1972) obtains a 12–13 per cent coefficient on years of schooling. The authors' method of allowing for 'ability' is to incorporate a separate dummy for each individual in the sample. Since they have two observations for each individual this is possible.

22. Note that it is the omitted variable's correlation with the included variables, not with the dependent variable, that is relevant. If an omitted variable is correlated with the dependent variable, but not with the included variables, $R^2$ will be lower but the included variables' coefficients will not be biased. Such a case is quite possible – $X$ can be well correlated with $Y$, and $Y$ with $Z$, without $X$ being correlated at all with $Z$ (Yule and Kendall 1950: 301).

23. Mantell presents data on mean ($\mu$) and coefficients of variation ($c$) of male earnings in 1969 in eight occupational categories: engineering, professional, technical, sales, blue-collar, services, white-collar and owner-manager. Looking at those with just high school, the rank correlation between $\mu$ and $c$ is 0.545; for those with an undergraduate degree it is even higher, 0.786.

24. Brown believes that other studies also fail to support the equalising differentials hypothesis. But most of the unfavourable studies he cites are simply unpublished Ph.D. theses.

25. In fact a coefficient of variation of $r$, $CV_r$, of greater than unity seems implausible (see Chiswick and Mincer 1972: S42 n.14).

It can be shown that

$$R^2 = \frac{1}{1 + CV_r^2/CV_M^2 + CV_r^2}$$

where $CV_M$ is the coefficient of variation of accumulated human capital. If $R^2 = 0.5$, which is a reasonable value, then it follows that

$$CV_M^2 = \frac{1}{\dfrac{1}{CV_r^2} - 1}.$$

Since $CV_M^2 > 0$, this means $1/CV_r^2 > 1$ and $CV_r < 1$.

26. The Bowles earnings function has the additional misspecification of failing to include experience terms.
27. In one set of results (1977) he does include marriage, which enters significantly. Married men tend to earn more than single men, *cet. par.*, and men with large families more than those with small − presumably because of motivational effects.
28. Leibowitz's further research (1977) finds mother's time to be clearly important.
29. See Boardman *et al.* (1977) for research into how background affects performance at school. Interestingly, given parents' education and occupation, motivation at school depends mainly on whether there are books at home, and whether parents talk about school (1977: Table 4).
30. This is using the formula $C = k/r$. If $C = 1.6x$ where $x$ is average income, then setting $r = 0.1$, $1.6x = k/0.1$ and $k = 0.16x$. Using Taubman's estimates of $r$, $r = 0.027$, the contribution of schooling is much lower, for then $k = 0.04x$. These calculations are only illustrative. The proper way to work out the contribution of schooling dispersion to earnings dispersion is to take the variance of a given earnings function; for example, given

$$\ln Y = \ln X + rS + u$$

we have

$$\text{var} (\ln Y) = \bar{r}^2 \, \text{var} (S) + \bar{S}^2 \text{var} (r) + \text{var} (s) \, \text{var} (r) + \text{var} (u).$$

Here it has been assumed that var (ln $X$) = 0, and the Goodman results used in formula [33] have been used to evaluate var($rS$). (This result requires that $r$ and $S$ be independent.) Nevertheless, the method used in the text gives the orders of magnitude.
31. The screening argument is applied more to higher education because many of the courses here are less obviously productivity-increasing. At the lower education levels productivity explanations reign supreme. R. Barrett helpfully commented on screening for me.
32. For example, the statement 'college degrees have been used as a means to allocate the cushy jobs regardless of the relevance schooling may have to the work' (Levitan 1981) implies educational discrimination. This requires a taste for such discrimination and the ability to exercise that taste (a monopoly position), the simultaneous occurrence of which is likely to be of limited extent in practice.
33. This is recommended in SCRAC (1980).
34. Including education's role in revealing innate abilities raises its weight in determining earnings above one-third. But the one-third figure is more relevant when considering policies which leave the ability distribution unaltered.

# References

Adamson, A. D. and Reid, J. M. (1980) The rate of return to post-compulsory education during the 1970s: an empirical study for Great Britain, SSRC Labour Studies Group: London School of Economics, mimeo.

Addison, J. T. and Siebert, W. S. (1979) *The Market for Labor,* Goodyear: Los Angeles.

Akerlof, G. A. (1981) Jobs as dam sites, *Review of Economic Studies,* **48**, 37−49.

Albrecht, J. W. (1981) A procedure for testing the signalling hypothesis, *Journal of Public Economics,* **15**, 123−32.

**Anderson, C. A.** (1979) Societal characteristics within the school: inferences from the international study of educational achievement, *Comparative Education Review*, **23**, 408–21.

**Arrow, K.** (1973) Higher education as a filter, *Journal of Public Economics*, **2**, 193–216.

**Bartel, A. P. and Borjas, G. J.** (1978) Specific training and its effect on the human capital investment profile, *Southern Economic Journal*, **44**, 333–41.

**Becker, G. S.** (1962) Investment in human capital, *Journal of Political Economy*, **70**, S9–S49.

**Becker, G. S.** (1975) *Human Capital: A Theoretical and Empirical Analysis*, NBER: New York (2nd edn).

**Ben-Porath, Y.** (1967) The production of human capital and the life cycle of earnings, *Journal of Political Economy*, **75**, 352–65.

**Berg, I.** (1971) *Education and Jobs: The Great Training Robbery*, Beacon Press: Boston.

**Blaug, M.** (1976) The empirical status of human capital theory: a slightly jaundiced survey, *Journal of Economic Literature*, **14**, 827–55.

**Blaug, M.** (1980) *The Methodology of Economics*, CUP: Cambridge.

**Blinder, A. S. and Weiss, Y.** (1976) Human capital and labor supply: a synthesis, *Journal of Political Economy*, **84**, 449–72.

**Boardman, A. E., Davis, O. A. and Sanday, P. R.** (1977) A simultaneous equation model of the educational process, *Journal of Public Economics*, **9**, 23–49.

**Bowles, S.** (1972) Schooling and inequality from generation to generation, *Journal of Political Economy*, **80**, S219–S251.

**Bowles, S. and Gintis, H.** (1975) The problem with human capital theory: a Marxian critique, *American Economic Review*, **65**, 74–82.

**Brown, C.** (1980a) Equalising differences in the labor market, *Quarterly Journal of Economics*, **94**, 113–34.

**Brown, C.** (1980b) The overtaking point revisited, *Review of Economics and Statistics*, **62**, 309–12.

**Butler, D. and Stokes, D.** (1974) *Political Change in Britain*, Macmillan: London.

**Campbell, D. and Siegel, B. N.,** (1976) The demand for higher education in the United States, 1919–1964, *American Economic Review*, **57**, 482–93.

**Carnoy, M. and Marenbach, D.** (1975) The return to schooling in the US 1939–1969, *Journal of Human Resources*, **10**, 311–31.

**Chiswick, B. R. and Mincer, J.** (1972) Time series changes in personal income inequality in the United States from 1939, *Journal of Political Economy*, **80**, S34–S66.

**Common, M. S.** (1976) *Basic Econometrics*, Longman: London and New York.

**Conlisk, J.** (1977) A further look at the Hansen – Weisbrod – Pechman debate, *Journal of Human Resources*, **12**, 147–63.

**Crewe, M. A. and Young, A.** (1977) *Paying by Degrees*, Institute of Economic Affairs: London.

**Denison, E. F.** (1962) *The Sources of Economic Growth in the US*, Committee for Economic Development: New York.

**Dorfman, R.** (1969) An economic interpretation of optimal control theory, *American Economic Review*, **59**, 817–31.

**Duncan, G. J. and Stafford, F. P.** (1980) Do union members receive compensating differentials?, *American Economic Review*, **70**, 355–71.

**Duncan, O. D. and Featherman, D. L.** (1973) Psychological and cultural factors in the process of occupational achievement, in Goldberger, A. S. and Duncan, O. D. (eds), *Structural Equation Models in the Social Sciences*, Seminar Press: New York.

**Edwards, I.** (1975) The economics of schooling decisions: teenage enrolment rates, *Journal of Human Resources,* **10,** 155–73.

**Ehrenberg, R. G.** (1971) *Fringe Benefits and Overtime Behaviour,* Heath: Lexington, Mass.

**Ehrenberg, R. G.** (1980) Retirement characteristics and compensating wage differentials in the public sector, *Industrial and Labor Relations Review,* **33,** 470–83.

**Freeman, R.** (1971) *The Market for Colleged Training Manpower,* Harvard University Press: Cambridge, Mass.

**Friedman, M. and Kuznets, S.** (1945) *Returns to Independent Professional Practice,* NBER: New York.

**Ghez, G. R. and Becker, G.** (1975) *The Allocation of Time and Goods over the Life Cycle,* NBER: New York.

**Glass, D.** (1954) *Social Mobility in Britain,* Routledge and Kegan Paul: London.

**Goldberger, A. S.** (1979) Heritability, *Economica,* **46,** 327–47.

**Goldberger, A. S. and Duncan, O. D.** (eds) (1971) *Structural Equation Models in the Social Sciences,* Seminar Press: New York.

**Goldthorpe, J. H., Helvelyn, C. and Payne, C.** (1980) *Social Mobility in Great Britain,* Clarendon Press: Oxford.

**Goodman, L. A.** (1960) On the exact variance of products, *Journal of the American Statistical Association,* **55,** 708–13.

**Gordon, A. and Williams, G.** (1979) Case Study: United Kingdom, in Harnquist, K. (ed.), *Individual Demand for Education,* OECD: Paris.

**Graham, J. W.** (1981) An explanation for the correlation of stocks of non-human capital with investment in human capital, *American Economic Review,* **71,** 248–55.

**Griliches, Z.** (1964) Research expenditures, education, and the agricultural production function, *American Economic Review,* **54,** 961–74.

**Griliches, Z.** (1977) Estimating the returns to schooling: some econometric problems, *Econometrica,* **45,** 1–22.

**Griliches, Z. and Mason, W. M.** (1972) Education, income and ability, *Journal of Political Economy,* **80,** 74–103.

**Haley, W. J.** (1973) Human capital: the choice between investment and income, *American Economic Review,* **63,** 929–44.

**Halsey, A. H. Heath, A. F. and Ridge, J. M.** (1980) *Origins and Destinations: Family, Class and Education in Modern Britain,* Clarendon Press: Oxford.

**Hanoch, G.** (1967) An economic analysis of earnings and schooling, *Journal of Human Resources,* **2,** 310–29.

**Hansen, W. L. and Weisbrod, B. A.** (1969) *Benefits, Costs and Finance of Public Higher Education,* Markham Publishing Co.: Chicago.

**Harnquist, K.** (ed.) (1978) *Individual Demand for Education,* OECD: Paris.

**Hartog, J.** (1980) Earnings and capacity requirements, *Review of Economics and Statistics,* **62,** 230–40.

**Hashimoto, M.** (1979) Bonus payments, on-the-job training, and lifetime employment in Japan, *Journal of Political Economy,* **87,** 1086–104.

**Haspel, A. E.** (1978) The questionable role of higher education as an occupational screening device, *Higher Education,* **7,** 277–94.

**Hause, J. C.** (1972) Earnings profile: ability and schooling, *Journal of Political Economy,* **80,** 108–38.

**Hausman, J. A. and Taylor, W. E.** (1981) Panel data and unobservable individual effects, *Econometrica,* **49**, 1377—98.

**Heckman, J. J.** (1976) A life cycle model of earnings, learning and consumption, *Journal of Political Economy,* **84**, 11—44.

**Hirsch, B. T.** (1978) Earnings inequality across labor markets: a test of the human capital model, *Southern Economic Journal,* **45**, 32—45.

**Horowitz, S. P. and Sherman, A.** (1980) A direct measure of the relationship between human capital and productivity, *Journal of Human Resources,* **15**, 67—76.

**Huffman, W. E.** (1981) Black—white human capital differences: impact on agricultural productivity in the US South, *American Economic Review,* **71**, 94—107.

**Jencks, C.** *et al.,* (1979) *Who Gets Ahead?,* Basic Books: New York.

**Johnson, G. E. and Stafford, F. P.** (1973) Social returns to quantity and quality of schooling, *Journal of Human Resources,* **8**, 139—55.

**Johnson, N. L. and Kotz, S.** (1970) *Distributions in Statistics: Continuous Univariate Distributions — 1,* Houghton Mifflin: Boston.

**Johnson, T.** (1970) Returns from investment in human capital, *American Economic Review,* **60**, 546—60.

**Johnson, T.** (1978) Time in school: the case of the prudent patron, *American Economic Review,* **68**, 862—72.

**King, R. H.** (1980) Further evidence on the rate of return to schooling and the business cycle, *Journal of Human Resources,* **14**, 264—72.

**Kneisner, T. J., Padilla, A. H. and Polachek, S. W.** (1978) The rate of return to schooling and the business cycle, *Journal of Human Resources,* **13**, 264—77.

**Kuratani, M.** (1972) A theory of training, earnings and employment: an application to Japan, Ph.D. dissertation, Columbia University.

**Landsberger, M. and Passy, U.** (1976) A note on the distribution of the shadow price of human capital, *Metroeconomica,* **28**, 137—45.

**Layard, P. R. G.** (1977) On measuring the redistribution of lifetime income, in Feldstein, M. (ed.), *The Economics of Public Services,* Macmillan: London.

**Layard, P. R. G. and Psacharopoulos, G.** (1974) The screening hypothesis and the returns to education, *Journal of Political Economy,* **82**, 985—98.

**Lazear, E. P.** (1979) Why is there mandatory retirement?, *Journal of Policital Economy,* **87**, 1261—84.

**Leffler, K. and Lindsay, C. M.** (1977) Do human capital investors form earnings expectations?, Graduate School of Management, University of Rochester, mimeo.

**Leibowitz, A.** (1974) Home investments in children, *Journal of Political Economy,* **82**, 110—29.

**Leibowitz, A.** (1977) Parental inputs and children's achievement, *Journal of Human Resources,* **12**, 242—51.

**Levitan, S. A.** (1981) Book review in *Journal of Economic Literature,* **19**, 146—8.

**Link, C. R. and Ratledge, E. C.** (1975) Social returns to quantity and quality of education: a further statement, *Journal of Human Resources,* **10**, 78—89.

**Lucas, R. E. B.** (1977a) Hedonic wage equations and psychic wages in the returns to schooling, *American Economic Review,* **64**, 549—58.

**Lucas, R. E. B.** (1977b) Is there a human capital approach to income inequality?, *Journal of Human Resources,* **12**, 387—95.

**Mantell, E. H.** (1974) Discrimination based on education in the labor market for engineers, *Review of Economics and Statistics,* **56**, 158—66.

**Medoff, J. L. and Abraham, K. G.** (1980) Experience, performance and earnings, *Quarterly Journal of Economics,* **95,** 703–36.

**Mennemayer, S. T.** (1978) Really great returns to medical education?, *Journal of Human Resources,* **13,** 75–90.

**Mill, J. S.** (1878) *Principles of Political Economy,* Longman, Green, Reader and Dyer: London.

**Mincer, J.** (1958) Investment in human capital and personal income distribution, *Journal of Political Economy,* **66,** 281–302.

**Mincer, J.** (1962) On the job training: costs, returns and some implications, *Journal of Political Economy,* **70,** S50–S79.

**Mincer, J.** (1974) *Schooling, Experience and Earnings,* NBER: New York.

**Mincer, J. and Jovanovic, B.** (1978) Labor mobility and wages, presented to the Universities – NBER Conference on Low Income Labor Markets, mimeo.

**Mincer, J. and Polachek, S.** (1974) Family investments in human capital: earnings of women, *Journal of Political Economy,* **82,** S76–S108.

**Muzondo, T. and Pazderka, B.** (1979) *Professional Licensing and Competition Policy,* Research Monograph no. 5, Bureau of Competition Policy: Ottawa.

**Office of Population Censuses and Surveys** (1973) *General Household Survey,* HMSO: London.

**Oi, W. Y.** (1962) Labor as a quasi-fixed factor, *Journal of Political Economy,* **70,** 538–55.

**Parsons, D. O.** (1972) Specific human capital: an application to quit rates and layoff rates, *Journal of Political Economy,* **80,** 1120–43.

**Parsons, D. O.** (1975) Intergenerational wealth transfers and the educational decisions of male youth, *Quarterly Journal of Economics,* **89,** 603–17.

**Peltzman, S.** (1973) The effect of government subsidies in kind on private expenditures: the case of higher education, *Journal of Political Economy,* **81,** 1–27.

**Perlman, R.** (1958) Forces widening occupational differentials, *Review of Economics and Statistics,* **40,** 107–115.

**Phelps Brown, H.** (1975) The contribution of human capital theory to the explanation of differences in earnings between occupations, in Lecaillon, J. (ed.), *Essais en l'Honneur de Jean Marchal,* Editions Cujas: Paris.

**Phelps Brown, H.** (1977) *The Inequality of Pay,* Oxford University Press: Oxford.

**Polachek, S.** (1975) Differences in expected post-school investment as a determinant of market wage differentials, *International Economic Review,* **16,** 451–70.

**Polachek, S.** (1981) Occupational self-selection: a human capital approach to sex differences in occupational structure, *Review of Economics and Statistics,* **63,** 60–9.

**Psacharopoulos, G.** (1972) Rates of return to investment in education around the world, *Comparative Education Review,* **16,** 54–67.

**Psacharopoulos, G.** (1977) Family background, education and achievement: a path model of earnings determinants in the UK, *British Journal of Sociology,* **28,** 321–35.

**Psacharopoulos, G. and Layard, P. R. G.** (1979) Human capital and earnings: British evidence and a critique, *Review of Economic Studies,* **46,** 485–503.

**Psacharopoulos, G. and Soumelis, C.** (1979) A quantitative analysis of the demand for higher education in Greece, *Higher Education,* **8,** 158–77.

**Raymond, R. and Sesnowitz, M.** (1975) The returns to investment in higher education: some new evidence, *Journal of Human Resources,* **10,** 139–54.

**Ribich, T. I. and Murphy, J. L.** (1975) The economic returns to increased educational spending, *Journal of Human Resources,* **10,** 56–77.

**Riley, J.** (1979) Testing the educational screening hypothesis, *Journal of Political Economy,*

87, 227–52.

**Rizzuto, R. and Wachtel, P.** (1980) Further evidence on the returns to school quality, *Journal of Human Resources,* 15, 240–54.

**Rosen, S. and Willis, R. J.** (1978) Education and self selection, presented to the UK/US Conference on Human Capital and Income Distribution, Cambridge, mimeo.

**Rottenberg, S.** (1961) The irrelevance of apprentice/journeyman ratios, *Journal of Business,* 34, 384–6.

**Ryan, P.** (1980) The costs of job training for a transferable skill, *British Journal of Industrial Relations,* 18, 334–52.

**Samuels, J. and Smythe, D.** (1968) Profits, variability of profits and firm size, *Economica,* 35, 127–39.

**Schiller, B. R. and Weiss, R. D.** (1980) Pensions and wages: a test for equalising differences, *Review of Economics and Statistics,* 62, 529–38.

**Schultz, T. W.** (1972) Optimal investment in college instruction: equity and efficiency, *Journal of Political Economy,* 80, S1–S23.

**Sewell, W. H. and Hauser, R. M.** (1975) *Education, Occupation and Earnings: Achievement in the Early Career,* Academic Press: New York.

**Siebert, W. S.** (1977) Occupational licensing: the Merrison report on the regulation of the medical profession, *British Journal of Industrial Relations,* 15, 29–38.

**Siebert, W. S. and Sloane, P. J.** (1981) Measuring sex and marital status discrimination at the workplace, *Economica,* 48, 125–41.

**Smith, Adam** (1776) *The Wealth of Nations,* reissued 1976, University of Chicago Press: Chicago.

**Spence, M.** (1973) Job market signalling, *Quarterly Journal of Economics,* 8, 355–74.

**Standing Conference of Regional Advisory Councils for Further Education** (1980) *Foundations for Working Life,* SCRAC: London.

**Stigler, G.** (1963) *Capital and Rates of Return in Manufacturing Industries,* NBER: New Jersey.

**Tannen, M. B.** (1978) The investment motive for attending college, *Industrial and Labor Relations Review,* 31, 489–97.

**Taubman, P.** (1975) *Sources of Inequality in Earnings,* North-Holland: Amsterdam.

**Taubman, P.** (1976a) Earnings, education, genetics and environment, *Journal of Human Resources,* 10, 447–61.

**Taubman, P.** (1976b) The determinants of earnings: genetics, family and other environments: a study of male twins, *American Economic Review,* 66, 858–70.

**Taubman, P.** (ed.) (1977) *Kinometrics,* North-Holland: Amsterdam.

**Taubman, P. and Wales, T.** (1974) *Education and Earnings: College as an Investment and Screening Device,* McGraw-Hill: New York.

**Thurow, L.** (1970) *Investment in Human Capital,* Wadsworth Publishing Co.: Belmont.

**Tobin, J.** (1981) Reagonomics and economics, *New York Review of Books,* 28(19), 11–14.

**Wallace, T. D. and Ihnen, L. A.** (1975) Full time schooling in life-cycle models of human capital accumulation, *Journal of Political Economy,* 83, 137–55.

**Weiss, Y.** (1972) The risk element in occupational and educational choices, *Journal of Political Economy,* 80, 1203–13.

**Welch, F.** (1970) Education in production, *Journal of Political Economy,* 78, 35–59.

**Welland, J. D.** (1980) Schooling and ability as earnings complements, *Canadian Journal of Economics,* 13, 356–67.

**White, W. D.** (1980) On-the-job screening and investments in general and specific training, *Southern Economic Journal,* 47, 14–19.

**Whittington, G.** (1971) *The Prediction of Profitability,* Cambridge University Press: London.

**Wilkinson, W.** (1966) Present values of lifetime earnings in different occupations, *Journal of Political Economy,* **74,** 556–72.

**Woodward, N. and Anderson, T.** (1975) A profitability appraisal of apprenticeships, *British Journal of Industrial Relations,* **13,** 245–56.

**Yamane, T.** (1968) *Mathematics for Economists,* Prentice Hall: Englewood Cliffs (2nd edn).

**Yule, G. U. and Kendall, M. G.** (1950) *An Introduction to the Theory of Statistics,* Griffin & Co.: London (14th edn).

**Ziderman, A.** (1973) Does it pay to take a degree?, *Oxford Economic Papers,* **25,** 262–74.

**Ziderman, A.** (1975) Costs and benefits of manpower re-training programmes in Great Britain, *British Journal of Industrial Relations,* **13,** 363–76.

# CHAPTER THREE

# Discrimination in the labour market

Peter J. Sloane

## Introduction

It was only with the growing public awareness of the extensiveness of discrimination against minority groups in the USA and the development of equality of opportunity policies there that economists began to approach the question in a systematic manner.[1] Gary Becker's *The Economics of Discrimination*, first published in 1957 and surely one of the most quoted doctoral dissertations ever published by an economist, proved to be a landmark.[2] Most subsequent studies concentrated initially on aspects of racial discrimination, but eventually sex discrimination and related issues of marital status were examined and a multitude of empirical studies, first in the USA and then elsewhere, attempting to estimate the degree of discrimination by industry, occupation or establishment began to appear in the journals.[3] This has occurred to such a degree that today it is probably true to say that there is little further to be gained by mere replication using new data sets. Rather what appears to be called for is a more precise definition of discrimination and clarification of hypotheses to be tested.

This survey focuses on race, sex and marital status, unlike an earlier survey by Marshall (1974) who considered only the first of these categories; though emphasising the neo-classical approach it makes some attempt to consider the contribution of radical theories;[4] and it also attempts to survey the empirical literature up to the present time. In order to keep the discussion within manageable proportions, the main focus is on aspects of behaviour within the labour market to the relative neglect of such important issues as pre-entry discrimination (education and occupational choice), household behaviour and female labour-force participation and the attempts of the courts to interpret the intentions of the policy-makers.

The survey begins by examining in general terms the characteristics of those groups against which discrimination is directed, and among which females and coloured workers are the most obvious example. Why is it that certain groups and not others are subject to discrimination and what it is that determines the degree of discrimination are relevant questions here, but ones to which there is no simple answer when viewed from an economic perspective. Here, too, the extent of group disadvantage both in terms of gross earnings inequalities and also of more specific measures of discrimination in net terms is summarised. For purposes of empirical investigation, an operational definition of discrimination is unequal treatment in terms and conditions of employment for groups of equally productive workers, and it is useful to keep this definition in mind considering the various estimates of discrimination referred to in the survey. However, it is clear that different perceptions of discrimination have guided various investigations of the phenomenon, and in section 3 a number of definitions are considered. Economists have developed utility-based models in which a taste for discrimination is an argument, but it is by no means certain that these are consistent with notions of inequity as reflected in the law. The question of precisely what constitutes discrimination and what does not is, therefore, not an empty one.

Equally important are the questions of who discriminates, how discrimination manifests itself in the labour market and why individuals or groups discriminate, which are considered among other things in section 4. The main agents here are employers, employees (and their representatives, the trade unions), consumers and the government. Employers may discriminate against workers because of their own discriminatory attitude, or simply because workers and consumers discriminate and not to do so may increase the costs of production or reduce sales. Alternatively, lack of information concerning the productivity of potential employees or erroneous stereotypes concerning them on the part of employers may act to the detriment of members of minority groups. Governments may possibly discriminate in favour of or against particular groups or prevent others from doing so according to ethical views or voting power. In particular, governments play a key role, via the educational process, in determining the endowments of human capital with which particular groups of workers enter the labour market and which, ultimately, will determine their position in the labour market with respect to occupation and pay. This will also be determined in part by the structure of the labour market itself, for members of minority groups may be crowded into certain low-paying occupations and excluded from high-paying primary jobs and internal labour markets. In turn, this may have consequences for the propensity to be unemployed and the process of job search.

A key question is who benefits in financial terms from discrimination or indeed whether all groups lose in absolute, as opposed to relative terms. The answer to this question differs according to whether a neo-classical or radical stance is taken and according to the assumptions made, emphasising the importance of testing the predictions of the various models. Some of the problems involved in attempting to estimate the precise extent of discrimination are discussed in section 5, which examines the results of various studies on a disaggregated basis, including measured rates of return to education, on-the-job training and experience for the various groups. For married women in particular, it is necessary here to take into account the effect on earnings of marriage and discontinuous labour-market experience. This section also attempts to assess the impact of trade unions and governments. Finally, section 6 examines various policy issues, such as whether equality of opportunity polices have had a real impact on the welfare of minority groups or whether alternative approaches, such as maintaining high levels of aggregate demand or offering subsidies to encourage the employment of minority group members, have more to offer.

## 2 The facts of labour-market disadvantage

Before a group can be subjected to discrimination in any systematic manner it must be clearly identifiable.[5] As Sowell (1975vi) suggests, races or ethnic groups 'are generally regarded, and regard themselves, as a socially distinct group with inherent characteristics that set them apart and cause them to encounter different attitudes and behaviour than those encountered by the general population'. Relevant characteristics might include sex, marital status, age, colour, language, religion, education, class, culture or, as in the case of the Irish, the mere fact that the group is large enough to be seen as distinct by the indigenous population and can be identified (e.g. by accent). Particularly where the real reason for exclusion from employment is the maintenance of real incomes through the exercise of monopoly power, it does not matter which group faces restrictions on entry provided only that there is a substantial impact on total supply, though personal prejudice may be utilised to rationalise the restriction. Where individuals possess several of the above attributes then severe problems may be encountered in obtaining a job. This will be particularly true of immigrants who lack knowledge of the operation of the labour market and who may also have language difficulties.

However, it is usually difficult from the empirical point of view to ascertain whether the inferior position of the immigrant is a consequence of discrimination or the possession of less productive attributes (see Mayhew and Rosewell 1978). It seems reasonable to suppose that these effects should become less important over time with respect to date of immigration. One study by Higgs (1971) found that in 1909 there was a positive association between the earnings of thirty-five immigrant groups in the USA and the percentage able to speak English and the percentage who were literate, these two variables together explaining almost four-fifths of the variance in average earnings among the groups. Further, the simple correlation between the proportion speaking English and the proportion having resided in the US 5 years or more was 0.94. The finding that these factors were also operative within each racial group (e.g. northern and southern Italians) tends to suggest that employer discrimination was not itself a major factor. More support has been found for the more recent period in North America by Chiswick (1978, 1979). For the UK, Chiswick (1980) has found in contrast that number of years since date of migration has no additional explanatory power in a regression model including variables for education, labour-market experience, weeks worked, marital status, location, colour and whether foreign born. This he attributes to the fact that a large proportion of immigrants have come from English-speaking or Commonwealth countries, perhaps reinforcing rather than refuting the proposition above. It has further been suggested (Williams 1978) that class is now more important than race in determining the relative labour-market position of blacks, because it is the more privileged blacks who have been assisted by affirmative action legislation, under which federal contractors are required to set goals and timetables for minority employment in job categories where minorities have previously been under-represented. Indeed, it appears that the black – white differential in the USA accounts for less than 3 per cent of the total variance in earnings (in logarithmic form), and that within racial groups earnings differences are greater for blacks than for whites (Smith and Welch 1979).[6]

The above points to the need to treat minority groups as heterogeneous rather than homogeneous entities. Yet this is rare in the literature. One notable exception is a paper by Gwartney and Long (1978) which analyses the relative earnings position of eight minority groups in the USA (Japanese, Chinese, Mexicans, Filipinos, Puerto Ricans, Cubans, American Indians and Negros). Dummy variables were added to a human capital model, in which earnings were held to be determined by the number of years of education, to indicate whether main language was non-English, whether foreign born and whether parents were foreign born. The regression analysis results for these variables were, however, mixed. The ratio of minority to white earnings ranged from 63.1 to 98.8 per cent in the case of men, and from 72.7 to 108 per cent in the case of women in 1969, with Japanese and Chinese faring better in the labour market, and Mexicans worse, than other minorities. Further, while for all male groups the minority/white earnings ratio increased in the 1960s, the size and source of the improvement varied considerably among groups. The authors conclude, therefore, that policies designed to improve the position of minority groups need to be related to the specific circumstances of each group.

Whether economic models are equally applicable to race and sex is even more in doubt, though following Becker many economists have assumed that theories developed specifically with race in mind are equally applicable to the case of sex. Indeed, as Koch and Chizmar (1976: 27) note:

> economic theories of sex discrimination are in fact hybrid offshoots of theories of racial discrimination. There has been very little theorising with respect to the economics of sex discrimination per se. Rather, theories of sex discrimination typically fit into the mold of racial discrimination models in which whites discriminate against blacks. Sex discrimination models amend this to deal with the case where men discriminate against women. This adaptation . . . is not always appropriate.

First, as both Marshall (1974) and Thurow (1976) note, it is very doubtful whether physical distance or social distance models (discussed in section 3) are applicable to sex discrimination. Second, as Madden (1973) points out, family status and decision-making roles must play a central role in the analysis of sex discrimination, but are barely relevant to discrimination against other groups. This is most clearly demonstrated in relation to Becker's international trade model (discussed in section 4) where the theory is developed on the assumption that male and female societies are independent of each other, oblivious of the fact that the majority of either sex become married to members of the other.[7] Third, genetic differences between the races are much smaller than between the sexes (Boulding 1976). Fourth, while most studies on achievement-related motivation find very similar patterns among blacks and whites, women and men do appear to be different, with the former being motivated relatively more by a desire for good interpersonal relations and working conditions, and the latter by opportunities for upward mobility and independence. Using psychological measures, differences in each of these aspects of motivation have rarely exceeded 10 per cent (Gurin 1977). Fifth, when we come to explain differences in earnings differentials by race and sex there are a

TABLE 3.1    Fractions of the wage gap between white men and other groups of workers in the USA explained by various factors

(All working households heads and wives, aged 18–64)

| | Black men % | White women % | Black women % |
|---|---|---|---|
| Formal education | 38 | 2 | 11 |
| Years of training completed on the current job | 15 | 11 | 8 |
| Other work history | 3 | 28 | 14 |
| Indicators of labour-force attachment† | −3 | 3 | −1 |
| Unexplained | 47 | 56 | 68 |
| Total | 100 | 100 | 100 |

†Time lost because of own illness or due to illness of others and restriction placed on job locations and work hours.
Source: Corcoran and Duncan (1979).

number of important differences. As Strauss and Horvath (1976) and Wolff (1976) note, several studies have confirmed the fact that within-occupation earnings inequality is more important in explaining sex earnings differentials than differences in occupational distribution, while the reverse is the case for racial differentials. Also as Table 3.1 indicates, differences in length of formal education appear to be more important in explaining the racial differential, and differences in work history more important in explaining the sex differentials. Similar differences have been found even within sectors. Thus, Long (1976) finds with respect to federal employment in the USA that for women the main problem has been to gain entry into any federal jobs, but for black males the main problem has been to achieve promotion to higher-paying jobs once entry has been made.[8] Finally, it needs to be determined whether sex and race discrimination are substitutes or complements. One attempt to test this by Haessel and Palmer (1978) suggests the latter to be the case. In other words, firms that discriminate in employment tend to do so on the basis of both race and sex. It is also worth noting that Grant and Hamermesh (1981) have produced estimates of white female/youth substitutability which imply strongly that the growth in white female labour-force participation has harmed the earnings prospects of young workers, suggesting that these two groups are substitutes in the labour market and that gains achieved by one group may be at the expense of another.

In order to isolate sex discrimination it is first necessary to estimate those differences in earnings which are more properly a function of family responsibilities. In particular, married women face the prospect of discontinuous work experience and constraints on their job mobility as discussed in section 5. Considerable problems arise in making adequate allowance for this where data sets do not contain information on actual work experience, and reliance has to be placed

TABLE 3.2   Interpretation of the unexplained earnings differential by sex-marital
status group

| Comparator groups | Interpretation |
|---|---|
| 1. Single women/married women | Family role of wife minus marital status discrimination |
| 2. Married men/single women | Family role of husband minus discrimination |
| 3. Married men/single men | Family role of husband plus discrimination |
| 4. Single men/single women | Discrimination |

on a proxy variable such as potential work experience, which is derived by deducting from the age of an individual employee his or her years of education and preschool years. This is likely to exaggerate the labour-force experience of married women in particular, from whom much of the remaining time may be spent on household activities. When results using the different measures (actual and potential work experience) are compared, it appears that the potential experience measure can seriously underestimate the effect of lower experience in diminishing female earnings relative to male (Jones and Long 1979b).

Particularly for this reason it would appear that the most suitable comparison to make for purposes of identifying discrimination is that between single men and women (Greenhalgh 1980; and Siebert and Sloane 1981), since attitudes to work and career orientation are closest in this case.[9] However, as Greenhalgh points out, marriage and career are complementary for men but may be competitive for women, so that women who work may on average be very able and highly motivated towards their work. Another caveat, pointed out by Long (1976), is that high female/male earnings ratios may simply reflect the youth of single workers. As noted below, the earnings gap is likely to widen with age, especially where women are channelled into jobs with limited prospects for advancement. For these reasons it might be better to accept this comparison as giving a lower-bound estimate of discrimination.

Out of the six possible comparisons among the sex/marital status groups it would appear that four are potentially useful for analysis of discrimination as illustrated in Table 3.2. In this table it is assumed that discrimination is always in favour of men and particularly of married men, though there may well be circumstances where discrimination goes in the opposite direction. Generally, it has been found that sex differences are least when single men and single women are compared. Indeed, in some studies comparable or even greater differences have been found to exist between the earnings functions of married and single men than between single men and women (e.g. Siebert and Young's study of librarians 1983).

To summarise, in order to isolate discrimination a considerable amount of disaggregation is necessary. It is essential to distinguish groups not only according to sex but also marital status, and in the case of race according to country or area of origin and native language, if we are to comprehend fully the forces at work.

Before discussing in detail precise definitions of discrimination some preliminary points on the magnitude of the problem are in order. Regardless of political or economic systems there is abundant evidence of differentiation or inequalities among groups in the labour market. Thus, Moroney (1979) points out that average earnings for women are well below those of men in virtually every country where statistics on wages classified by sex are available (though this is not necessarily evidence of discrimination). In the predominantly English-speaking countries such as the USA, UK, Canada and Australia, women have tended to earn on average less than 60 per cent of male average earnings, while in such diverse countries as Czechoslovakia, Finland, France, Hungary, Israel, Norway and Poland the figure lies between 65 and 70 per cent. Further, fragmentary evidence suggests that the picture is not vastly different in the Soviet Union, China and Cuba, casting at least some doubt on the radical economists' view that discrimination is a function of the capitalist system.

Corresponding data by race are much harder to come by at the international level, but detailed statistics are available in the USA, which also has relatively long-standing equal opportunities legislation. Many studies, such as those of Freeman (1973a and b), Welch (1973) and Smith and Welch (1979) report a substantial narrowing of the black–white wage differential over recent years, which has been most pronounced among young workers. Thus, James P. Smith in Lloyd *et al* (1979) shows that the median wage income ratio rose from 0.54 in 1947 to 0.73 in 1975 for black males relative to white males, and from 0.34 to 0.97 for black females relative to white females. He notes that: 'the increase has been so persistent and continous that it dominates all business cycle movements and time-series changes in the standard set of characteristics typically included in wage functions'. (p. 175) Yet it would be premature to conclude that this outcome points to the effectiveness of equality of opportunity or affirmative action programmes. Over the 1960s for instance, Haworth *et al.* (1975) find that roughly one-half of this improvement in the relative position of black workers is due to the departure from the labour force of older black workers with relatively low earnings, together with the entry into the labour force of younger and better educated black workers with relatively high earnings. Also, as Reich (1980) points out, the differential advantage in favour of white workers with respect to rates of unemployment and labour-force participation has widened since the 1950s, and more recent data may show that some of the gains referred to above have been eroded. The very marked improvement in the relative position of black women must also be considered in the light of the continuing decline since 1940 in the earnings of all females relative to those of males, despite the introduction of equal opportunities legislation for women. Finally, it may be necessary to focus on lifetime earnings rather than current earnings. As Lazear (1979a) notes, employers may have reacted to the inability to discriminate in the form of wages by offering black workers fewer opportunities for on-the-job training. This would reflect itself in the form of an upward adjustment in the recorded earnings of young black workers (more of whom no longer sacrifice current earnings in order to undertake training). Hence lifetime earnings opportunities for black workers may actually be worsening despite the improvement in their short-term position. This shows one must be cautious in using aggregate earnings to draw inferences with respect to discrimination in the labour market.

Discrimination may not be accurately reflected in variations in gross earnings differentials and it is useful to summarise here the results of various studies estimating discrimination by multiple regression techniques, explained more fully in section 5. These attempt to control for differences in personal characteristics among the various groups (such as endowments of education, training and experience), so that discrimination is measured as the 'unexplained' residual. Since the assumption is made that characteristics should be equally rewarded among the various groups, this is equivalent to saying that discrimination occurs where equally productive workers receive different levels of pay. Caution is required, however, in interpreting these estimates of discrimination. As more and more differences in the nature of work are controlled for, the unexplained wage differential will become smaller. Since difference studies include independent variables which differ in number and form, estimates of discrimination will also vary for this reason. Similarly, we might expect the measured extent of discrimination to decline as the degree of disaggregation increases, being lowest of all at the level of the individual establishment. Rosenbaum (1980) finds, for instance, in his study of sex discrimination in an individual firm in the USA, that he is able to explain 65 per cent of the variance in earnings (far from atypical at this level), while macro-level analyses tend to explain 20–40 per cent. He suggests that the defects of the macro studies may arise from inadequate controls (i.e. omitted variables) rather than from defects in the empirical model as such. Earlier it was argued that in order to estimate sex discrimination the most appropriate comparison to make was that between single men and single women. Using the British Household Survey, Greenhalgh (1980: 771) finds that

> in 1975 discrimination of the order of 10% was operating between adult single persons and the same figure was obtained for younger persons. The unexplained differential between single and married women is quite large (12%), so that the total labour market disadvantage of married women vis-a-vis single men was about twice that of single women. Married men obtained a 10% differential over single men. Thus the overall variation in earnings between husbands and wives with similar characteristics can be expressed as a multiple of three roughly equal ratios; married to single men; single men to single women; single women to married women; each ratio being close to 1.1.

These results appear to be comparable with those found by other investigators, such as Siebert and Sloane (1981) and Siebert and Young (1983) in Britain, Malkiel and Malkiel (1973), Gunderson (1975), Ferber et al. (1978), Robb (1978), and Osterman (1979) in North America, among others; and thus they can be regarded as reasonably representative.

The substantial differences observed between married and single men suggest that marital status (whether ever married and with dependent children) should also be held constant when estimating racial discrimination, but this is not always the case. Studies in the USA using conventional standardisation procedures estimate that race discrimination leads to black workers receiving between 13 per cent (Smith 1980) and approximately 20 per cent (Hansen *et al.* 1970; Griliches and Mason 1972) less than equivalent white workers, while Haworth *et al.* (1975) noted an improvement in the relative position of blacks between 1959 and 1969 (19.5 to 17%). For the UK, McNabb and Psacharopoulos (1981a) found that coloured workers earned 20 per cent less than white, and Chiswick (1980) that immigrants earned 25 per cent less than native-born men, *cet. par.* The latter study uses a dummy variable for colour in the regression, while the former suggests that there are important differences between the races, so that separate regressions should be run for the two groups. This fact and the very small sample size suggests that we should be cautious before drawing the obvious conclusion that race differences will narrow somewhat as a higher proportion of the coloured population is native born.

# 3. What is discrimination?

When we examine the gross annual earnings differential between two groups of workers − majority and minority − it is possible in theory to distinguish between those differences which are a consequence of:

(a) differing attitudes, some of which will be acquired prior to entry into the labour market;
(b) differences in occupational level given attributes, often referred to as occupational discrimination;
(c) differences in pay given occupations, referred to as income or wage discrimination;
(d) differences in participation in the labour force in terms of time in employment over the year. This will be a function of hours of work and time spent unemployed or out of the labour market and is referred to as participation discrimination by Tsuchigane and Dodge (1974).

To assume that all these differences are 'discriminatory' makes no allowance for the fact that tastes may differ between the two groups (e.g. women may prefer fewer hours and less demanding jobs on average than do men). Further there may be constraints on the minority workforce which apply less strongly to members of the majority. For instance, married women's potential labour mobility is restricted by family commitments, making them more susceptible to monopsonistic labour markets, which may drive down their wages.

One approach is to assume that all differences are in the long run discriminatory. Thus Tsuchigane and Dodge (1974: 5) begin their analysis of sex discrimination on the assumption that:

> men and women are equal in their capabilities in almost every respect, provided that women are given the same opportunities for training, employment

and promotion as men. It is also assumed that if men should come to accept responsibility for raising the young, caring for the sick or elderly, and looking after the home, the participation of women in the labour force would be essentially equal to that of men.

Similarly some would include in their definition of discrimination the effects of social and cultural conditioning which lead members of the minority group to seek employment only in careers that are traditional to that minority (Zincone and Close 1978). However, if the focus is upon discrimination in the labour market, it seems preferable to take as given distinctions which might otherwise be regarded as discriminatory, such as differential access to education.[10] For one thing, it is often difficult to differentiate social conditioning from individual preferences, and for another the cause of the difference is immaterial to the employer who is concerned to maximise his profits. This approach places discrimination clearly on the demand side of the labour market – it represents a preference by the purchaser of labour for one group over another, holding constant the productivity of the two groups and the price at which they are prepared to work. Thus, monopsonistic exploitation, which leads some workers to be paid less than others because of differences in supply elasticities, is not discrimination according to this perspective. This too is essentially the approach of the human capital school, which sees the groups as investing in disparate quantities of human capital with the expectation that outcomes will be inherently different, because men and women or black and white workers have different biologically determined family roles or social and cultural traditions.

In a sense all pricing is discriminatory because it reflects the preferences of the purchaser (Mermelstein 1970). Further, in the labour market with its various imperfections it must be recognised that inequalities of remuneration exist even within well-defined majority or minority occupational groups, so that it is not always clear where the most appropriate comparison is to be made. Meanings of discrimination extend then from the making of innocent distinctions to depriving people of benefits because irrelevant criteria are used (Sowell 1975), but it is clear that discrimination as a term of opprobrium must include some notion of prejudice, inequity or the use of irrelevant criteria in the treatment of particular individuals or groups in the labour market. Lloyd and Niemi (1979) counsel, however, against treating 'prejudice' and 'discrimination' as synonymous terms since either may be present in the absence of the other. The former may be regarded as representing a desire to discriminate, or intent, which in practice may be unfulfilled, while the latter may be regarded as an outcome, which could occur without a conscious desire to treat one group more unfavourably than another. Notions of equity are found in the distinctions made by Tsuchigane and Dodge (1974) between justified and unjustified discrimination. Thus, while pure market discrimination is never justified, discrimination on the grounds of physiological or psychological differences in capabilities can be held to be always justified. They also allow that discrimination based on the fact that social and cultural conditioning adversely affects the development of capabilities among the minority groups can be justified temporarily. Erroneous discrimination could itself be a function of some prejudice which causes an individual to believe that a minority group is in fact more inferior with respect to a particular characteristic than is actually the case. Disconfirming experience should, however, in this case remove the discrimination.[11]

The neo-classical theory, developed by Becker, is based upon the notion of personal prejudice or aversion. Thus it is assumed that an employer is prepared to pay a premium (or sacrifice profits) in order to avoid associating with members of minority groups at the work-place. Similarly, discriminatory employees will be prepared to accept a lower wage to avoid employment with such minorities, or perhaps more realistically demand a higher wage where workforces are racially or sexually mixed than where they are segregated. This notion is not without its critics.

Some authors have taken issue with the idea that discrimination is related to physical distance or the frequence of contact between members of majority and minority groups at the place of work, which is far from clearly explained in Becker's original formulation. Is physical distance a function of employment in a particular establishment or in a particular occupation, or does this itself depend upon the particular minority group against which discrimination is directed? For instance, it might be postulated that racial discrimination is more establishment-based and sex discrimination occupationally based. Shepherd and Levin (1973) and Medoff (1980a) have suggested that it is more appropriate to test physical distance models by concentrating on white-collar patterns as far as employer discrimination is concerned, since it is this group that is in closest contact with management, and it is hard to see why managements should be concerned over the employment of minorities in blue-collar occupations with which they share relatively little contact (other than as a response to employee segregation). A similar argument can be put forward in relation to firm size. Since small establishments are likely to have fewer production processes, we would expect relationships between managers and employees to be closer than in large establishments with their relatively impersonal relationships, so that larger establishments should discriminate less than small on this basis. However, if workers are the chief source of discrimination this may not follow. Again, it should follow that capital-intensive methods of production which involve a low level of personal interaction (Franklin and Tanzer 1968) will give rise to low levels of discrimination relative to labour-intensive production processes. Further, if physical proximity is important we would expect market discrimination to be greatest against the most highly educated members of minority groups.

An alternative approach would be to assume that discriminators, rather than being adversely disposed to members of the minority group, are merely favourably disposed to members of their own group. As Toikka (1976) has demonstrated, this is a non-trivial issue, as a taste for favouritism model has very different welfare implications than a taste for discrimination one.[12] Thurow (1976) argues that a desire for social distance rather than physical distance is the source of discrimination (though it should be pointed out that Becker himself refers to the former as well as the latter). That is, the discriminator insists on specifying the relationship under which contact at the work-place is made. In the case of sex, for instance, he suggests that physical distance makes no sense at all, for the implication is than men are discriminating against other men's or even their own wives. Alexis (1973) has developed a model in which employer discrimination is a function of envy or malice rather than aversion, but as Dex (1979) notes, no explanation is given as to why discriminators should wish to exhibit envy or malice.[13] As Marshall (1974) states, status seems to be a more plausible explanation than envy or malice in explaining discrimination. Once one recognises, however, the possibility that discriminators may well gain from the act of discrimination, the need to base its existence on envy or malice disappears. This will be the case when lack of competition enables one group to collude and exert its power over the minority group in order to raise the income of its members. As Siebert and Addison (1977) note, the concept of a taste for discrimination is then redundant.

As noted earlier, for operational purposes discrimination may be defined most simply as the receipt of lower pay for given productivity (Aigner and Cain 1977; Siebert and Sloane 1981), but this obscures the fact that equally productive workers may receive different levels of pay because of differences in supply conditions (e.g. monopsony), which have nothing to do with the prejudices of the employer other than a desire to maximise profits. It also necessarily ignores the circumstances under which different levels of attributes or performance were determined. A further step is to define discrimination as any form of unequal treatment between groups which does not directly result in cost minimisation in relation to labour utilisation, or with respect to employee discrimination which does not directly result in the maximisation of the total wage bill (Chiplin and Sloane 1976a). A problem here is to unravel prejudice from pecuniary advantage where discriminators gain from the weakened market power of the minority group. Even this definition may not be consistent with equitable outcomes as it leaves open the possibility of 'statistical discrimination'. This may be defined as a situation in which potential employees are screened on the basis of the characteristics of the group of which they are a member. This is most clearly seen in relation to the employment of the sexes. Let us suppose, for example, that employers prefer men to women on account of the lower absenteeism or higher productivity of the former as a group, but *a priori* it is not possible to assess the potential absenteeism of any one member of either group. Then an individual woman with a high potential attendance rate or level of performance may be excluded from employment on grounds which are quite rational in terms of cost minimisation, but are inequitable in terms of her own potential performance. Any attempt to make such behaviour by the employer unlawful would, however, be inefficient from the point of view of maximising potential output (Stiglitz 1973).

There are a number of difficulties attached to the concept of discrimination. First, there is an apparent lack of agreement on the most appropriate definition of discrimination, though in general it is assumed that discrimination manifests itself on the demand side of the market. Second, it is estimated as a residual, after accounting for all other known relevant variables causing income differences. That is, discrimination is inferred rather than observed directly. For these reasons the simplest approach is to define labour-market discrimination as lower pay for given productivity, regardless of the difficulties alluded to in the preceding paragraph and noting the attempts to measure pre-entry discrimination referred to in section 4. This has the advantage, too, of being reasonably consistent with legal interpretations of discrimination under British and North American equal opportunities laws.

## 4. Forms of discrimination and related aspects of labour-market differentiation

### PRE-ENTRY VERSUS POST-ENTRY DISCRIMINATION

Differences may arise before a worker has entered the workforce, because of factors such as differential educational opportunities (pre-entry discrimination), or because of post-entry discrimination resulting from factors acting within the labour market, which is the main focus of this survey. It is in order to say something about pre-entry discrimination, however, before proceeding.

Individual incomes will in part be determined by the amount of education received prior to entry into the labour market. In the USA, for example, white men average 13 years' education compared to 11 years for black men (Corcoran and Duncan 1979), and the educational profile of women is quite different from that of men. Similar differences apply in the UK and elsewhere. It is important then to determine those factors which explain differential access to education by racial and sex group. However, if members of minority groups anticipate entry barriers to certain jobs or discrimination in pay, then they may rationally choose to invest less in education for this reason and educational differences are not a consequence of pre-entry discrimination, but should themselves be included in any estimate of market discrimination. If, on the other hand, differences in educational attainment are the result of innate differences in preferences or of biological or cultural differences, it would overstate the amount of market discrimination if such differences in educational attainment among groups were included. King and Knapp (1978) attempt to explain racial differences in educational attainment by means of the following sequential three-equation model

$$
\begin{aligned}
ED &= F_1(SES) & \text{[a] [1]} \\
PSI &= F_2(SES, ED) & \text{[b]} \\
LE &= F_3(SES, ED, PSI) & \text{[c]}
\end{aligned}
$$

where   $ED$  = final educational attainment;
        $SES$ = socio-economic background;
        $PSI$ = discounted stock of post-school human investments;
        $LE$ = discounted lifetime earnings.

Since blacks on average come from lower socio-economic backgrounds than whites (as well as having parents of lower educational attainment and being members of families of above average size), this is an important factor contributing to their lower lifetime earnings. That is, lifetime earnings are influenced by the $SES$ that determines the levels of education and post-school investment for each racial group. By substituting black socio-economic background factors into the white equations, King and Knapp estimate that between 64 and 75 per cent of inter-racial differences in lifetime earnings are a consequence of this factor. Further, Shaffer and Wilson (1980) report some results which suggest that blacks tend to invest less in education due to expectations of direct discrimination in hiring (though they can find no similar pattern in the case of women). If one examined only the race coefficient in their structural equation results one *could* underestimate the effect of discrimination on occupational level by as much as 30 per cent. This negative feedback mechanism or indirect discrimination is related to preference formation and not only to the economic consequences of fixed preferences as in Becker's model. As Franklin and Tanzer (1968) point out, another implication is that the motivation to work productively will itself be diminished by discrimination, making it difficult to isolate pure discrimination from that based on productivity differentials.

It is still likely, however, that tastes and biological or cultural factors differ among the various racial and sex groups. Relevant to this, Allison and Allen (1978) developed a model of occupational choice in which the number of entrants into professional jobs is a function of absolute salary levels and salaries in alternative occupations, and salaries in turn are a function of supply and demand. Since this model is only able to explain 25 per cent of the variance in entrants for either sex, it appears that a purely economic theory of occupational choice possesses limited explanatory power. However, the salary elasticities for new entrants are roughly equal for both sexes, implying that women are just as economically motivated as men. How then do we explain the propensity of women to join the lower-paying professions? The two possibilities offered by Allison and Allen are that women are steered into certain occupations through career counselling or they are excluded from certain jobs by discriminatory hiring practices. Yet is it just as plausible to suppose that tastes for certain occupations and abilities differ between the sexes and concentration of women's job choice on relatively few occupations depresses salaries there. Further light is cast on this by Polachek's study of sex differences in choice of degree subjects (1978). It is postulated that choice of degree subject is a function of abilities, intended labour-force participation and sex. Thus the following model is estimated

$$M = F(X_1, X_2, S) \qquad [2]$$

where
$M$ = a vector of dummy variables representing choice of degree subjects;

$X_1$ = a vector of ability variables including various forms of aptitude test and parents' level of education;

$X_2$ = a vector of proxies representing expected life-cycle labour-force participation, including marriage and number of children intentions at time of college entry and time out of the labour force since leaving school;

$S$ = sex dummy variable.

Thus once factors such as $X_1$ and $X_2$ have been accounted for, any remaining sex effect could be attributable to discrimination by colleges, future market discrimination or sex differences in tastes. In fact in each major field apart from social sciences and the fine arts, the sex variable was significant, consistent with discrimination or differences in tastes, though sex differences were somewhat less in the early 1970s compared with the 1950s. Finally, it has been suggested that the narrowing earnings differential between college-educated black and white males might partly be a consequence of an increasing tendency for blacks to graduate in predominantly white institutions. However, Burnim (1980) has found no evidence for this 'white-college hypothesis'.

The above studies point to the fact that we cannot rule out the possibility of indirect discrimination and feedback effects influencing the relative position of minority groups in the labour market, though it is uncertain how much allowance should be made for this.

## EMPLOYER DISCRIMINATION

Discrimination by the employer has received more attention in the literature than any other form, though there is no clear evidence that it is the most important manifestation of discrimination in terms of extent and effect. Broadly speaking, Becker's analysis can be split into macroeconomic and microeconomic approaches. The former is intended to be a straightforward application of international trade theory. Let us suppose that we have two societies, one white (or male) and one black (or female). The white society is assumed to be capital abundant and the black society to be labour abundant. This is most easily illustrated by means of an Edgeworth–Bowley box diagram as in Figure 3.1, which represents the isoquant maps of the two societies. It is assumed that white capitalists restrict the export of

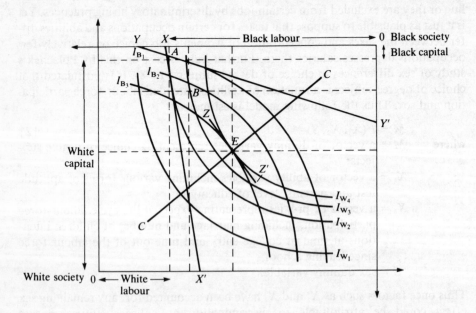

FIG. 3.1   Edgeworth–Bowley box model of discrimination

capital to the black sector so that we start from a position of zero (or restricted) trade at $A$, where the one product is produced by relatively capital-intensive methods in the white society and relatively labour-intensive methods in the black society. The price lines $XX'$ and $YY'$ show that capital is relatively expensive in the black society and labour relatively expensive in the white society. Free trade in factors of production between the two societies would lead to a position on the contract curve $CC$, which joins all points of tangency between the isoquants of the two societies, thereby maximising their joint output. If the white society were to allow the free export of capital, the price of capital would fall in the black society (and rise in the white society) until factor prices became equalised, as shown by the price line $ZZ'$, with higher wages in the black society and lower wages in the white society.

It is only on the contract curve that marginal technical rates of substitution between the inputs are equal. Other points such as $A$ or $B$ represent a misallocation of factor inputs, and this is precisely what will happen if say the white society discriminates against the black by refusing to 'export' its abundant factor, capital. $A$ or $B$ represent a lower output of goods for the white society than does $E$ which is on the contract curve. Thus, Becker argues, the discriminator, as well as the society subject to the discrimination, pays a penalty for discrimination in terms of reduced output, though white (male) labour and black (female) capitalists gain.[14] This last point in fact seems to emphasise the importance of employee rather than employer discrimination, since it is in the interests of white workers to force white capitalists to restrict the export of capital to the black society. The move from $A$ to $E$ also implies that white capitalists would have to employ some black labour if full employment of white workers existed at $A$. As Madden (1973) and Koch and Chizmar (1976) note, there are eight explicit or implicit assumptions in the Becker model:

1. The white (male) and black (female) societies are independent.
2. There are only two factor inputs, capital and labour.
3. The two societies trade capital and labour, but not the single output.
4. There are constant returns to scale with given technology.
5. The white (male) society is capital abundant and the black (female) society labour abundant.
6. The factor supply curves of the two societies are perfectly inelastic with respect to factor prices.
7. The white (male) society has a taste for output and discrimination, while the black (female) society has a taste only for output.
8. There is perfect factor mobility between the two societies.

The appropriateness of some of these assumptions in the context of discrimination has been challenged. For instance, is the assumption of independent societies compatible with a situation in which most blacks work for white employers, and in which it is often difficult to determine the race of the owners of capital? It is even less appropriate in the context of sex discrimination, as mentioned earlier, where the independent status of the sexes is altered through marriage. Also, it has been argued that the discriminator might well gain financially. As Krueger (1963) and

Thurow (1969) point out, optimal tariff theory suggests that it is possible for a discriminator to increase his income even where there is retaliation, so that the elimination of discrimination might raise the combined output of the two societies, but lower it for the discriminatory society. As Thurow (1976: 159) puts it in relation to the USA:

> In most cases whites will gain from practising discrimination. Discrimination is being practised in a country where whites predominate numerically and are possessed of much larger stocks of both physical and human capital on a per capita basis. Given these circumstances, blacks have no option but to trade with (i.e. work in and borrow from) the white community. Of necessity blacks offer a relatively elastic supply curve.

The implication here is not simply that the parties under conditions of discrimination operate off the contract curve in the Edgeworth–Bowley box diagram, but that the stronger party forces the other on to a lower isoquant (level of production) than would occur in the absence of discrimination. This requires that the majority acts collectively as a monopolist or cartel, perhaps through the exclusion of blacks from professional licensing bodies and trade unions. In any event, as Toikka (1976) demonstrates, Becker's argument is essentially circular as discriminators are assumed to be worse off simply because they have a taste for discrimination as opposed to a taste for favouritism. He shows that a taste for favouritism towards white (male) labour by white (male) capitalists leads to the identical equilibrium as a taste for discrimination against black (female) labour, but has very different welfare implications. In fact there is no clear prediction as to the effects on the income of the discriminator. All that can be said is that those groups subjected to discrimination will lose.

The Becker micro model assumes that an individual employer forfeits profits by refusing to recruit members of the minority group, even under competitive conditions and where the marginal value product is in excess of the marginal cost of hiring an additional unit of that labour. The extent to which this happens, or the market discrimination coefficient ($d$), is measured by

$$d = \frac{W_{MAJ} - W_{MIN}}{W_{MIN}} \qquad [3]$$

where $W_{MAJ}$ is the equilibrium wage rate for members of the majority group and $W_{MIN}$ that for the minority group.

Let us assume that:

1. All firms possess identical utility and production functions.
2. Members of the majority and minority groups are perfect substitutes in the production of a single commodity.
3. Supplies of majority and minority labour are perfectly inelastic.
4. We are in a short-run situation in which capital is given to the firm, so that output is a function of employment, i.e. $f(MAJ + MIN)$ where $f$ is strictly concave and increasing.

5. Employers are assumed to maximise a utility function $U(\pi, MAJ, MIN)$, where $U_{MAJ} > 0$ and $U_{MIN} < 0$. That is, employers derive positive utility from profits and the employment of workers of the majority group, and negative utility from the employment of members of the minority group.

Then following Arrow (1972, 1973), profits for the firm are given by

$$f(MAJ + MIN) - W_{MAJ}MAJ - W_{MIN}MIN \qquad [4]$$

where $W_{MAJ}$ and $W_{MIN}$ are the wage rates for members of the majority and minority groups respectively.

Substitution into the utility function yields

$$U = U\{(f(MAJ + MIN) - W_{MAJ}MAJ - W_{MIN}MIN), MAJ, MIN\}. \qquad [5]$$

Maximisation with respect to $MAJ$ and $MIN$ respectively gives

$$U_\pi(f' - W_{MAJ}) + U_{MAJ} = 0 \qquad [6]$$

and

$$U_\pi(f' - W_{MIN}) + U_{MIN} = 0. \qquad [7]$$

Hence

$$U_\pi(f' - W_{MAJ}) + U_{MAJ} = U_\pi(f' - W_{MIN}) + U_{MIN} \qquad [8]$$

and

$$f' = W_{MAJ} - \frac{U_{MAJ}}{U_\pi} = W_{MIN} - \frac{U_{MIN}}{U_\pi}. \qquad [9]$$

Letting $-U_{MAJ}/U_\pi = d_{MAJ}$ and $-U_{MIN}/U_\pi = d_{MIN}$, where $d_{MAJ}$ and $d_{MIN}$ are Becker's discrimination coefficients for members of the majority and minority groups respectively,

$$f' = W_{MAJ} + d_{MAJ} = W_{MIN} + d_{MIN}. \qquad [10]$$

Under the assumption of discrimination against the minority group

$$d_{MIN} > 0, \qquad d_{MAJ} < 0.$$

Hence

$$W_{MAJ} > f' > w_{MIN}. \qquad [11]$$

Though in this model wage rates are given to the firm, it treats the price of minority labour as the minority wage rate plus the discrimination coefficient ($d$). In other words, the demand curve for minority labour must lie to the left of that for majority labour according to the size of the discrimination coefficient ($d$), and with inelastic supply curves wage differences must result. If $W_{MAJ} = W_{MIN}$ by arbitrary assumption, then the forces which yield [11] would be reflected in hiring policies, that is, fewer, if any, minority workers would be hired. In general, however, it is assumed that in equilibrium members of the majority group will

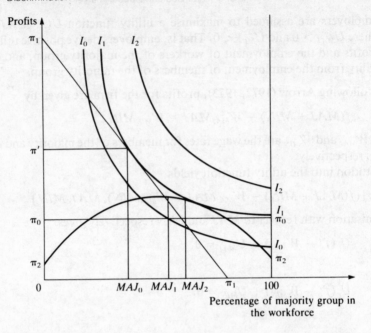

FIG. 3.2   Employer discrimination

receive higher payment than those of the minority, even though they are perfect substitutes. With discrimination against the minority and no favouritism towards the majority, the latter will receive a wage equal to the value of their marginal product and the minority somewhat less.

The above is illustrated graphically in Figure 3.2 where the indifference map indicates the employer's tastes for combinations of profits and majority group employment. Initially assume that majority and minority workers are perfect substitutes with equal wage rates. In this case profits are given by the horizontal line $\pi_0\pi_0$, since they are independent of the sex/race composition of the workforce and the rational employer would employ only majority workers in order to attain the highest possible level of utility. Now, if we allow minority wage rates to fall below those of the majority, profits will be given by a downward-sloping schedule such at $\pi_1\pi_1$, and $0MAJ_0$ would measure the percentage of the majority group in the workforce at a cost of $\pi_1\pi'$ profits which would have accrued to the employer if he had engaged an entirely minority membership workforce. Thus it appears that wage differences are necessary to encourage the employer to take on members of the minority group. Here, $\pi_2\pi_2$ describes the case in which the two groups of workers are imperfect substitutes. That is, if there is an optimal sex mix which implies a combination of majority and minority workers, profits will rise and eventually fall as minority workers are taken on. In this case the employer hires a higher percentage of majority workers ($0MAJ_2$) than would maximise his profits ($0MAJ_1$).

A clear implication of this theory of employer discrimination is that

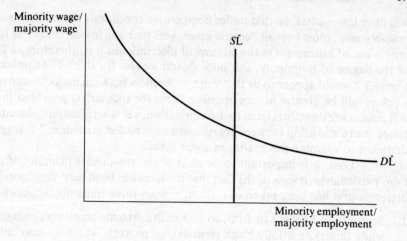

FIG. 3.3   Relative minority demand function

there will be an inverse relationship between minority/majority wage rates and minority/majority employment ratios. Rather than showing discrimination as a leftward shift in the demand curve for minority labour, a direct test of the model is provided by the existence or otherwise of a *relative* minority demand function as shown in Fig. 3.3. As the wage difference between the majority and the minority widens, the aversion of the employer to taking on minority applicants will weaken and the percentage of minority workers in the workforce will increase. The relative demand curve may be written as

$$W_{MIN}/W_{MAJ} = F(MIN/MAJ, X)$$ [12]

where $W_{MIN}$ and $W_{MAJ}$ = the wage rates of minority and majority labour;
   $MIN$ and $MAJ$ = the quantities of each type employed;
      $X$ = a vector of other determinants of demand.
Thus the hypothesis to be tested is that

$$d(W_{MIN}/W_{MAJ})/d(MIN/MAJ) < 0.$$ [13]

Studies attempting to confirm this hypothesis have, however, yielded mixed results (Ashenfelter 1972; Flanagan 1973; Landes 1968). Medoff and Dick (1978) point out that these studies are marred by the use of state rather than industry data to which Becker's original hypothesis relates, and by the use of earnings data (influenced by hours worked) rather than wage rates. Their own results, free of these defects, do find a negative relationship, as postulated, but one which is only significant at the 10 per cent level.

The majority of tests of the employer discrimination model have, however, been indirect, testing the relationship between discrimination and market structure on the grounds that discrimination is unlikely to persist under competitive conditions. As Becker suggests, given a dispersion of discrimination coefficients and identical production functions, employers who discriminate less will have lower costs, so that under competitive conditions the lowest coefficient, possibly zero, must prevail because employers with the lowest costs will force the others out of business. On this argument discrimination is, therefore, a function of the degree of monopoly. But how should we test for this? The implication of Figure 3.2 would appear to be that wage differences between majority and minority workers will be greater in monopolistic firms (or industries) provided that wage differences are directly related to discrimination, yet several empirical studies have tested the relationship between *segregation* and market structure.[15] It is necessary therefore to examine this matter in some detail.

First, it is important to be clear about the precise meaning of segregation, particularly in view of the fact that the term has been used very loosely in the literature and has been taken to refer to at least three quite distinct phenomena:

1. Segregation by plant or firm, so that at the extreme employers engage wholly white (male) or wholly black (female), employees, which we may refer to as *enterprise segregation*.
2. Segregation by occupation, so that in the extreme cases all non-manual workers, say, are white and all manual workers black, or all accountants male and all typists female, which can be described as *occupational segregation*.
3. Partial segregation by occupation or firm such that the proportion of blacks (females) to whites (males) is less than it would have been in the absence of discrimination, which is perhaps more accurately referred to as *partial exclusion*.

While, doubtless, cases can be found of establishments which are predominantly male or female, enterprise segregation is probably more significant in relation to race than to sex, where occupational segregation appears to predominate.

The argument for testing for employer discrimination by examining the relationship between monopoly and segregation runs as follows. Assuming that there is no discrimination other than employer discrimination[16] and that the different groups are perfect substitutes, the necessary condition for 'cost minimisation' for the discriminatory employer is

$$\frac{MP_{MIN}}{MP_{MAJ}} = \frac{W_{MIN}(1+d)}{W_{MAJ}} \qquad\qquad [14]$$

where $MP_{MIN}$ and $MP_{MAJ}$ = the marginal productivities of minority and majority
workers respectively;
$W$ = the wage rate;
$d$ = the discrimination coefficient.

Masters (1975) and Medoff and Dick (1978) point out that employers with a discrimination coefficient less than the mean $(d)$ will hire only minority workers and employers with a coefficient greater than this hire only majority employees, so that we end up with segregated firms in the long run.[17] Note, however, that even here we may end up with enterprise segregation, but no detectable difference at the industry level at which the hypothesis is generally tested. Further, the crowding hypothesis, referred to below, suggests that minorities will be excluded from high-paying industries and depress wages in industries from which they are not excluded, thus again yielding wage differences. The argument for segregation depends upon the assumptions that employers exhibit a distribution of discrimination coefficients and competition is sufficient to reduce the output of those employers with the higher discriminatory coefficients.[18] Yet the empirical tests relate to *non-competitive* product markets. However, Medoff (1980a) argues that Becker himself makes no predictions concerning the structure of the product market and the degree of wage discrimination across industries as the latter assumes competitive labour markets, finding a relationship between the number of non-whites employed and the degree of competition within industries.[19] Or in Johnson's (1978: 78) words

> on closer reflection, it is clear that such theories of discrimination are theories of employment discrimination for firms which face exogenous wage rates in a competitive labour market and can exercise their discriminatory tastes only by adjusting the racial composition of the workforce. The black/white wage differential should be the same for all firms in a given labour market and will reflect the preponderance of discriminatory tastes among all employers in the market.

How far the assumption of a perfectly elastic supply curve of labour is an appropriate one is, however, debatable. As Fujii and Trapani (1978) point out, a perfectly elastic supply curve of labour implies that labour is completely unspecific to the industry, there are readily available job opportunities elsewhere, and negligible costs of mobility exist in relation to inter-firm and inter-industry movement. Where this is not so, any reduction in minority employment will be a function of the elasticity of supply and demand as well as market power, with the danger of specification error.[20] Further, it should be noted that models of employee and consumer discrimination, as outlined below, also predict segregation as the outcome of discriminatory tastes, and here there is no reason to expect any relationship between the degree of discrimination and product market structure.

In the light of the above it is hardly surprising that tests of the relationship between 'employer' discrimination and market structure have tended to be inconclusive as revealed in Table 3.3. Shepherd (1970) and Comanor (1973) both find a significant relationship between the ratio of racial employment and market power, but the former uses a profit variable rather than a concentration variable and the latter does not standardise for other variables. When Medoff restricts the analysis to white-collar employees a positive relationship emerges, but for a similar group Shepherd and Levin (1973) find only a weak relationship. As for racial wage differences, Haessel and Palmer (1978) and Medoff and Dick (1978) (the latter using a profits variable) find a positive relationship between discrimination and market structure, but Fujii and Trapani (1978) and Johnson (1978) find no such relationship. In the case of sex, only Luksetich (1979) reports a strong significant relationship with the expected sign, but in his case there are no standardising variables. Indeed in several of these studies 'a suspicion arises ... that the diversity of results may in part be due to the effect of left-out variables' (Fujii and Trapani 1978: 556).

TABLE 3.3  Tests of the relationship between discrimination and market power

| Investigator | Group | Dependent variable | Assumed supply/ curve of labour | Standardising variables | Market power relationship |
|---|---|---|---|---|---|
| Shepherd (1970) | Race | Negro/white employment ratios in managerial jobs in USA | — | — | Significant positive relationship between degree of discrimination and concentration |
| Comanor (1973) | Race | Ratio of black to total employment in specific US occupations and industries | Perfectly elastic | Age, education, motivation (head of household), large firm, unionisation, large city, location | Significant positive relationship between degree of discrimination and profitability |
| Medoff (1980a) | Race | Ratio of black to total employees in white-collar occupations in USA | Perfectly elastic | Elasticity of demand (capital intensity), elasticity of supply (union membership), employer size, region | Significant positive relationship between degree of discrimination and concentration in all four occupations |
| Fujii and Trapani (1978) | Race | Ratio of black and white earnings for married adult males, 25–54, working full time with no health problems in USA | Upward sloping | Elasticity of demand, elasticity of supply (unionisation) | No significant relationship between degree of discrimination and concentration |
| Johnson (1978) | Race | Difference in wages between blacks and whites in USA | Upward sloping | Education, experience, union membership | Competitive and oligopolistic industries most discriminatory |

| Medoff and Dick (1978) | Race | Relative wage ratios of black and white males for five educational levels in USA | Upward sloping | Significant positive relationship between profits and degree of discrimination |
|---|---|---|---|---|
| Shepherd and Levin (1973) | Race and sex | Male blacks or females as percentage of all employees in upper-white-collar jobs in 200 large US enterprises | — | Only weak relationship between discrimination and market structure for race and sex |
| Haessel and Palmer (1978) | Race and sex | Relative wages by occupations in USA | Perfectly elastic | Concentration significant in 10 out of 11 occupations for race, and 5 out of 9 for sex |
| Oster (1975) | Sex | Female/male employment ratio by industry/occupation in USA | — | No significant relationship between degree of discrimination and concentration |
| Chiplin and Sloane (1976a) | Sex | (a) Absolute male/female earnings differences in UK by industry (b) Percentage of males in labour force in UK by industry | (a) Region, shift-work, unionisation/strikes, percentage of males (b) Shift-work, strikes, skill, capital/labour ratio | (a) No significant relationship between degree of discrimination and concentration (b) Significant relationship, but with wrong sign |
| Luksetich (1979) | Sex | Percentage of women in white-collar employment in USA | — | Significant relationship between degree of discrimination and concentration |

A further problem may be model misspecification. Thus Medoff (1980a) suggests that a double-log, rather than standard linear, model should be used where there is reason to believe that the threat of state intervention modifies the propensity of monopolistic employers to behave in a discriminatory fashion, in order to allow for the diminishing marginal rate of substitution between market power and discrimination. Where there is reason to believe the labour supply is less than perfectly elastic it is also more appropriate to use two-stage least squares rather than ordinary least squares (Medoff and Dick 1976). Another possibility is that market power is a poor proxy for ability to discriminate because there is a trade-off between discrimination and other forms of managerial discretion. Indeed, Shepherd and Levin (1973) argue that the result under market power is indeterminate, since some senior managers may even exercise their discretion positively in relation to the employment of minority groups, or in fact ultimately there may be no structure–discrimination relationship at all.[21] The failure to find a consistent relationship between market structure and discrimination should not be taken to imply, however, that discrimination itself is absent. Thus, Becker himself, and Comanor (1973) using 1966 data, find for instance, that racial segregation is pervasive throughout all major sectors of the US economy, and Smith (1979) using 1973 data finds the same for wage discrimination.

## EMPLOYEE DISCRIMINATION

Some economists have found discrimination by employees to be more plausible than employer discrimination (e.g. Chiswick 1973; Gordon and Morton 1974; Marshall 1974; Welch 1975). One reason for discriminatory behaviour would be the fact that white men, who make up the majority of union members, dislike associating with coloured or female workers in the work-place, particularly where minorities or women gain access to supervisory posts. The analysis then parallels the employer taste for discrimination model. A second, and possibly more potent reason for discriminatory behaviour would be that minorities and women are seen as a potential threat to job and income security through their possible impact on labour supply in particular occupations. In either case the majority employee utility function would take the form illustrated in Fig. 3.4 where short-run wages are traded off against the benefit of excluding minority workers, either to avoid contact with the minority at work or to maximise long-run wage levels. $I_0I_0$, $I_1I_1$ and $I_2I_2$ represent majority employee indifference curves for various combinations of wages and majority employees in the labour force. If majority and minority employees are perfect substitutes with identical wage rates, employment of integrated labour forces will raise the employer's costs. Thus a rational, non-discriminatory employer will hire a completely segregated labour force, cet. par. Competition will ensure that any wage differences are removed, for were minority wage rates to fall below those of the majority, competition by the non-discriminatory employers would force up the price of such labour until equality was achieved. Thus, we end up with completely segregated firms and efficient resource allocation in the long run.

The above, however, implies that the employer is able to treat the labour

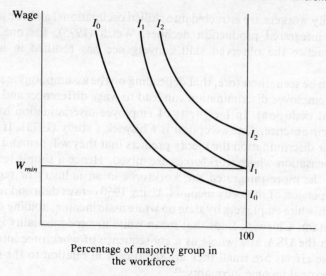

FIG. 3.4   Employee discrimination

force as though it were completely flexible. As Arrow (1972) notes, there are costs of hiring and firing workers and these costs of adjustment may inhibit firms from replacing white (male) employees by blacks (females). There is bound to be white (male) resistance to such a policy which will be all the greater where there is unionisation. Further, a policy of replacing all workers at once by members of the minority group, which might avoid this problem, will not allow firms to amortise fully their fixed recruiting costs and may thus be sub-optimal. As Gordon and Morton (1974) point out, we do not observe in practice situations in which firms hire only members of one group in an attempt to reach a segregated position. To the extent that such forms of adjustment are restricted, wage differences between majority and minority workers are likely to remain. But, as Masters (1975) notes, if wage discrimination persists for any length of time there should be enough new firms entering the industry to eliminate such wage differentials.

A second reason why integration might occur is that majority and minority workers, rather than being perfect substitutes, are complements in production (e.g. foremen and labourers).[22] It is possible that if a firm initially employs only majority workers and then adds minority workers to its establishment, the marginal productivity schedule of majority workers will be raised to a degree that more than offsets the extent to which majority wages have to be increased to overcome the distaste for working with minority workers. Where affirmative action legislation applies and firms are required to reach a particular target for the employment of minority workers, there may be a similar effect, even though workers are perfect substitutes in terms of production (Chiswick 1973). Further, if we suppose that a higher proportion of minority labour is unskilled, the equilibrium outcome implied is one in which higher wages will be paid for the relatively scarce skilled minority workers and lower wages for unskilled minority relative to majority unskilled workers. Over time there should be skill convergence as more minority workers are attracted into skilled occupations, and consequently the extent of integrated production declines. Welch (1975), for one, doubts whether in practice the observed skill convergence has resulted in increased segregation.

It can be seen, therefore, that depending on the assumptions made, both employer and employee discrimination can lead to wage differences and segregation (or partial exclusion). In fact, tests of employee discrimination have been notable by their absence. One exception is Chiswick's study (1973). If workers have a taste for discrimination the theory predicts that they will demand a higher wage as compensation where workforces are mixed. Hence a simple test of this model is that the more integrated the workforce in an industry or region, the greater the dispersion of majority incomes. Using 1960 census data and regressing percentage non-white employees by state on white male income, holding other key variables constant, Chiswick finds that mean white income inequality is 2.3 per cent greater in the USA as a whole as a consequence of workforce integration. Although these effects are small they are significant in relation to the observed stability of personal income inequality.[23]

Trade unions may act to reduce or to reinforce the prejudices of their members. While females are less likely than males to be members of a union, coloured workers are more likely than whites to be members, though in part this is a function of their occupational distribution (Antos et al. 1980). The behaviour of unions will, however, be influenced by whether their power depends largely on their ability to recruit a substantial proportion of the labour force (e.g. industrial unions), or whether it is a function of their ability to restrict supply (e.g. craft unions) (Ashenfelter 1972). In the latter case one can distinguish between referral and non-referral unions, at least in the USA. Referral unions operate hiring halls which function as private employment agencies for particular employers and which are open only to union members, so that exclusion from the union may effectively debar a worker from a job. In the case of craft unions (and particularly referral unions), discrimination may take the form of exclusion of minorities from union membership, while industrial unions may admit such workers, but discriminate against them once they have become members by excluding them from positions of power in the union, failing to process their grievances, or operating discriminatory seniority and promotion systems (Gilman 1965). The effect of trade unions on the overall majority–minority earnings ratio will be determined by three factors: the difference in the percentage of each group which is unionised or subject to a collective agreement, the difference in the percentage mark-up in each of the groups resulting from union membership, and the depressing effect of unionisation on the wages of non-union members. Further discussion of this is postponed until the next section.

## CONSUMER DISCRIMINATION

In parallel to the above forms of discrimination, prejudiced consumers may refuse to purchase goods and services from members of minority groups unless goods are cheaper than when purchased from majority employees. Thus Gunderson (1975) suggests that discriminatory customers account for the large male—female differential in the trade sector. This feature is likely to be particularly strong where professional services are offered (e.g. doctors and lawyers). Fuchs (1971) found, for instance, using 1960 US census data, that the ratio of female to male hourly earnings was lowest for self-employed women and that far fewer women than men were found in this category. This he attributes to the relatively close contact the self-employed have with consumers. Shepherd and Levin (1973) argue, in contrast, that firms dealing exclusively with women's goods will have strong incentives to employ women in decision-making positions (and presumably on the sales staff). On average they find that female employment in the three highest occupational classifications is some 7 per cent higher in women's industries than in non-producer durable goods industries. In fact, given *men's* preference for attractive women it is clear that women in certain occupations gain from consumer discrimination though this will not necessarily be the case for racial minorities. In general, however, consumer discrimination will lead to employment segregation. Further, even unprejudiced employers may require minority employees to accept lower wages in order to compensate for lost sales (the same being true with respect to employee discrimination and the increased wage bill).

## GOVERNMENTAL DISCRIMINATION

Governments can influence the relative position of minority groups in the labour market in three particular ways, either positively or negatively. First, there is the question of the provision of education and particularly the quality of education, which governs the acquisition of human capital by minority groups. Secondly, there is the question of employment in the public sector itself, or in industries regulated by or under the direct influence of government. Thirdly, there is the ability of governments to implement legislation designed to limit the freedom of the majority group to discriminate against the minorities in terms of earnings and employment opportunities.

Becker (1957) points out that in a political democracy we would expect governments to act on the basis of the median taste for discrimination among the electorate. Thus the size of the minority group relative to the total population will be important in terms of the number of votes at stake, which suggests that discrimination will decline as the size of the minority group increases.[24] Becker, on the other hand, argues that the extent of discrimination may increase as the size of the minority group increases, and it becomes more of a perceived threat to the majority in terms of job competition and influence on the wage rates of particular occupations. Yet, if the issue of minority rights is a crucial one for minority voters but a minor issue as far as majority voters are concerned, more votes would be gained by pressing for an extension of minority rights than will be lost as a result of moderate opposition from the majority. This might explain, for instance, why in the UK legislation against racial discrimination preceded that against sex discrimination, despite the fact that there are many more female than coloured workers in the labour force. Borjas (1982) has formalised this into a vote maximisation hypothesis which predicts that the economic status of minorities in federal agencies will depend on how important such minorities are to the political support generated by the particular agency.

Johnson (1978), using 1972 data, divided US industries into the government sector and other sectors. In terms of discrimination, regulated and non-profit firms fell somewhere between the government sector at the one extreme and the competitive and oligopolistic sectors at the other, and this may reflect the fact that though regulated industries have fewer economic constraints they are more subject to political constraints (Sowell 1975). Thus we may observe rapid changes in the treatment of minority groups in this sector when the political emphasis changes towards anti-discrimination policies, as was illustrated in the US telephone, electricity and gas industries in the 1960s.[25]

## STATISTICAL AND ERRONEOUS DISCRIMINATION

Statistical discrimination, unlike the above forms, does not derive from any taste for physical or social distance, but is a consequence of imperfections of informtion in the labour market. As Phelps (1972: 659) put it:

> the employer who seeks to maximise expected profit will discriminate against blacks or women if he believes them to be less qualified, reliable, long term etc. on the average than whites and men respectively, and if the cost of gaining information about the individual applicants is excessive. Skin colour or sex is taken as a proxy for relevant data not sampled. The a priori belief in the probable preferability of a white or male over a black or female candidate who is not known to differ in other respects might stem from the employer's previous statistical experience with the two groups (members from the less favoured group might have been, and continue to be, hired at less favourable terms); or it might stem from prevailing sociological beliefs that blacks or women grow up disadvantaged due to racial hostility.

Therefore, statistical discrimination is an inevitable part of profit maximisation under conditions of uncertainty. However, it might easily give rise to erroneous discrimination, if employers underestimate the productive abilities of the minority group relative to the majority. This is particularly likely where circumstances change, but employers continue to hold outdated stereotypes about particular groups of employees. Thus, for instance, the very rapid increase in female labour-force participation rates has meant that the difference in time spent out of the labour market between this group and other groups is much less than it was. Employers may not, however, have fully adjusted to these changed circumstances, and in the short run discrimination may occur through error. Given competition, such discrimination should, however, disappear in the long run (McCall 1973). Statistical and erroneous discrimination are separate (though related) forms of discrimination, since the former will continue in the long run even under competitive conditions, while the latter should disappear through the learning process.

Models of statistical discrimination developed by Phelps (1972) and Aigner and Cain (1977) assume that employers may have a preference for white males in hiring workers because, while they are uncertain about any particular worker's productivity, they know or believe coloured workers or women are less productive as a group than white males. Suppose hiring decisions are based upon some performance test, $y$, which measures the true performance level, $q$, but only imperfectly. Then

$$y = q + u \qquad\qquad [15]$$

where $u$ is a normally distributed error term, and $q$ is also assumed to be normally distributed and to have a constant variance. Here, three factors may give rise to statistical discrimination: differences in the means of abilities between the groups, differences between groups in the variance of ability, and differences in the ability to predict accurately the true performance of groups from test scores (i.e. in the variance of $u$). Let us suppose majority workers have higher mean ability than the minority. Then the employer is likely to hire a majority worker rather than a minority worker even though they have the same test score. This is illustrated by the following equation

$$\hat{q} = (1 - \beta)\alpha + \beta y + u' \qquad \text{where } 0 < \beta < 1 \qquad [16]$$

where $\hat{q}$ = predicted value of $q$;

   $\alpha$ = mean performance level;

   $\beta$ = a regression coefficient measuring the reliability of the test.

Another possibility is that $\alpha$ is the same for majority workers as for minority workers, but that $\beta$ is greater for majority workers. Then it can be demonstrated that at low test scores majority workers will be predicted to perform better than minority workers, while at high test scores the reverse will be the case.[26] In such cases there is no group discrimination since the probability of being hired is related to average rates of productivity for the groups. Within-group or individual discrimination is, however, inevitable, wherever true performance can only be assessed by observation on the job (i.e. after the workers have been hired).

The importance of statistical discrimination depends on how far majority and minority groups do differ in terms of their actual performance or net worth to employers. The major factors to consider here are differences in motivation between groups and, particularly in relation to sex, differences in rates of turnover and absenteeism. As noted earlier in section 2, there is some evidence that men and women exhibit different motivational patterns which could impinge on their performance at the place of work. In contrast, conclusions from most of the achievement-related motivation studies for the races indicate very similar patterns among blacks and whites. One attempt to compare the degree of initiative displayed by black and white middle-aged men using US National Longitudinal data is that of Andresani (1977). He adapts Rotter's Internal–External Scale which places individuals on a continuum from the highly internal, who perceive success as highly dependent upon personal effort, to the highly external, who place little value on initiative as they perceive success as being unrelated either to effort or ability. His results indicate that young and middle-aged black men consistently tend to be less internal in outlook than white men of the same age, but such differences are too small to account for the substantial differences in labour-market experience that exist between the races. Several investigators have examined the relative performance of blacks and whites using data from the AFQT test, which is a qualification test for entry into the armed services in the USA (Hansen *et al.* 1970; Griliches and Mason 1972), and Masters (1975) concludes that differences in these scores are an important component of the racial earnings gap, though the results themselves could be affected by cultural bias.[27]

Direct comparisons of actual performance are often difficult to make because of the nature of the productive process, or because of the difficulty of holding all other relevant variables constant. However, professional baseball is one industry in which it is possible to obtain meaningful data on individual performance. Pascal and Rapping (1972) and Scully (1974) find that black players in major league baseball are more productive (in terms of the baseball production function) than their white counterparts, suggesting barriers to entry exist for black players, and pointing to the fact that there may well be certain occupations where minority workers are more, rather than less, productive than members of the majority. As for female—male comparisons, there have been a large number of attempts to examine the relative performance of male and female academics (see for instance Katz 1973; Koch and Chizmar 1976; Strober and Quester 1977; Ferber and Kordick 1978; Ferber *et al.* 1978; Ferber and Green 1982). In general, the results suggest that women are less productive than men in terms of scholarly publication and related performance measures. More generally Tsuchigane and Dodge (1974: 34—5) assert

> although the productivity of women in office or factory work is substantially the same as that of men, there is less conclusive evidence that women in business and executive positions are as productive as men. In scholarly productivity women appear to be less productive, even if the results are corrected for under-estimation. ... Women's lower productivity is partially attributable to discrimination against women and partially to the time and momentum lost due to career interruption. If women and men were in similar professional environments, women's productivity might be more similar to that of men.

Yet that male and female productivity can be substantially different even under supposedly identical conditions is illustrated by the study by Battallio *et al.* (1978). Men and women working on the same manual task were compared under experimental conditions, being given the freedom to choose their own duration and intensity of work rate. Average hours worked for females were only 82 per cent of the male hours and average hourly output only 78 per cent. The difference here was explained in terms of fatigue and a lower demand for money income on the part of women.[28] On the productivity side, therefore, differences appear to be more marked in the case of sex than in the case of race.

Studies in a number of countries have shown that women have higher quit and absenteeism rates than men, though the differences vary according to the country, industry, occupation and over time (Lewis 1979). Gaumer (1975) and Goldfarb and Hosek (1976) have developed similar models to show the relationship between quit rates and wage differentials between the sexes. Using the latter model we assume that the employer will attempt to equate the net returns from labour with the costs ($c$) of hiring and training that labour. Thus, we have

$$\sum_{t=0}^{T} (MP - W) \left(\frac{1 - s}{1 + r}\right)^t = C \qquad [17]$$

where $T$ = employer's time horizon;
$\quad MP$ = marginal product of labour;
$\quad W$ = employee's earnings per period;
$\quad s$ = employee's probability of separation;
$\quad r$ = market rate of discount.

If we assume $T$ is sufficiently large we can replace [17] by

$$(MP - W) \frac{(1 + r)}{(r + s)} \simeq C \qquad [18]$$

and assuming the sexes have identical marginal products but different quit propensities we obtain

$$W_M - W_F = \frac{C}{(1 + r)} (s_F - s_M) \qquad [19]$$

where subscript M refers to males and subscript F to females. Thus men and women with identical marginal products will receive different wages if their quit rates differ. If equal pay legislation rules out wage differences, some firms will adopt high/low turnover strategies (employing males) and others low wage/high turnover strategies (employing females).[29]

Goldfarb and Hosek, using data on total separation rates for the sexes and rough figures of initial hiring and training costs, proceed to estimate sex wage differentials on the basis of plausible values of $(s_F - s_M)$ and $c/(1 + r)$. However, comparing these with actual occupational male/female differentials indicates that this factor cannot explain a major part of the differential. Gaumer, similarly, finds that tenure accounts for only 6–10 per cent of the observed differential in his model. Further, in the USA Viscusi (1980) has detected a considerable narrowing of the quit rate differential between men and women between 1958 and 1968, and also points out that apart from the initial work period women are actually more stable employees than men.[30] This suggests that previous discussions of sex differences in quitting may have been exaggerated. How far this is true of other countries remains to be determined, particularly in the light of Viscusi's finding that male and female quitting have different causal explanations[31] and cannot be captured by adding a sex-specific constant term to the analysis. Further, recent work by Ragan and Smith (1981) conflicts with the above findings. By pooling time-series industry turnover rates, by sex, with 1970 US census data, they estimate the effect of past industry turnover on current earnings and find that when such differences in turnover are taken into account the proportion of the male/female earnings gap explainable by human capital and other variables is increased by about 50 per cent.

Evidence on racial differences in turnover rates is relatively sparse and also conflicting. Director and Doctors (1976), for example, found in each of three firms that crude turnover rates were higher for non-whites, but holding factors such as age, education and occupation constant the regression coefficient on the non-white dummy was negative in three out of four cases and was significant in one of them. Probably the safest statement to make is that there is no clear evidence of substantial differences in quit rates by race.

Female absenteeism rates appear to be generally higher than male. Goldfarb and Hosek adapt their quit rate model to deal with this case and find that allowing for differences in absenteeism, *cet. par.*, men would earn nine cents an hour more than women rather than seven. Further, for all occupations in the USA it appears that the additional cost per year of female absenteeism is small ($8.00), hardly sufficient to explain much of the sex wage differential (Tsuchigane and Dodge 1974). Regardless of these facts, Osterman (1979) has attempted to test Aigner and Cain's model of statistical discrimination by examining rates of absenteeism by sex in one company. He concludes that there is no support either for the difference in means or reliability of tests versions of the model. The latter judgement is based on the fact that the coefficients of determination, corrected for degrees of freedom, are greater for women than for men, which he takes to imply that men's absenteeism is more difficult to predict than that of women. Kahn (1981) has pointed out, however, that the appropriate test is the variance of the error term ($u'$ in our equation [16]), and Osterman's data suggest that this variance is indeed higher for women, consistent with Aigner and Cain's model. Clearly, further empirical work using larger data sets is required here. As for race, Corcoran and Duncan (1979) using 1976 data examine the hypothesis that blacks earn less than whites because of higher absenteeism due to poorer health. Time lost per year due to *own* illness was 36 hours for white men, 43 for white women, 50 for black men and 58 for black women. However, absenteeism had virtually no effect on the wages of any of the four sub-groups of workers. All in all, the empirical evidence provides support for the note of caution expressed by Aigner and Cain (1977: 186) in the conclusion of their paper to the effect that 'we are reluctant however to claim too much for these models'.

There remains the possibility that employers might exaggerate any such differences as exist. Such a possibility was in fact suggested by Arrow (1972) on the grounds that discriminators may, albeit subconsciously, attempt to rationalise their prejudice, following the principle put forward by Festinger in his theory of cognitive dissonance (1957), which deals with the way in which individuals attempt to maintain a degree of consistency between their opinions and attitudes and their actual behaviour. Some substantiation for this is found in Lewis's (1979) interviews with personnel managers in twenty-four firms in Australia. These indicate that employers consistently underestimate the quit rates of males and overestimate those of females, and furthermore these errors are statistically significant. No information is provided, however, on the nature of competition in the markets in which these employers are found, and a time-series approach is perhaps called for here in order to establish whether errors diminish over time.

## RADICAL AND OTHER APPROACHES TO DISCRIMINATION

The radical approach differs from the neo-classical approach in a number of ways. First, while in the latter tastes for discrimination are exogenous, in the former they are endogenous, being part of a conscious decision-making process of an employer. Second, unlike Becker, radical economists hold that discrimination is widespread because various interest groups, in particular capitalists, benefit from it. Third, it is held that group power processes or class interest, rather than individual acts, are an essential element in perpetuating discrimination,[32] and that discrimination is directed at particular groups because capitalists find it easier to exploit certain groups rather than others. Fourth, the economy is not competitive enough to ensure that less discriminatory tastes predominate.

The central notion of radical theories is that capitalists deliberately segment labour markets in order to divide workers and prevent them from forming a cohesive group to challenge management. Segmentation does not imply segregation, however. The idea is that the employment within an establishment of both majority and minority workers will cause conflicts within the workforce, and reduce its cohesiveness and bargaining power. More specifically, in direct contrast to Becker, it is assumed that individual employers deliberately integrate their workforces racially in order to reduce the capability of striking. According to Roemer (1979: 695) such a divide and conquer strategy will force down the wages of both black and white workers, so that 'capitalists gain and all workers lose from discrimination, which is a conclusion much at variance with Becker's neo-classical theory'. The model also depends upon employer discrimination which allows a wage differential to emerge in mixed workforces. Again in contrast to Becker, it is assumed that discrimination is a function of profit-maximising behaviour on the part of the employer, together (presumably) with non-wage bill maximising behaviour on the part of workers. Figure 3.5 illustrates the relationship between

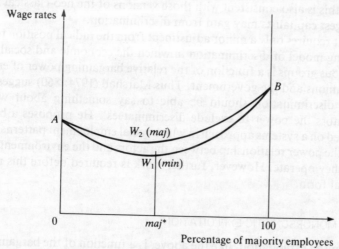

FIG. 3.5   A Marxian model of discrimination

the cost of labour and the extent to which the labour force is integrated. Majority workers must be paid a wage of at least $W_2(MAJ)$ and minority workers a wage of at least $W_1(MIN)$. If the workforce is segregated (i.e. only one of the groups is hired), this increases the bargaining power of the workers and a higher wage will be obtained, at $A$ if only minority workers are employed and at $B$ if only majority workers are employed. As Roemer notes, since majority workers are more expensive, equilibrium will occur at the point at which sufficient minority workers are hired to trigger the 'dissension effect'. There will also be a point such as $MAJ^*$ where wages are lowest and the wage differential between minority and majority employees the greatest. Where such wage discrimination is illegal the effect will simply be embodied in a low general wage rate.[33] Whether it is realistic to suppose that workers' bargaining power is lower where members of majority and minority workers are employed together is debatable. For instance, are workers stronger in small non-integrated and non-unionised establishments?

It is possible to test these competing predictions of the Becker and radical models by examining the distribution of income among the majority population. If Becker is correct in assuming that majority capitalists lose financially and majority workers gain from discrimination, and in assuming that majority capitalists have higher incomes than majority workers, then more discrimination should be associated with greater majority income inequality. The radical theory leads to the opposite prediction. Reich (1970) has attempted to test this 1960 US census data for forty-eight large standard metropolitan statistical areas, using the ratio of black to white median family income as a measure of discrimination and the percentage share of total white income accruing to the top 1 per cent of white families and the Gini coefficient as measures of income inequality. Controlling for industry, occupation, region, average income and proportion black, he finds that a 1 per cent increase in the ratio of black/white median incomes leads to a 0.2 per cent decrease in white inequality – consistent with the radical hypothesis. However, this is also consistent with those versions of the neo-classical approach which suggest capitalists may gain from discrimination.

It requires only a minor adjustment from the radical position to develop a bargaining model of discrimination in which the economic and social situation of the various groups is a function of the relative bargaining power of employers, workers, unions and the government. Thus Marshall (1974: 860) suggests that 'a theory of discrimination should be able to say something about what gives discriminators the power to exclude discriminatees'. He proposes a bargaining model based on a systems approach in which racial employment patterns are determined by the power relationship between the actors and the environmental context in which they operate. However, further work is required before this model has operational form.

## MONOPSONISTIC EXPLOITATION

Monopsonistic exploitation, like the above, is a function of the bargaining power of the employers relative to the workers, but is determined by forces on the supply side of the labour market rather than demand (since its basis is lack of perfect mobility of labour) and thus is not properly a theory of minority group discrimination as such.[34]

A number of economists have, however, given monopsony a central role in explanations of male–female earnings differences (Madden 1973; Gordon and Morton 1974; Koch and Chizmar 1976; Cardwell and Rosenweig 1980). Monopsonistic exploitation is a function of monopsonistic power or upward-sloping supply of labour schedules, the ability to segment labour into different categories and the existence of different wage elasticities for the two groups. If men and women are perfect substitutes in production, equilibrium requires that the male and female marginal revenue products are equated. Thus, the profit maximisation condition can be expressed as

$$W_M(1 + 1/E_M) = W_F(1 + 1/E_F) \qquad [20]$$

where $W_M$ and $W_F$ = male and female wage rates respectively and $E_M$ and $E_F$ = the elasticities of supply for the two groups.

Sex 'discrimination' will occur if $E_M \neq E_F$ even under conditions of profit maximisation, since the marginal wage costs rather than the wage rates of the two groups of workers will be equated. Thus in Fig. 3.6 $0N_W$ women and $0N_M$ men out of a total labour force of $0N_T$ will be employed at wage rates $0W_W$ and $0W_M$ respectively. If $E_F < E_M$ then $(dE/dM)/(dE/dF) < W_M/W_F$ and females will be

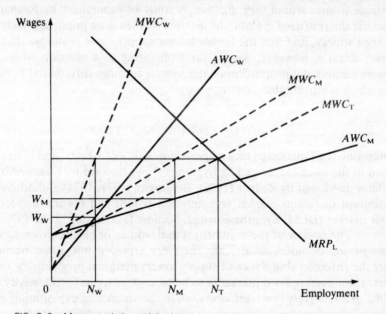

FIG. 3.6   Monopsonistic exploitation

$MWC_W$ = marginal wage cost of women;
$AWC_W$ = average wage cost of women;
$MWC_M$ = marginal wage cost of men;
$AWC_M$ = average wage cost of men;
$MWC_T$ = combined marginal wage cost (men and women)
$MRP_L$ = marginal revenue product of labour

discriminated against. In general, the group with the lower elasticity of supply will receive the lower wage and be 'discriminated against'.

To estimate the overall impact of imperfect labour markets on the relative position of females requires a substantial amount of data. As Cardwell and Rosenweig (1980: 1103) note, 'the little empirical work that has been done is indirect and only loosely tied to the theory. . . . Several studies measure concentration ratios among employers, relate concentration to wages or consider labour shortages. These studies thus present corroborating evidence; none is a direct test of the existence of monopsonistic exploitation.' What are really required, however, are data on firm level supply elasticities and these are rarely available. Unfortunately, too, Cardwell and Rosenweig's own study is marred by weaknesses similar to those in the other studies to which they refer. They combine micro data from the US 1970 Public Use Samples with aggregate Standard Metropolitan Statistical Areas data to estimate supply elasticities for white males and white never-married females, finding that the latter receive lower wages due to monopsony, especially in those areas characterised by high levels of union activity and occupational segregation. How far reliance should be placed on regional supply elasticities and wage rates rather than firm level elasticities is a moot point, particularly in the light of the very low explanatory power of their model. Further, the use of monopsony power rests on the participation of married women rather than the single women whom they analyse. A study of economists by Reagan (1975) finds that the restricted mobility of married women is an important factor affecting their supply, and that the female labour supply curve is steeper than that of males.[35] Clearly, however, we are far from being in a position where we can estimate reliably the proportion of the overall earnings differential between the sexes which is attributable to monopsony.

### THE CROWDING HYPOTHESIS AND LABOUR MARKET SEGMENTATION

Monopsony is a function of lack of perfect mobility of labour, and in this sense is related to the so-called 'crowding hypothesis' put forward by Edgeworth in 1922 and later developed by Zellner (1972), Bergmann (1971, 1974) and others, and to the concept of labour market segmentation (LMS) and the more specific dual labour market (DLM) hypothesis which became fashionable in the 1970s.

The essence of the argument is that women or blacks are excluded from higher-paying occupations and are therefore crowded into other occupations, where the enforced abundance of supply lowers marginal productivity and hence wages. If an overcrowded market is to be cleared, marginal productivity must be pushed to a relatively low level, and even in the absence of exploitation members of the minority groups will receive lower wages than members of the majority, even though they have the necessary skills to perform the higher-paid jobs. Chiswick (1973) suggests the crowding hypothesis can be divided into two analytically distinct sub-hypotheses. First, the labour supply hypothesis suggests that the presence of minority workers will increase income inequality among the majority population by raising the rate of return to education. This depends on the plausible assumptions that minority workers have a low endowment of education, and are closer substitutes to unskilled majority workers than the latter are to skilled majority workers. Secondly, the job-rationing hypothesis (also suggested by Stiglitz 1973) suggests that some firms attempt to cream the market by offering higher than the going rate of pay and creating a job queue within particular occupations. These jobs will all be allocated to members of the majority group. If as a consequence we assume there is a normal distribution of wage offers within any occupation, an increase in minority workers in that occupation will reduce majority wage inequalities as shown in Fig. 3.7. As the number of employed minority workers increases from 0A to 0B, the remaining distribution of wage offers to majority workers shrinks from AC to BC. Chiswick's own empirical work is, however, consistent with the employee discrimination model, as shown above (p.102–4), and not with the job-rationing hypothesis.

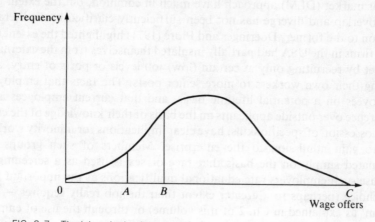

FIG. 3.7   The job-rationing hypothesis

Occupational crowding has been found in a number of studies of employment distribution by race and sex. In the latter case in particular, attempts have been made to construct indices of sex segregation (see for instance Blau and Hendricks (1979) for the USA and Hakim (1979) for the UK), and these suggest long-run stability in the distribution of the sexes by occupation. The extent to which women lose as a result of overcrowding will depend on the wage elasticity of demand in overcrowded occupations (where their earnings will be artificially depressed) and in the under-represented occupations (where earnings will be artificially raised for those few women who manage to gain entry). If demand is inelastic in the under-represented occupations and elastic in the overcrowded occupations, the total female wage bill might actually increase as a consequence of crowding. This will depend on the elasticity of substitution between male and female labour.[36] Further, as Bergmann (1974) points out, any desegregation of jobs might well lead to a greater wage reduction for men than a rise in wage levels for women, particularly if the effect of easing the entry of women into a larger range of jobs encourages a substantial increase in female labour-force participation. However, using UK General Household Survey data, Pike (1982) finds that if occupational segregation could be eliminated, gains in national income would be sufficient to prevent any substantial reduction in male earnings as a consequence of the entry of women into previously male-dominated jobs.

Women may lose out in other ways than just pay. Dillingham (1981) finds that virtually all of the differential in observed differences in male and female injury rates is due to sex differences in the occupational distribution of employment. Similarly, there is evidence that there are disproportionate numbers of non-whites in hazardous jobs. Further, Leigh (1981) finds that non-whites appear to receive lower compensating wages for the same jobs.

Lack of potential mobility of labour is an essential ingredient also of the LMS theories. Two separate approaches can be distinguished in the work on structured labour markets. The internal labour market (ILM) approach and the dual labour market (DLM) approach have much in common, but the extent to which they overlap and diverge has not been sufficiently clarified in the literature. In relation to the former, Doeringer and Piore (1971) highlighted the extent to which large firms in the USA had partially insulated themselves from the external labour market by recruiting only at certain (low) job levels or ports of entry, and promoting their own workers to more senior posts. The facts that employers seek employees on a potential lifetime basis, and that current employees are given preference over outside applicants on the basis of their knowledge of the enterprise and possession of specific skills, have clear implications for minority workers who fail to gain admission to the enterprise. Members of such groups may be eliminated simply on the basis that race or sex is used as a screening device, because such employers rate eduational qualifications as the important factor in job choice (perhaps to a greater extent than the job really requires – 'credentialism' as explained in Ch. 2 of this volume) or through the use of employment tests which are sex or culture biased. Few empirical studies have, however, been undertaken either in North America or Europe which enable us to assess with any degree of accuracy the extent to which ILMs are an important feature of the labour market, or operate discriminatory hiring procedures in the ways outlined.[37]

The simple DLM theory suggests that the labour market can be divided into two quite distinct sectors: a primary market where 'good' jobs and majority workers predominate, and secondary markets where 'bad' jobs and minority workers predominate. In contrast to the assumptions of human capital theory, it is argued that racial differences in earnings are not so much the result of differing endowments of human capital, but rather of differing rates of return in consequence of the entrapment of minority workers in the secondary sector. Further, it is argued that because of discrimination inter-sectoral mobility will be lower for minority workers, that because of the absence of promotion opportunities in secondary jobs the rate of return to service will be lower for minority workers, and that because of considerable job instability in the secondary sector there will be higher unemployment rates for minority workers. There are therefore a number of predictions that can be tested empirically. In the USA Osterman (1975), using 1967 Survey of Economic Opportunity data, and Rumberger and Carnoy (1980), using the 1 per cent sample of the 1970 Census of Population, claim some support for the DLM theory, the former on the grounds that there are substantial differences in earnings functions between the segments of the labour market, and the latter on the grounds that there is less upward mobility for blacks than for whites and that human capital attributes (education and experience) are essentially unrewarded in the secondary sector. However, doubts arise as to the validity of the procedures adopted in these studies which may lead to the truncation of the dependent variable (logarithm of earnings), so biasing downwards the absolute values of the coefficients on age and schooling in the secondary sector (Cain 1976; Kruse 1977). Further, an attempt to replicate Osterman's results with another data set, the 1970 Census of Population Public Use Sample Tapes (Langley 1978), contradicted these results, finding, indeed, that the rate of return to education was higher in the secondary sector than in the primary sector.

Other studies have failed to find any clear evidence supporting the DLM hypothesis. Thus, Andresani (1976), using a cohort of males aged 14–20 from the 1966 National Longitudinal Survey, found that though there was more upward mobility for whites, such mobility was still substantial for blacks, that for both races investment in human capital increased the probability of being in a primary job, and that for both groups the rate of return to education was as high in the secondary as in the primary sector. Leigh (1978a, 1978b) found no clear evidence of differential rates of return for the races or of differential inter-firm and inter-industry mobility. Rosenberg (1980) criticised earlier studies for the way in which they had assigned workers to primary and secondary sectors. He defined labour-market duality on the basis of four job dimensions, vocational preparation, educational development, job discretion and wage levels, and traced the career patterns of male workers living in low-income areas in four USA cities. The results suggest that explanations based upon differential human capital characteristics of individual workers are helpful in explaining initial career position, but less so in explaining upward occupational mobility. However, the DLM theory is not wholly satisfactory in this respect either.

Attempts to test for the existence of a DLM in the UK, following a poorly specified attempt by Bosanquet and Doeringer (1973), have produced similarly negative results. Psacharopoulos (1978) and McNabb and Psacharopoulos (1981b) used General Household Survey data for men and distinguished between primary and secondary sectors on the basis of pay and a general desirability occupational ranking scale. Performing a number of tests using individual, industrial and occupational data, together with a number of different definitions of the lower segment of the market, they were unable to detect any evidence of a structural break in the earnings determination mechanism. Finally, Mayhew and Rosewell (1979), using data on over 10,000 men from the Oxford Social Mobility Survey, found that there was substantial mobility between various segments of the market, and that human capital variables were important deter-minants not only of the segment in which an individual starts his career, but also of upward mobility between segments. Thus empirical evidence in North America and the UK suggests that the human capital model is a better predictor of success in the labour market than various versions of the DLM hypothesis, though there is evidence that the labour market is segmented in the classical sense of non-competing groups.

UNEMPLOYMENT AND JOB SEARCH

To the extent that hiring practices do exclude members of minority groups disproportionately and wages are rigid we would expect this to be reflected in unemployment rates. Yet

> to date, theoretical models of sex and race discrimination have concentrated on the resulting wage differentials and neglected the possibility of differential unemployment rates. This is because wage flexibility and supply inelasticity have been implicitly or explicitly assumed. However, in the presence of imperfect information and wage ridigities, the preference for discrimination cannot be completely satisfied via differential wage rates. Unemployment differentials will result as well.

(Lloyd and Niemi 1979: 193)

The authors go on to suggest that no research so far has been successful in measuring the quantitative significance of discrimination as a factor in explaining unemployment differentials. Gross unemployment rates for racial minorities are significantly higher than those of white employees both in North America and the UK, and the same is true for women in North America.[38] Gilman (1965) found that standardising for differences in education, age, occupation, industry and region only accounted for about half the racial differential in unemployment, and attributes at least part of the residual to wage rigidities. This is, if employers are unable to satisfy their hiring preferences (which may in part be discriminatory) by offering lower wages to minority workers, as would be the case where equal opportunities legislation or perhaps minimum wage laws apply, then we would expect employment opportunities to decline more for minority workers relative to the majority. Gilman goes on to argue that higher unemployment differentials in less skilled occupations in states other than in the South and in the most recent period are all consistent with the wage rigidity hypothesis. Also Medoff (1980c) has found that the unemployment differential is significantly lower in states that have ratified the Equal Rights Amendment, which would amend the United States Constitution to outlaw discrimination on the basis of sex by federal, state or local government officials, rules or statutes. This he explains as resulting from the fact that market discrimination is greater in ratified states, while higher female/male wage rates in non-ratified states lead women to invest more time in job search there. The implication is then that the more favourable position of women in the labour market may be bought at the cost of greater unemployment. This also appears to be born out by the experience of black employees in the USA. Levy (1980) reports that being out of the labour force is increasingly long term for some black males. In 1950, for example, about 50 per cent of black teenagers were employed but by 1978 the figure had fallen to about 25 per cent. Thus it is misleading to judge changes in the relative position of minority groups only by reference to their earnings/occupational distribution.

Several authors have suggested that discrimination against minority groups will raise the costs of job search for them (e.g. McCall 1973; Gordon and

Morton 1974; Dex 1980). This would arise where the probability of rejection is greater for a minority group member. Amsden and Moser (1975) note that equal opportunities legislation might itself increase women's search costs if it causes employers to interview minority applicants for the sake of appearances, without any intention of hiring them. If, therefore, one finds that, controlling for quality, the ratio of interviews to follow-up job offers differs between majority and minority group members, discrimination cannot be ruled out. In their analysis of men and women economists in 1973/74, Amsden and Moser find no significant difference in this ratio between men and women, suggesting that search costs are not different between the sexes. Gordon and Morton (1974) use a separate argument for differential search costs for women. It is argued that the psychological costs of search are higher for women because they have been socialised to be passive and because bargaining for a higher wage is not a feminine trait. Further, since fewer women than men drive a car, their physical costs of search will be higher.

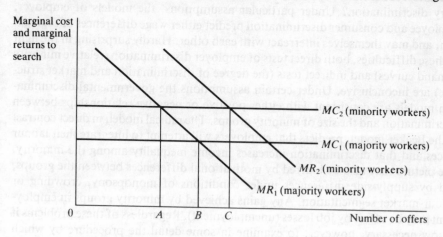

FIG. 3.8   A job search model

Can higher search costs explain the higher unemployment rates experienced by minority workers? The simple job search model suggests that a searcher's behaviour will be a function of the cost of search and the dispersion of wage rates in the market where search is undertaken. In fact, if the cost of search increases (i.e. the marginal cost curve shifts up from $MC_1$ to $MC_2$ in Fig. 3.8) then the amount of search undertaken will diminish from $0B$ to $0A$. The expected gain from search, on the other hand, will increase as the dispersion of wage offers increases. Thus for this particular model to explain the observed differences in unemployment experience between majority and minority members requires that the dispersion of wage offers is sufficiently greater for minority workers to shift the marginal returns to search to the right (from $MR_1$ to $MR_2$) at $C$ to outweigh the additional search costs incurred (the increase from $MC_1$ to $MC_2$). An alternative argument suggested by Dex (1980) is that the probability of rejection actually increases the duration of search, as minority workers are forced to continue searching longer than majority workers before any offer is forthcoming, the assumption of one offer per time period in the above model being inappropriate. Further, we must remember that the opportunity cost of search is lower for minority workers if their potential earnings in employment are lower than for majority workers. In her study of West Indian and white school-leavers in London and Birmingham in 1972/73, Dex suggests that the explanation for the observed results might be the inferior awareness of the market on the part of the West Indians, as illustrated by the different methods by which they obtained their first job compared to the white group.

### SUMMARY

This section has argued that there are ambiguities or conflicts in the predictions of the various economic models of discrimination. How far, for instance, should we take into account the possibility of pre-entry discrimination in estimating post-entry discrimination? Under particular assumptions, the models of employer, employee and consumer discrimination predict either wage differences or segregation, and may themselves interreact with each other. Hardly surprising in the light of these difficulties, both direct tests of employer discrimination (relative minority demand curves) and indirect tests (the degree of discrimination and market structure) are inconclusive. Under certain assumptions the governmental discrimination models are consistent with either positive or negative relationships between discrimination and the size of minority groups. The radical model, in direct contrast to the Becker model, predicts that employers will attempt to integrate their labour forces and that discrimination increases income inequality among the majority. The picture may also be blurred by motivational differences between the groups, and by supply-side differences under conditions of monopsony, crowding or labour-market segmentation. Any gains achieved by minority groups in employment may be offset by job losses (unemployment). Regardless of these problems it is now necessary, however, to examine in some detail the procedure by which discrimination, whatever its cause, is estimated, and some further empirical results.

## 5.   Measuring discrimination — some problems and further results

### PROBLEMS IN ESTIMATING DISCRIMINATION

The starting-point for estimating discrimination is Mincer's 'basic schooling model' which is explained in Chapter 2 of this volume. From this model the following estimating equation is derived[39]:

$$\log W_t = a + b_1 S + b_2 X + b_3 X^2 + \varepsilon \tag{21}$$

where $W_t$ = earnings at age $t$;
$S$ = years of schooling;
$X$ = years of experience;
$\varepsilon$ = stochastic error.

Some authors have attempted to measure discrimination by inserting a dummy variable for the minority group in the above equation. Johnson (1978), Lloyd and Niemi (1979), Smith (1979) and others have pointed out that this procedure will give biased estimates to the extent that significant interactions exist between membership of a minority group and various other characteristics which are not themselves a function of discrimination. A superior approach is to estimate separate regressions for each racial/sex/marital status group. This allows membership of a particular group to affect the coefficients of personal characteristics as well as to shift the wage function. As Johnson notes, this is particularly important if there is reason to believe that factors such as quality of education or marginal returns to experience vary systematically among groups.

Earnings are then decomposed into differences resulting from varying endowments and coefficients, and the unexplained differential arising in the constant term. Thus, taking as an example men $(M)$ and women $(F)$ the crude mean wage differential $(R)$ can be decomposed as follows:

$$\bar{W}_M - \bar{W}_F = (a_M - a_F) + (\bar{X}_M - \bar{X}_F)b_M + \bar{X}_F(b_M - b_F) \qquad [22]$$
$$(R) \quad = \quad (U) \quad + \quad (E) \quad + \quad (C)$$

where $\bar{X}$ = mean characteristics;
   $(U)$ = the proportion explained by differences in the intercepts;
   $(E)$ = the proportion due to differing personal characteristics;
   $(C)$ = the proportion due to differing coefficients.

Discrimination $(D)$, a residual, is normally taken to be equal to $C + U$.[40] This implies that no part of $C$ is non-discriminatory, for example resulting from division of labour in the household. Further, it has been suggested that the residuals and particularly the constant term might be best thought of as a measure of our ignorance, so that more direct tests are required before any confidence can be placed in the estimates of discrimination (Lloyd et al. 1979). There is a tendency in regression analysis not to interpret differences in the constant term as they may be considered to be arbitrary (Jencks et al. 1979). This becomes particularly crucial in the estimation of discrimination, however, and particularly so in the light of Jencks's own and other findings that the main difference between white and non-white earnings equations is the difference between constants. Two extreme interpretations, that any such difference measures discrimination or that it represents non-discriminatory differences in motivational factors excluded from the model, seem equally arbitrary and unsatisfactory.

This decomposition procedure is explained in more detail by reference to Fig. 3.9. Let us suppose that the comparison is between male and female employees in a particular productive unit. Then it is necessary to compare the average earnings that would be received by men and women if they were paid according to the same earnings function, while recognising that they possess different attributes or endowments.

There are two possible measures of discrimination. One may assume that men and women are paid according to the male earnings function in the absence of discrimination, or that they are both paid according to the female function (Oaxaca 1973). In the former case, estimated female average earnings $(\bar{F}_e)$ are

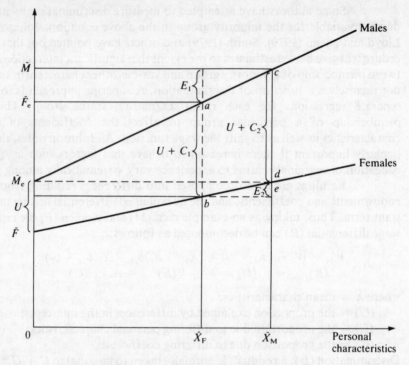

FIG. 3.9    Measuring discrimination; the index number problem
$\bar{X}_F$ = average female characteristics (or endowments);
$\bar{X}_M$ = average male characteristics
$\bar{M}$ = average male earnings
$\bar{F}$ = average female earnings;
$\bar{F}_e$ = estimated average female earnings if paid according to the male earnings function;
$\bar{M}_e$ = estimated average male earnings if paid according to the female earnings function

given by

$$\bar{F}_e = W_M(\bar{X}_F)$$

where $W_M$ represents the male earnings function and $\bar{X}_F$ is a vector of the mean level of personal characteristics of females. In this case the difference in actual male average earnings ($\bar{M}$) and actual female average earnings ($\bar{F}$) can be decomposed as follows:

$\bar{M} - \bar{F}_e$ = the difference in average earnings attributable to differences in average characteristics ($E_1$);

$\bar{F}_e - \bar{F}$ = residual difference not accounted for by characteristics ($C_1$). This is our measure of discrimination, made up of differences in the intercept ($U$) and differences in the slope of the earnings functions.

An alternative is to estimate average male earnings ($\bar{M}_e$) by

$$\bar{M}_e = W_F(\bar{X}_M)$$

where $W_f$ represents the female earnings function and $\bar{X}_M$ is a vector of the mean level of personal characteristics of men. In this case the difference between $\bar{M}$ and $\bar{F}$ is decomposed as follows:

$\bar{M}_e - \bar{F}$ = the difference in average earnings attributable to differences in average characteristics $(E_2)$;

$\bar{M} - \bar{M}_e$ = residual difference not accounted for by characteristics $(C_2)$.

It can be seen, therefore, that provided the male earnings function lies above the female function and is of steeper slope, for which there is some empirical evidence, then the second approach will always give a larger estimate of discrimination than the first. In the diagram $(C_2 + U)/(C_2 + E_2) > (C_1 + U)/(C_1 + E_1)$ since $C_2 > C_1$ and $C_1 + E_1 = C_2 + E_2$. The question then arises as to which estimate is the more appropriate one to use.[41] Boulet and Rowley (1977) have argued that an estimate of discrimination should be skew-symmetric; that is, it should indicate that discrimination against the $i^{th}$ group relative to the $j^{th}$ group is identical (though of opposite sign) to labour-market discrimination against the $j^{th}$ group relative to the $i^{th}$ group. As Masters (1977) points out, however, there is asymmetry in the context of discrimination. If discrimination implies an aversion to the minority group, but no favouritism towards the majority, then the majority workforce will be paid a wage in accordance with its marginal revenue product and the minority somewhat less. Here the elimination of discrimination would imply that all workers would be paid the value of their marginal revenue product, and the appropriate procedure would be to use the male earnings function as the basis of comparison. Given the presence of favouritism towards the majority group, on the other hand, the elimination of discrimination might imply that the outcome would lie somewhere between the two functions, but given their numerical superiority in the labour force the outcome is likely to be closer to the earnings function of the majority. Most authors, however give estimates for both procedures, while others, such as Greenhalgh (1980), take an average in order to obtain a single measure (For a further discussion of these issues see Chiplin and Sloane 1982).

The above index-number problem is one reason for treating estimates of discrimination with caution. There are, however, others. First, and this is particularly so where aggregated data are used, there is a danger of omitted variable bias (De Tray and Greenberg 1977; Fujii and Trapani 1978; Simeral 1978; Vrooman and Greenfield 1978 among others). If important explanatory variables are excluded from the estimating equation this will affect the decomposition of the wage differential, in particular the shift coefficient, and thus the amount of discrimination indicated by the equation. If the omitted variables are positively correlated with the included variables the true level of discrimination will be underestimated. This is likely to be the case with market work motivation, which does not directly enter into the equation. However, this will be counterbalanced to an unspecified degree if the average values of the omitted variables are higher for the majority than for the minority group. We cannot, therefore, be certain whether the estimate of discrimination represents an upper or lower limit to its true level.[42] As De Tray and Greenberg (1977) note, few if any data sets contain sufficient information to ensure that omitted variable bias will be absent, and in certain cases it may have a major impact on reported results. Thus, in their analysis of productivity of men and women working under experimental conditions, Battallio *et al.* (1978) found that if the residual approach had been routinely applied to their data the entire difference between male and female earnings would have been (mistakenly) attributed to discrimination rather than motivational and related factors.

These and similar problems of under-adjustment have led Kamalich and Polachek (1982) to propose an alternative procedure which examines qualification differentials rather than wage differentials. To quote,

> this method referred to as reverse regression, compares the job qualifications (which serve as productivity proxies) of members of different race or sex groups, who are earning the same wage. If discrimination exists, one would expect to find blacks and women to have higher mean qualifications for any given wage level (p. 540).

The appropriate reverse regression is obtained by having each productivity proxy as a dependent variable, and wages and other standardising variables as independent regressors. Hence in the simplest formulation with wages ($W$), years of schooling ($S$) and experience ($X$) as independent variables we have

$$S = a_0 + a_1 W + a_2 X \qquad\qquad [23]$$
$$X = b_0 + b_1 W + b_2 S \qquad\qquad [24]$$

Running separate regressions for each sex/marital status group, we can examine differences in each productivity proxy, holding the wage constant. In their initial formulation Kamalich and Polachek merely insert sex and race dummies, so that differences in the coefficients on these variables measure discrimination, and add an interaction term between sex (race) and the wage to allow for the fact that discrimination may vary according to the wage level. However, as we have argued earlier, it seems preferable to run separate regressions for each group. The reverse regression approach has the advantage of measuring discrimination directly rather than as residual. As Kamalich and Polachek admit, however, it may not itself be free of bias, since there may be problems of simultaneity when wages are used as an explanatory variable, and multicollinearity with regard to sex (race) and wages, although appropriate tests did not reveal these to be major problems in relation to their own data set.

One might add that differences in the productivity proxies do not necessarily indicate discrimination. For example, Frank (1978) has pointed to the probability of differential overqualification in relation to married women as a consequence of family income maximisation (see section 5d below). Using data on over 4,500 individuals in the University of Michigan Panel Study of Income Dynamics 1976, Kamalich and Polachek found using the residual approach to the measurement of discrimination that women earned 35 per cent less than men after adjusting for schooling, experience and tenure, while the figure was 13 per cent in the case of race. When, however, the reverse regression approach was adopted there was no clear-cut evidence of discrimination. Using the simple model, strengths in particular qualifications compensated for weaknesses in others. Thus, women had more education, but less experience and tenure, and blacks less education but more experience and tenure, compared with white males. In the more complex model there was even a suggestion of reverse discrimination for higher-earning blacks. Therefore, this evidence must cast some doubt on estimates of discrimination in earlier studies, and perhaps suggests that residual and reverse regression approaches should be used together to provide upper- and lower-bound estimates of discrimination.

The index-number approach also takes no account of differences in occupation or job level. Brown *et al.* (1980a) show that this is immaterial if the same characteristics that determine wages also determine occupation. But occupational status may be subject to separate or additional constraints such as environmental influences, personal choice or discriminatory restrictions on entry to particular occupations. Some studies have attempted to deal with this by including dummy variables for occupation in the earnings regressions or estimating earnings within levels (Rosenbaum 1980), which assumes implicitly that there is no discrimination in access to the various occupation levels and that any discrimination that exists is pure wage discrimination. That does not appear to be an entirely satisfactory assumption. Mincer (1979) has also objected on the grounds that job level is merely a grouped variant of the dependent variable and therefore illegitimate. The only alternative, therefore, is to develop a separate theory of occupational attainment.[43] Whether job level is included or excluded, it should be remembered that cross-sectional studies of earnings reflect the influence of past as well as current discriminatory practices. As equality of opportunities policies bite deeper, employers' attitudes and policies may be adjusting over time. If so, from the point of view of policy it may be more appropriate to focus on *current* hiring and promotion decisions.

Following on from the above it is likely, as noted earlier, that the tastes of each group for particular occupations may differ for non-discriminatory or biological and cultural reasons (Simeral 1978). Thus, differences in regression coefficients may be related to differences in labour supply dependent upon factors such as household decision-making. If so $(U + E)$ will be an overestimate of the amount of discrimination. As Blinder (1973) points out, in these circumstances we need to estimate a simultaneous system by two-stage least squares or similar techniques, with separate structural equations for supply-side and demand-side variables. A reduced form equation can then be estimated, based on characteristics which are completely exogenous. An alternative is to measure directly the wage offers of the employer (Chiplin 1979a, 1981) as opposed to the wage outcomes, which may reflect both demand-side and supply-side influences. What is then relevant is whether the probability of receiving a job offer or promotion is identical for members of the majority and minority groups with identical characteristics, irrespective of whether or not that job offer is accepted. While this approach is appealing, it is very demanding in terms of data requirements, because we require details of the number of offers made for each vacancy as opposed to acceptances.

We must now turn to some of the estimates that have been made of discrimination, more specifically to the differences in components such as education and experience, then to the effects of marriage on the earnings of women and finally to the impacts of both trade unions and governments.

### RATES OF RETURN TO EDUCATION

The amount of education received and the rate of return obtained from it are central to the human capital model. As illustrated in Fig. 3.10, ignoring the question of state subsidies for education, we can draw an upward-sloping schedule $S$ showing that as an individual increases his or her investment in education the cost of funds increases (possibly because small amounts of education can be funded from personal savings, while larger amounts require external borrowing). Also there will be a downward-sloping schedule $D$, indicating the fact that as an individual increases his investment in education there will be decreasing rates of return. It is plausible to suppose that minority members have a lower demand for education, that is given amounts of education ($D_{MIN}$), than majority members ($D_{MAJ}$). This could be because of expectations of future discrimination or (in the case of women) anticipated family commitments. Given identical supply curves (representing the terms under which funds for education are available), in equilibrium minority members would then receive a lower rate of return to education. However, it is also possible that the supply curve for minority members ($S_{MIN}$) lies to the left of that for majority members, so that we observe differences in the amounts of education received ($0E_1$ and $0E_2$), but little if any difference in rates of return. Minority supply schedules might be raised because of anticipated discrimination, the difficulty of obtaining grants or loans or because of family background considerations. Thus contrary to what might be thought, similar rates of return to members of minority and majority groups are quite compatible with

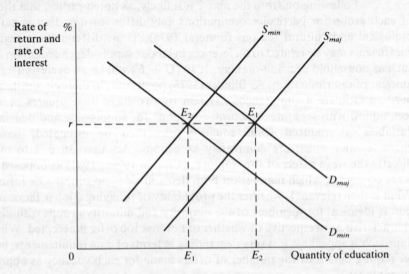

FIG. 3.10   Demand and supply schedules for education

the presence of discrimination in the labour market. In fact, we do observe significant differences in the amounts of education obtained by white men relative to women and black workers, but similar rates of return.

As far as rates of return to education are concerned, it appears from US evidence (Table 3.4) that rates of return for men and women increase with years of schooling in virtually every racial group.[44] The rate of return for white men is higher than for other men apart from the Japanese and Chinese. Within each racial group, apart from the Cubans and Chinese, the rate of return is generally higher for women than for men (more so when women are compared with white men only). For the UK, data are less complete, but analysis of the General Household Survey suggests than men and women receive similar increments for qualifications (Greenhalgh 1980), and that coloured men obtain as favourable or more favourable returns to education than their white counterparts, mean years of schooling in fact being greater for coloured workers in this sample (McNabb and Psacharopoulos 1981a); but that coloured immigrants obtain a much smaller rate of return (Chiswick 1980). Cross-section analyses may conceal changes over time in the relative pay-off from education. Haworth et al. (1975), adopting a cohort approach, find that in the USA the relative education/earnings pay-off is definitely related to age, with the white/non-white earnings education ratio declining with age, suggesting either that there has been a substantial improvement over time in the education received by non-whites or discrimination in the labour market is weakening.

Welch (1973) argued that differing quality of education was a major factor in explaining differences in rates of return to education for blacks and whites, since the quality of education is in general higher for whites, and in particular that received by young blacks and whites is much more equal than is the case for older cohorts, which is consistent with Haworth et al.'s findings reported above. Attempts to include educational quality variables in human capital models

TABLE 3.4   Percentage rate of return to education in 1969 by years of schooling in the USA

| Group | Male Years of schooling | | | Female Years of schooling | | |
|---|---|---|---|---|---|---|
| | 8 | 12 | 16 | 8 | 12 | 16 |
| White | 4.04 | 5.40 | 6.76 | 5.13 | 7.21 | 9.29 |
| Japanese | 3.11 | 5.03 | 6.95 | 5.58 | 7.74 | 9.90 |
| Chinese | 3.22 | 7.22 | 11.22 | 5.32 | 7.00 | 8.68 |
| Filipino | 1.90 | 3.18 | 4.46 | 0.89 | 4.89 | 8.89 |
| Mexican | 3.31 | 4.03 | 4.75 | 4.38 | 6.30 | 8.22 |
| Cuban | 1.19 | 3.19 | 5.19 | 2.09 | 1.29 | 0.49 |
| Puerto Rican | 2.69 | 4.53 | 6.37 | 2.94 | 6.22 | 9.50 |
| Negro | 2.67 | 4.35 | 6.03 | 4.28 | 10.28 | 16.28 |
| American Indian | 0.87 | 2.15 | 3.43 | 0.26 | 8.42 | 16.58 |

Source: Gwartney and Long (1978).

have been made by Link *et al.* (1976, 1980), Hoffman (1979) and Akin and Garfinkel (1980). The last of these use data for 1968–72, including educational expenditure per pupil as their measure of labour quality and income and education of father, IQ and an achievement motivation index as controls. They find that the percentage returns to education for whites are approximately 3 percentage points greater than for blacks at every working age. Link *et al.* (1980), using a different data set, find in contrast that returns to schooling of young blacks are comparable to those of young whites, but less favourable for blacks in older cohorts, supporting Welch's original claim. Therefore, we cannot say for certain how important differences in educational quality are in explaining differences in rates of return to education for black and white workers, which suggests there is a need for further research. Welch himself (1980) suggests, however, that state average pupil expenditures may not be a good indicator of school quality, and doubts whether the case for school quality can be proven as there are 'too many competing but observationally equivalent explanations' (p. 182). Similar problems would be found in any attempt to compare male and female educational quality, though here the fact that types of education (skills or disciplines) received vary considerably between the sexes is undoubtedly of some significance.

Radical economists have challenged the claim of human capital theorists that education itself makes the individual inherently more productive in the labour market. Gintis (1971), for instance, suggests that education increases earnings not so much by increasing knowledge as by repressing unstable personality traits of individuals which reduce their productivity, or by acting as a screening mechanism. He also argues that the inclusion of an achievement measure in the human capital model should enable one to test whether this is so through comparison of the relative magnitude of the schooling and achievement coefficients. This in fact has been done by Vrooman and Greenfield (1978), using data from the University of Texas which measures functional competency within five knowledge areas. Results using this variable are, however, mixed, suggesting that ability to score well in these tests is associated with increased earnings for white males and black females, but not for black males and white females, while the schooling coefficient is significant for all samples other than black females. Again much work remains to be done before we are clear about the precise way in which education sustains differences between majority and minority workers. (For a fuller discussion of the screening hypothesis, see Ch. 2 of this volume.)

## RATES OF RETURN TO ON-THE-JOB TRAINING AND EXPERIENCE

There is abundant evidence that the earnings of women increase at a slower rate for each year of experience than do those of men, and the same appears to be true of black men relative to white men, but as Duncan and Hoffman (1979) point out, the proper interpretation of the effects of experience on earnings is even less clear than for education. One particular problem of interpretation arises from the rise in female labour-force participation. If this is a consequence of an influx of inexperienced workers average experience will fall, but if it is a consequence of longer stays in the labour force for women average experience will rise (Mallan

1982). Many of the data sets used in analyses of race and sex differences are inadequate as they measure work history by a single variable or estimate experience indirectly. The ninth wave of the Panel Study of Income Dynamics 1976 does, however, provide a direct measure of on-the-job training and experience for the USA. This reveals that white men had obtained almost twice as much on-the-job training as had black men, white women or black women. Compared with white men, the average white woman had 3 years' less labour market experience with other employers and a similar difference in her current employment, and comparable differences applied to black women in comparison to black men. Duncan and Hoffman find that when an earnings equation is estimated, using direct measures of work experience rather than a single work experience variable, the results change dramatically. The estimated returns to training reveal no evidence of direct discrimination, since the coefficients show an increase of 5.4 per cent in the wages of white men for an additional year of training, 5.9 per cent for black men, 8.5 per cent for white women and 6.6 per cent for black women. If the minority groups had the same amount of training as white men, rewarded at the same rate, the earnings gap would diminish by 18.6 per cent for black men, 9.4 per cent for black women and 12.0 per cent for white women. Unfortunately similar longitudinal data are not available in the UK, but McNabb and Psacharopoulos (1981a) find, using General Household Survey data, that earnings increase by 7.5 per cent for each year of experience for coloured male workers and 9.1 per cent for white male workers. Greenhalgh (1980) obtains a similar result for women relative to men. Broadly comparable results have also been found in studies of individual establishments in the USA and the UK, but since the experience variables used are generally inferior to those of Duncan and Hoffman less reliance can be placed upon them.

The conventional wisdom with regard to the assumed relationship between earnings experience and performance according to the human capital model has recently been challenged by Medoff and Abraham (1980, 1981). Examining data for managerial and professional staff in four large US corporations, they find that although there is a strong positive association with grade levels between experience and relative earnings, there is either no association or even a negative association between experience and rated performance. Assuming that such performance rating is an accurate indicator of actual productivity, it would seem that the on-the-job-training human capital model is unable to explain a substantial part of the observed rate of return to labour-market experience, which, were these findings to apply more widely, would have major implications for the measurement of discrimination. For example we know that on average women have less experience than men, and on the assumption that this experience is related to productivity we make an allowance for these differences in measuring discrimination as a residual. If, however, the extra experience which generates extra earnings does not add to productivity, then we are underestimating the true extent of discrimination against women. In the context of British equality of opportunity legislation, differential pay for experience would amount to indirect discrimination. But it should be noted that Medoff and Abraham's analysis relates to within-grade performance rating and one might, plausibly, argue that the more able will be promoted faster to higher grades, so those who are left in lower grades (with more experience) are in fact the less able. Medoff and Abraham defend themselves against this criticism by pointing out that this does not explain the failure of the estimated within-grade returns to labour-market experience to move towards zero when performance-related controls are introduced, but none the less it would have been better to compare performance ratings across grades. Clearly, further work is required on this important issue.

## THE IMPACT OF MARRIAGE ON THE EARNINGS OF WOMEN

The first effect of marriage may be to limit the job horizon of the woman, a factor emphasised among others by Turnbull and Williams (1974), Ferber and Kordick (1978), Frank (1978) and Corcoran and Duncan (1979). As Frank notes, the search for a pair of jobs is constrained geographically. Only rarely will a range of wage offers produce a best offer in the same location for both husband and wife. In other cases a compromise will have to be made, and given that on average husbands possess a large stock of human capital and work longer hours, family income maximisation demands that husbands make smaller compromises than their wives. Hence, on average married women will earn less than married men endowed with identical personal characteristics, and there will be differential overqualification between the sexes in given occupations in the sense that individuals have qualifications in excess of the requirements of the job.[45]

There are a number of ways in which we might attempt to determine how much of the gross wage differential is attributable to family locational decisions. First one might compare the earnings of married and single women since the latter should be relatively free of locational constraints. Thus, for instance, Turnbull and Williams (1974) find that married female teachers in England fare substantially worse than their unmarried female colleagues, and attribute this to the more restricted area over which they can search for jobs on account of their husbands' employment, rather than to the effects of breaks in service. Corcoran and Duncan (1979) find, however, that self-imposed limits on job choice have a negligible effect on the earnings of four groups of workers (white men, black men, white women and black women). Perhaps, as Frank argues, other undetected differences between married and single women blur any differential overqualification measure. Frank himself postulates that the extent to which wives are overqualified for the jobs they occupy will be a function of the size of market in which they are located. Using 1967 data for individuals in professional and related groups who have moved location since husband was age 17, he finds that wives in small Standard Metropolitan Statistical Areas can earn nearly 8 per cent less than husbands with the same measured levels of education and experience (or a quarter of the unexplained earnings differential between the two groups). Ferber, Loeb and Lowry (1978) in their analysis of the earnings of Ph.D. graduates in the USA attempt to construct a job mobility index. This values positively an individual's moves to another location to further his or her career and pay increases or promotion in response to an offer elsewhere, and negatively moves made because spouse was moving, either having already obtained a job or without having found a job (the latter given a double weighting) and rejected chances of changing jobs or of using an offer for bargaining purposes on account of the spouse's inability or unwillingness to leave. In both selected cohorts the mobility index is significantly higher for men than for women (0.54 and 0.32 compared with 0.27 and 0.24 respectively), but this only explains a small proportion of the gross earnings differential (14.7 and 15.0% respectively). As Ferber and Kordick (1978) note, one implication of the above is that monopsonistic exploitation does play some role in determining the inferior position of women in the labour force, as discussed earlier.

A second aspect of marriage is the raising of children and its effect on labour-force participation. Most data sets do not contain information on number and age of children, which are both likely to influence the decision whether or not to work in the labour market and also the extent of such work. Greenhalgh (1980), using British General Household Survey data, finds that children are associated with lower earnings for women, but higher earnings for men. Osterman (1979) finds the same in a large US publishing company where the inclusion of a marriage and children variable in the regression equation reduces the unexplained differential by almost half (from 32 to 19%). In a most detailed analysis of the variable Hill (1979) finds that the large negative wage effects of number of children for white women are reduced to insignificance once refined statistical controls for work history (such as lessened work experience, investment in the labour market and labour-force attachment) are introduced. Yet in the case of black women and white men the insignificant *positive* effects of children become large and significant when refined controls for work experience and training are introduced. Further, Siebert and Young (1983) found for librarians in the UK that married male librarians without children earn between 9 and 12 points less than married men with children, which they attribute to the greater stability and reliability of the latter.

In the case of marital status, on the other hand, the wage effects remain stable despite the introduction of more refined controls for each of the sex/race sub-groups. In fact there is a strong positive wage effect of marriage of 25–30 per cent for white men and 25 per cent for black men, while there are apparently no detrimental effects of marriage *per se* for either white or black women.[46] Hill (1979) suggests that these somewhat surprising results considerably weaken strict human capital explanations of the wage effects of marital status. But human capital theory emphasises certain consequences of marital status rather than status itself, and it is more appropriate to look directly at measures of labour-force attachment. In the case of children, for instance, their effect on female participation may depend less on their number and ages than on the availability or otherwise of child-care facilities or relatives willing and able to substitute for the mother.[47]

There has been considerable discussion in the literature over the effects of discontinuous labour-force experience on married women (which is well summarised in Weiss and Gronau 1981). O'Kelly (1979) reports that in the USA in 1967 and subsequent to equal pay and civil rights legislation, the smallest female/male earnings ratio (73%) related to adult women who had worked continuously, while those working between 75 and 99 per cent of their adult lives earned only 55 per cent of male average earnings and those who worked the least reached only 22 per cent of male earnings. The counter argument is that female participation rates have been increasing in the USA (as in other countries), exceeding 50 per cent for all women over 16 and approaching 70 per cent for those aged 20–25 (Lloyd and Niemi 1979), so that the gap should be narrowing over time.[48] An early attempt to take account of the discontinuous labour-market experience of women in a human capital framework was that of Mincer and Polachek (1974). Their model is based on three propositions. First, even those women who have identical current personal characteristics (other than experience) as males will have lower wages where past experience is shorter. Second, the total investment of such women will be smaller also because those who spend less time in market work invest less per year worked. Third, the interruption of work for any significant length of time causes the value of human capital to depreciate or 'atrophy'. Hence, women are likely to choose occupations with low atrophy. Mincer and Polachek analysed the wages of women aged 30–44 using data from the 1967 US National Longitudinal Survey with the following equation:

$$\log W = a + b_1 E_1 + b_2 E_2 + b_3 E_3 + b_4 H_1 + b_5 H_2 + \sum_{i=1}^{n} C_i Z + \varepsilon \qquad [25]$$

where $W$ = hourly rate of pay;
    $E_1$ = years of work experience until birth of first child;
    $E_2$ = years of work experience after first child until current job;
    $E_3$ = years of work experience on current job;
    $H_1$ = home time after first child;
    $H_2$ = all other years of home time;
    $Z$ = vector of other variables related to earnings (schooling, health, migration, etc.).

Mincer and Polachek's results confirm the hypothesis that female human capital will depreciate in periods of absence from the labour market, and also reveal that investment while on current job is greater than in earlier periods when intermittent labour-force participation may have been anticipated. Sandell and Shapiro (1978) cricitised this latter result on the grounds that the estimates for years of work experience up to the birth of the first child cover only general experience, while number of years with current employer includes the combined return to both general and specific training, both of which influence the results. Further, their own estimates suggest that differences in the work experience of men and women account for only a quarter of the difference in wages between the two groups rather than one-half, as found by Mincer and Polachek. In reply, the latter (1978) analysed further the effects of interrupted work experience between 1967 and 1971, and found that this factor explains 19 per cent of the wage gap in their ordinary least squares regression and 49 per cent in their two-stage least squares regression. Corcoran (1979) cricitised the restriction of the analysis to the 30–44 age group. Many in this particular group are likely to have only recently re-entered the labour market and through misinformation about job opportunities may have their earnings temporarily depressed, thus leading to overestimates of the amount of depreciation in skills. Corcoran uses data from the Panel Survey of Income

Dynamics which, unlike the National Longitudinal Survey, has unrestricted age ranges and precise measures of timing, frequency and duration of withdrawals from the labour market. The only negative and significant coefficient for years out of the labour force is for white women, and suggests that wages fall only 1 per cent for each year out of the labour force (Corcoran and Duncan 1979). Likewise, Jones and Long (1979b) find when they take account of the hours dimension of market work that the net depreciation rate is small (only 0.5% p.a.). In their study of English teachers Turnbull and Williams (1974) found that both men and women who returned to teaching after a break of 2 years or more suffered no loss of earnings when compared to other teachers with a similar length of completed service, though this may be a function of the salary structure as much as anything else. These findings suggest that the importance of depreciation of skills through lack of use may have been exaggerated.

Another important question not directly tested by Mincer and Polachek is how the frequency and timing of labour-force withdrawals influence wages. Corcoran notes, for instance, that men's withdrawals are short, concentrated at the start of their careers and often involve the acquisition of skills; while those of women are often long, spread out over the working life and rarely involve skill acquisition. Obviously this factor is worthy of further investigation.

There is evidence that intermittent labour-force participation influences the amount of training undertaken. Duncan and Hoffman (1979) find that past labour-force interruptions lead to significantly lower amounts of training for black women; past part-time work has the same effect for white women; and the expectation of children reduces the likelihood of training for women by 6 per cent. This can explain why, together with the fact that differences in experience are necessarily small in the early years, the wage gap widens over the life cycle. King (1977) finds, for instance, using US 1970 census data, that on average earnings of women increase by less than 1 per cent p.a. while those of males increase by almost 3 per cent p.a. It appears from King's analysis that the flatter earnings—experience profiles of women are only to a minor extent due to the pattern (i.e. occupational distribution) of female employment. Consistent with this, Ferber and Kordick (1978) explain the flatter earnings profiles of women with Ph.Ds as a consequence of their inability (or unwillingness?) to take lower-paying jobs in more prestigious institutions in comparison to men.

Recently Polachek (1981) has taken the above a stage further by hypothesising that intermittent labour-force participation will influence occupational choice and that the impact of lifetime labour-force participation on the probability of entering a given occupation will vary with that occupation's rate of atrophy. Using National Longitudinal Survey data for women aged 30—44 years he finds a strong relationship between lifetime labour-force participation and occupational choice, even after adjusting for marital status, age and education. For example, it is estimated that if women were to have a full commitment to the labour force, the number of professional women would increase by 35 per cent. Further, there is some evidence that women avoid occupations with the highest rates of atrophy. However, using the same NLS data for women aged 30—44 years, but categorising their occupations according to their sex composition,

England (1982) finds that women are not penalised less for time spent out of the labour force if they choose female occupations. In addition, there is no evidence that women with more continuous work histories are less likely to be found in predominantly female occupations. Examination of longitudinal data might help to resolve this issue.

The positive wage effects of marriage referred to above require in particular further comment. One interpretation is that married men are more work-motivated than single men because of their additional family responsibilities. As Hill (1979) notes, however, large positive wage effects of marriage for men persist even when numerous (but still crude) controls for productivity are introduced. It could be that employers engage in some form of statistical discrimination, or that their decisions are based upon paternalistic attitudes which lead them to reward those with greater financial responsibilities with higher wages.[49]

## THE IMPACT OF TRADE UNIONS

As pointed out in section 4, trade unions may be a negative or positive influence on the degree of discrimination. A number of studies in the USA have attempted to determine the effects of trade unions on the relative position of minority groups in terms of wage differences, the degree of exclusion or some combination of the two. Time-series analyses have been carried out by Rapping (1970), Ashenfelter and Godwin (1972) and Moore and Raisian (1980). Rapping attempted to estimate the impact of unions on the percentage change in non-white male employment relative to the total change in male employment and unionisation in the periods 1910–30 and 1930–60, but was unable to find conclusive evidence that the presence of unions had increased racial barriers. Ashenfelter and Godwin examined the hypothesis, which they were able to confirm, that industrial unionism had a less discriminatory effect on the black–white wage ratio over the period 1900–67 than did craft unionism. Moore and Raisian showed that over the period 1967–74 union relative wage effects were subject to considerable cyclical variations, but the fact that results for blue-collar and white-collar workers were affected differently suggest that factors other than cyclical forces were at work.

Results from some of the several cross-section analyses undertaken in the USA are summarised in Table 3.5. These results are not entirely consistent. Oaxaca (1975) for instance, finds that differentials are highest among black males and white females, while Ashenfelter (1976) finds that females and white males obtain roughly the same wage advantage from union membership and black males significantly more. The significant increase in the differential shown by Ashenfelter's figures for 1967–75 might indicate the increasing effect of unions in the recession, since unemployment was increasing over this period. When mark-up figures for the effects of unionisation on the level of earnings are combined with data on unionisation, it is possible to measure the overall effect on aggregate majority/minority wage differentials. Thus, Ashenfelter finds, using 1975 data, that unionisation may narrow overall white/black wage differentials by 2.3 per cent but widen the male/female differential by 2.9 per cent. The mark-up results for women contrast with Canadian and British findings. For Canada Gunderson

TABLE 3.5  Cross section estimates of percentage union/non-union wage differentials by race and sex in the USA

| Source | Year of investigation | Group | | | | |
|---|---|---|---|---|---|---|
| | | White males | Black males | White females | Black females | All workers |
| Oaxaca (1975) | 1967 | 11.3 | 25.1 | 21.6 | 7.3 | 15.7 |
| Ashenfelter (1976) | 1967 | 9.3 | 21.5 | 14.4 | 5.6 | 11.6 |
| Ashenfelter (1976) | 1973 | 15.5 | 22.5 | 12.7 | 13.2 | 14.8 |
| Ashenfelter (1976) | 1975 | 16.3 | 22.5 | 16.6 | 17.1 | 16.8 |
| Kiefer and Smith (1977) | 1973 | | | | | |
|     North | | 17.9 | 15.0 | 13.4 | 10.4 | – |
|     Border | | 36.6 | 24.0 | 30.7 | 20.7 | – |
|     South | | 31.4 | 49.2 | 28.3 | 22.6 | – |
| Lee (1978) | 1976 | 16.2 | 28.5 | 2.8 | 12.7 | 14.0 |
| Leigh (1978a) | 1969 | *Craft / Other†* | *Craft / Other†* | | | |
|     Craftsmen | | 38.1 / 13.3 | 12.9 / 20.1 | | | |
|     Operatives | | 29.9 / 18.3 | 17.8 / 27.2 | | | |
|     Non-farm labourers | | 38.6 / 32.4 | 48.1 / 33.9 | | | |
| Leigh (1980) | | *Adjusted‡ / Unadjusted* | | | | |
|     Young men | 1971 | 37.2 / 24.6 | | 28.0 | 22.0 | |
|     Middle-aged men | 1969 | 36.2 / 9.2 | | 45.2 | 31.5 | |
|     Middle-aged men | 1971 | 45.9 / 13.2 | | 105.0 | 37.6 | |
| Antos et al. (1980) | 1976 | | | | | 21.0 |

† The other union category includes industrial unions, government employee/white-collar unions and miscellaneous unions.
‡ Adjusted for selectivity bias (i.e. the fact that wages determine union membership).

Source: Jain and Sloane (1981).

(1975) found that unions had a substantial effect in raising the wages of women relative to men. Specifically, holding occupation and establishment constant, unions raised the ratio of female to male wages from 0.82 to 0.90. In the UK, Nickell (1977), holding constant environmental, labour quality and other effects, found that the union mark-up for men was 5 per cent and for women 14 per cent in 1966, and 18 and 19 per cent respectively in 1972. Neither of these studies implies, however, that trade unions necessarily operate to the advantage of women, since the relative wage effect may be swamped by the tendency of unions to exclude women from the membership in high wage industries.

It would be erroneous to assume that the effect of unions is common across regions and occupations. In the former case Kiefer and Smith (1977) found that unions had the effect of reducing racial wage differentials in the southern USA, while leaving them virtually unchanged in other regions, and of increasing male/female differentials in each of the three regions examined. In the latter case it has generally been found that the union mark-up is greater for less skilled workers. Leigh (1978a) finds that not only is there an inverse relationship between level of skill and size of differential, but that blacks enjoy larger mark-ups than whites in blue-collar occupations. He also finds that while the effect of industrial unions on the black–white wage differential is positive, that of craft unions is negative, reinforcing Ashenfelter's conclusion that craft unions are more discriminatory than industrial unions. In construction, Landon and Peirce (1971) found support for the hypothesis that the ratio of wage rates for skilled electricians relative to labourers would be negatively correlated with the extent to which black labourers were excluded from employment, and Ashenfelter (1973) found that there were significant differences in union–non-union wage differentials in this industry compared with other industries. Finally, Shapiro (1978) found that in the public sector there was no evidence of a positive wage effect of unions except for black blue-collar government employees who obtained a union mark-up of approximately 12 per cent.[50]

Generally, differences in the size of estimates of the effects of unions on the degree of discrimination in different samples, using different econometric techniques and over time, suggest we must be cautious before giving precise estimates. It does appear that on balance unions change the relative wage differential in favour of black workers and against women in the USA (though in favour of women in Canada and Britain), but that the overall impact is relatively small.

## THE IMPACT OF GOVERNMENT

A number of studies in the USA have attempted to estimate the impact of government on the relative position of minority groups. Smith (1976) is alone in finding that, while black and white workers earn more in federal government employment than in the private sector, discrimination against blacks if anything was slightly greater in the federal sector than in private industry in 1970. However, Long (1976), Smith and Welch (1979), Johnson (1978) and Alton Smith (1980) all found the reverse when more controls were added. The last of these investigators' results reported in Table 3.6(b) below show that it is dangerous, as with unions, to treat

TABLE 3.6(a)    Proportion of workforce employed in the government sector by race/sex group USA 1975

| Level of government | Black males | Black females | White males | White females |
|---|---|---|---|---|
| All government | 0.213 | 0.318 | 0.178 | 0.240 |
| Federal | 0.063 | 0.064 | 0.047 | 0.032 |
| State | 0.036 | 0.058 | 0.038 | 0.048 |
| Local | 0.114 | 0.196 | 0.093 | 0.160 |

TABLE 3.6(b)    Estimates of proportionate government/private sector wage differentials

| Level of government | Black males | Black females | White males | White females |
|---|---|---|---|---|
| Federal | 0.172 | 0.174 | 0.166 | 0.211 |
| State | 0.155 | 0.064 | −0.039 | 0.064 |
| Local | 0.034 | 0.043 | −0.060 | −0.007 |

Source: Smith (1980).

government as a monolithic entity. The mark-up is higher at the federal level compared to the state level and lowest at the local level (holding constant education, experience, marital status, occupation, region, union membership and city size). Further we must also consider the probabilities of gaining employment in the public sector (Table 3.6(a)). On average women and blacks are over-represented in government employment. Indeed almost one-thi ' of employed black women are employed in the government sector. Combining these wage and employment effects, Smith estimates that the relative wages of black workers as a whole have been raised by about 2 per cent through government employment. These results do not, however, imply that the government sector overall does not discriminate, merely that such discrimination as exists is less than that of the private sector. Thus Long finds that federal black employees earned only 76 per cent and women 74 per cent as much as comparable white employees. However, for single (never married) black males and females, which it was suggested earlier are the most relevant groups for purposes of estimating discrimination, earnings were over 90 per cent of those of (single) whites. Further, in the male comparison the relative earnings ratio was highest for the youngest age group 18−34 (87.1%), implying that current discrimination was less than past discrimination.

Finally, Borjas (1982) finds, consistent with his vote maximisation hypothesis, that the wage of black males relative to white, and of women relative to men, is higher in federal agencies with major black constituencies and in those which have substantial expenditure on the enforcement of affirmative action programmes in the private sector.

Having considered the extent to which discrimination against minority groups persists, it is now necessary in the final section to consider a number of possible ways in which the problem might be or has been tackled.

## 6. Policy issues

The case for intervention in the labour market rests on the supposition that pure discrimination is not only present, but has a sizeable effect on the position of minority groups. Few would argue that policies should be aimed at equality of outcomes as opposed to opportunities, but the difficulty of identifying pure discrimination raises the possibility that intervention may exceed the optimal degree required to achieve equality of opportunity and result in reverse discrimination. There is, therefore, a potential clash between equity objectives (equalising opportunities) and efficiency (ensuring that labour is put to its most productive uses). Further, some of the theories outlined above suggest that the majority groups may gain financially as well as deriving psychic or non-pecuniary income from discrimination against minority groups in the labour market. The elimination of discrimination may, therefore, reduce the income of the majority, perhaps by a significant amount in certain cases. This will reinforce the tendency for any laws against discrimination to be resisted, and evasion on a wide enough scale may make legislation an ineffective tool.

There are, however, a number of approaches to the improvement of the relative position of minority groups in the labour market. A number of economists (such as Masters 1975; Blau 1977; Lloyd and Niemi 1979) have stressed the importance of maintaining high levels of aggregate demand, since employment discrimination is likely to be inversely related to the tightness of labour markets, and affirmative action policies in particular are likely to be easier to implement when jobs are plentiful for majority workers. An alternative approach is to direct temporary employment programmes at specific groups in the labour market, thus offsetting some of the disadvantages of depressed economic conditions. The 1971 US Public Employment Programme, for instance, attempted to give preferential treatment to groups particularly disadvantaged in the labour market.[51] One of the problems facing members of minority groups is their comparative lack of human capital, so that another approach is to direct training programmes at members of minority groups in order that they should be qualified to apply for a wider range of jobs. Andresani (1977) has found, however, that formal training programmes have had little or no effect in improving the level of occupational attainment of black youth. The neo-classical approach, following Becker, is to attempt to change tastes for discrimination, and efforts to increase the degree of competition in the economy would have a central role here, though the empirical evidence considered above casts doubt on the efficacy of this approach. Subsidiary to this would be the provision of information to diminish any erroneous discrimination. At the other extreme, the radical approach would emphasis the need for fundamental changes in, or the abandonment of, the capitalist system (neglecting the absence of any clear evidence showing that discrimination is greater in capitalistic economies). This implies the need for substantial development of the political power of minority groups and their alliance with groups sympathetic to their cause. Equal opportunities legislation can be seen as lying somewhere between these two extremes.

As Beller (1978) has pointed out, the efficiency of legislation will be a function of the actual costs of compliance compared with the expected costs of violating the law. The former will in part depend upon the nature of the legislation. If the law is able to differentiate efficiently between 'pure' discrimination and other non-discriminatory differences in the treatment of majority and minority workers, productive efficiency might actually increase. At the other extreme, the imposition of quotas might raise costs considerably where certain firms were faced with inadequate supplies of minority workers to enable them to meet quota targets. Then minority wage rates will increase and firms will contract in size as a consequence. Here avoidance, which might take the form of shifting the location of production, changing the skill mix or adopting more capital-intensive techniques, is particularly likely. The costs of compliance are also likely to be related to the level of economic activity. In the recession the demand for labour and voluntary turnover will both decline increasing the costs of attaining any given target or quota for minority employment. At the same time the reduced availability of jobs is likely to make majority workers and unions more resistant to the hiring of minority workers (Beller 1980). The costs of violating the law are a function of the penalties imposed for violating the law multiplied by the probability of detection.

An alternative approach to the above, though one which has not been implemented by governments, is to subsidise employers who take on minority workers or tax employers who fail to do so (Bell 1971). The use of subsidies can be illustrated in a diagram similar to Fig. 3.2. Assume a bonus is paid in inverse relation to the percentage of majority workers in the enterprise, that wage rates of majority and minority workers are identical, the two groups are perfect substitutes within each occupation, and there is a rigid skill mix. Then in the absence of bonus, depending on the absolute level of wages, equilibrium for a discriminatory employer would occur at a point such as $e$ in Fig. 3.11 with no minority workers employed. The effect of a bonus ($ea$) is to enable the employer to reach a higher indifference curve such as $I_3$, and in equilibrium ($e_1$) some minority workers will gain employment. However, increases in the bonus rate will not always increase the employment of minority workers. Depending on the slope of the indifference curves, a relatively low bonus such as $ea'$ might maximise the number of minority workers employed (at $e_2$). Further, such a policy tends to reward most those who previously were most discriminatory. A quota, in contrast, will always make a discriminatory employer worse off, as indicated by $q_0$, but has the undesirable feature of raising employers' costs when fixed at an inappropriate level for the circumstances of the local labour market.[52] The difficulty that a bonus system potentially provides rewards to the most culpable could be diminished by a modified tax/subsidy system which rewards employers whose employment of minority workers exceeds some specified norm (such as $q_0$) and taxes those whose employment of majority workers exceeds this norm (as indicated by the line $bc$). In this case the impact is greatest upon those whose initial employment ratio was most discriminatory. On the other hand this is likely to be administratively complex, as it would hardly be appropriate to fix the same norm for all firms regardless of their particular circumstances.

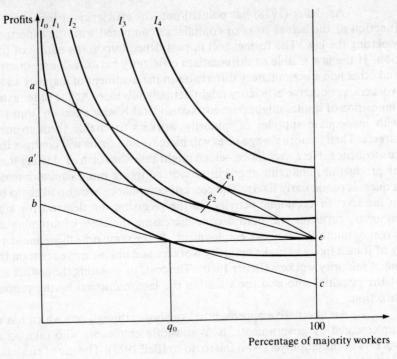

FIG. 3.11  Employer discrimination, subsidies, taxes and quotas

Irrespective of its form, it seems likely that legislation will lead to some inefficiency by inducing the placement of workers in jobs at which they are not most productive, or by forcing firms to cease the operation of economically efficient hiring practices and to undertake less efficient ones.[53] It is also possible that equal opportunities legislation will redistribute incomes from rich to poor families in the majority group. Papps (1980) points out, for instance, that women are on average less skilled than men and thus will enter relatively low-wage jobs in greater numbers than is the case with high-wage jobs as a consequence of equal opportunities legislation, thereby depressing wage rates for less skilled workers and widening skill differentials. This, she argues, may explain why the Women's Liberation Movement has greater support among more educated men and women (who may gain as a group), and suffers hostility from less educated men and women (who may lose as a group).[54] Finally, some minority workers may suffer if the inability of employers to discriminate in terms of wages leads them to discriminate in other ways, such as access to on-the-job training (Lazear 1979a).

There have been a number of attempts to test empirically the success or otherwise of equal opportunities or affirmative action programmes in improving the relative position of minority workers. These take the form of a time-series approach in which the time trend in the majority/minority earnings differential is related to the enforcement of legislation, holding constant economic conditions, and a cross-section approach in which firms subject to contract compliance under affirmative action programmes are compared to other firms not so affected. Cross-section studies of the enforcement of racial anti-discrimination laws in the USA have produced mixed results. Various analyses (see Hildebrand *et al.* 1976) suggest that there has been a significant increase in minority employment in contract compliance firms,[55] but the results are quantitatively small and the effect in terms of occupational advancement has been negligible. Beller (1978) utilises a cost of adjustment model in which the incidence of enforcement is measured by the ratio of number of charges of discrimination to employees in covered firms 1968–70. She finds that the enforcement of the employment provisions of Title VII of the 1964 Civil Rights Act, which prohibits discrimination on grounds of religion, sex or national origin, increased both relative black employment and wage rates, but this was more than offset by the negative effects of enforcing the wage provisions.[56] Thus it appears that legislation was unsuccessful in combating racial discrimination in the 1960s. These results contrast with the time-series results of Masters (1975). He utilises the following model of Rasmussen (1970), which takes into account the effect of cyclical and trend factors on black–white income ratios:

$$Y_t = a\,\%\Delta GNP + bU_{t-1} + cT_1 + dT_2 + eD + \varepsilon \qquad [26]$$

where $Y_t$ = the ratio of non-white to white median male income;
$\%\Delta GNP$ = percentage rate of growth of the gross national product;
$U_{t-1}$ = aggregate rate of unemployment, lagged one year;
$T_1$ = time trend prior to 1964;
$T_2$ = time trend beginning in 1964;
$D$ = dummy beginning in 1964.

Applying this model to annual data for the period 1964–71, Masters finds that the black–white income ratio has been increased by 9 percentage points from 0.52 to 0.61 in 1971. However, as he himself acknowledges, it would be dangerous to infer that all of this improvement was a direct consequence of the Civil Rights Acts.

Beller (1979) has also attempted to assess the effects of the strengthening of Title VII of the Civil Rights Act in 1972 on the male/female earnings differential, using a vector of enforcement variables assigned to each individual on the basis of geographical area, class of worker, and industry of employment (for federal contract compliance). Her findings are less pessimistic than earlier studies, for the enforcement of sex discrimination provisions is found to have reduced the male/female earnings differential by about 7 percentage points between 1967 and 1974. On the other hand, the revised provisions seem also to have reduced the earnings of men. She also finds (1982) that between 1967 and 1974 both Title VII of the Civil Rights Act of 1964 and the federal contract compliance programme increased the probability of an employed woman being in a male occupation relative to a man's probability. This she takes to imply that the earlier situation reflected discrimination. In a further study (1980), Beller finds that these results were influenced by the level of economic activity. More specifically, women's earnings would have been higher in 1974 and the sex differential smaller had the unemployment rate been lower. The downward influence of Title VII on male earnings would also have been reduced. If the unemployment rate is sufficiently low it appears from this analysis that legislation is a relatively costless tool (to male workers) for narrowing the sex differential in earnings.

It should be noted that unlike the case of race, Lazear (1979b) has found that the wage growth component of earnings (reflecting the amount of on-the-job training) has improved more markedly for young women than has the ratio of mean wages relative to young men. This implies that the male/female earnings ratio will diminish further in the long run. Finally Chiplin *et al.* (1980) have attempted to use a time-series model similar to that of Rasmussen and Masters to explain variations in the male/female earnings ratio in the UK. These results suggest, in contrast to Beller, that relative female earnings do not improve as labour markets tighten, that female earnings were worsening over time (the time trend being negative), and that in 1975 the female/male hourly earnings ratio was some 8 percentage points higher than it would have been but for a change in the underlying relationship. However, it appears that the influence of flat-rate incomes policies during this period has combined with equal pay and opportunities legislation in achieving this result.[57]

To conclude, therefore, it appears that the labour-market experiences of minority and majority group employees are influenced by a large number of factors which make it difficult to detect the extent to which discrimination plays a role in determining outcomes. Indeed, there can be few areas in economics where so many conflicting findings have been produced in empirical work based on various methodologies and data sets. On the most plausible assumptions, the removal of discrimination might raise the earnings of women by as much as 10 per cent and those of racial minority workers by rather more, but some differences in earnings and occupational distributions would still remain because of differing human capital endowments among the various groups. Equal opportunities legislation appears to have had some impact in moderating these influences, but its precise effect remains in doubt and its optimal form and the extent to which it should be combined with other approaches, if at all, remain a matter of debate.†

## Notes

1. Madden (1973: Ch 2, p 1) suggests that 'economists have a tradition of belated response to discrimination problems' and goes on to suggest that part of the problem is a lack of agreement on an appropriate definition of discrimination.
2. In his introduction to the first edition Becker writes:

   In view of the importance of discrimination, it may seem surprising that economists have neglected its study. One can only speculate about the reasons for this neglect. Other social scientists, notably the sociologists and anthropologists, by their early entrance into this field may have established it as their property. The inability of economists to deal in a quantitative way with non-pecuniary motives could have been a sufficient deterrent, since

†The author is grateful for helpful comments by the editors, an anonymous referee, W.S. Siebert and A. Young on an earlier draft of this survey.

such motives constitute an essential aspect of discrimination in the market place. They have lacked a systematic theory with which to interpret the economic differentials between majority and minority groups, a theory that could weave together discrimination toward minority groups with free choice of enterprise and occupation (p. 10).

It is no longer true to say that economists have neglected this field, nor is there a shortage of theories to explain the phenomenon — rather the number of competing theories and the elusiveness of a precise measurement of discrimination render interpretation difficult.

3. These studies have relied heavily on the development of the theory of human capital, to which Becker himself was an important contributor.

4. For a critique of the neo-classical approach and advocacy of a radical/Marxist approach, see Lord (1979).

5. We assume that the discriminators will be members of the majority group and those subject to discrimination will be members of a clearly identifiable minority group, except under very special circumstances such as control of the functions of state by a tightly knit minority (e.g. South Africa). There remains the possibility of retaliation by the minority against the majority. However, Chiswick (1973) has found no evidence for the hypothesis that non-white male workers act as if they have a taste for discrimination against white workers, despite evidence for the reverse case.

6. Another factor which is often neglected in comparing gross earnings differentials is the relatively low mean age of black workers compared with white.

7. Becker's model also assumes that both men and women have perfectly inelastic labour supply curves, which is particularly inappropriate in relation to sex discrimination given the intermittent labour-force participation of married women.

8. Governments may also influence the allocation of female labour in the market by passing factory legislation which limits their number of hours of work and the locations in which they may work.

9. Robb (1978:351) attempts to isolate discrimination by comparing the earnings of all males with those of single females of 30 years of age and over (as well as the earnings of all males and all females), on the grounds that this group is 'more like males in terms of career motivation and labour force attachment'. Similarly, Zincone and Close (1978) compare earnings for all males with those of females, single females with all males, and single females with married males. These approaches are likely to confuse sex discrimination with marital status discrimination.

10. That is not to say that there is no recognition of the possibility that there may be feedback effects which influence supply. An early paper by Formby (1968) distinguished cumulative discrimination, reflecting the impact of past discrimination on current levels of productivity within a minority group.

11. Lloyd and Niemi (1979:201) suggest that theories of discrimination based on erroneous beliefs are very close to those based on prejudice: 'In fact, the line between ignorance and deliberate prejudice is often unclear: As Arrow indicates, productive capacity may be deliberately (although not necessarily consciously) underestimated as a way to provide a more socially acceptable rationalisation for what is really an unacknowledged prejudice.'

12. See section 4 below.

13. The same criticism may be made of Becker's model since tastes for discrimination are

exogenous. As Wallace and LaMond (1977:Ch.8, p.8) point out: 'By defining discrimination as an exogenously given "taste", neo-classical economists have merely traced the economic consequences of discriminatory preferences. This approach ignores the inter-relation between market outcomes and the formulation of individual attitudes, and thus adds little to our understanding of the process of ending discrimination.' This leads them to conclude that the development of a general theory of discrimination requires the integration of economic analysis with sociological and psychological research findings, though precisely how such an integration is to be achieved is not explained.

14. For a formal exposition of this see Appendix 6-A in Addison and Siebert (1979).

15. Welch (1975:70) points to the absence of empirical tests to verify that the profits of firms depend upon the racial composition of their workforces. 'Further', he states, 'I think this omission itself is evidence that we fail to take seriously the most obvious implication of employer discrimination.' Comanor (1973) does, however, include a measure of profitability in his regression equation, postulating that as profits increase firms practise greater discrimination, provided that discrimination is not an inferior good. He finds that the regression coefficients on profitability are always positive and significant. More specifically, an increase of 1 percentage point in the reported industry profit rate in the USA is associated with an increase of 2 percentage points in the measure of discrimination. Medoff and Dick (1978) include a profits measure as a proxy for market power in their equations explaining wage ratios of black males relative to white, and find that there is a negative relationship, significant at the 10 per cent level. In other words, market discrimination is again greater, the greater are industry profits.

16. If, for instance, there is employee discrimination, employers may find it impossible *not* to discriminate in order to stay in business.

17. Non-convexity of the indifference surface of the employer with respect to profits and ratios of black (female) to white (male) employees would also tend to lead either to enterprise or occupational segregation, and Arrow (1973) has in fact suggested that indifference curves cannot be convex everywhere, where utility depends only on the ratio of black (female) to white (male) employees. However, this issue must again remain in some doubt as Chiplin (1976) has shown that Arrow's mathematical proof of the above proposition is in fact invalid.

18. Note, however, if the non-discriminatory firms attempt to take over the whole market, their marginal costs will increase as they have to hire white labour and this effect will be more marked where there is employee discrimination. Only if the supply of black labour to the industry is perfectly elastic at the discriminatory wage will Becker's conclusion (on p. 44) necessarily follow, i.e. that 'the firm with the smallest DC would product the total output'.

19. However, in the theoretical sections of the *Economics of Discrimination* Becker does discuss the relationship between the structure of the product market and the size of the discrimination coefficient. It is in his tests of the theory that he looks at the extent of segregation.

20. Haessel and Palmer (1978) examine wage ratios on the assumption that firms face perfectly elastic supply curves of labour in two separate markets for male and female labour. The assumption of different wages and perfect labour markets only makes sense either if the wage is measured incorrectly or there are hidden quality differences within the groups (Medoff 1980a).

21. Empirical studies such as the above have found that large employers discriminate less than small (Medoff 1980a; Medoff and Dick 1978) — though not apparently large firms relative to average (Shepherd and Levin 1973); discrimination is greater in the case of skilled than semi- and unskilled workers (Comanor 1973); that discrimination is greater in the South (Medoff and Dick 1978; Smith 1979); and that the higher the educational level the greater the degree of discrimination (Medoff and Dick 1978).

22. As with employer discrimination, employee discrimination would predict an increase in wage differences at higher educational levels. Not only will the resistance of majority workers to the employment of members of the minority group be greater the higher the occupational classification, but the actual costs of compensation will be greater because a greater number of workers will be found below that classification.

23. Unfortunately Chiswick's measure of income inequality is total money income of adult males, which includes non-labour income, rather than the more appropriate wage income.

24. For discussion of the role of political power in determining the structure of opportunity for minority groups in industrialised societies see Swinton (1975).

25. In the telephone industry in the northern states one-third of new employees hired between 1966 and 1968 were Negro. See Anderson (1970).

26. See Chiplin and Sloane (1976a) and Aigner and Cain (1977).

27. Gwartney (1970) and Kiker and Liles (1974) among others have examined the relationship between scholastic achievement and black/white earnings differences. It appears that scholastic achievement is far more important than years of schooling in explaining observed white–black earnings and employment differentials, using a weighted regression model.

28. Battallio *et al.* point out that there are also substantial differences in performance between the two male groups examined, and this must temper any attempt to make general inferences about productivity differences between the sexes on the basis of their own results.

29. Using a similar kind of simulation model, Watts (1978) produces results which suggest that firms employing high turnover/low productivity women will pay higher wages than those employing relatively more males but with the same size of labour force. This is suggestive of reverse discrimination.

30. This perhaps surprising finding might be explained by the observation that while labour-force exits are more frequent for women, quitting to move to another job within the labour market is more common for men (Barnes and Jones 1974).

31. In contrast, Viscusi's elasticity values of quit rates with respect to wages are remarkably similar for the sexes. Further, if female earnings levels were raised by $1.31 per hour the predicted quit rates would be equal for the sexes.

32. On this point see Silver (1968).

33. Roemer's model is couched in terms of racial discrimination, but presumably can be applied to sex discrimination in the same way as Becker's model.

34. Gordon and Morton (1974) develop the monopsony model to incorporate discrimination by assuming not only that supply curves of labour to the firm are upward sloping for women and horizontal for men, but also that men dislike working with women. Then the employer will continue to hire women not up to the point at which the female wage is equated to the marginal revenue product, but up to the point at which the female wage plus the increase in the wage bill from the pay-

ment of the higher wage to existing female employees plus the increase in the wage bill necessary to bribe male employees to work with the additional women equals the male wage and marginal revenue product.

35. The presence of monopsonistic exploitation in the case of Ph.D. women is also reported by Ferber and Kordick (1978). Contrary to Reagan's findings, Ekelund et al. (1981) report that recent empirical findings suggest that women have higher reservation wages and respond more to wage changes than men, cet. par. Taken together with the fact that women receive lower wages than men, cet. par., this is inconsistent with the linear monopsony price discrimination model, though possibly consistent with a non-linear model.

36. An analysis of the British New Earnings Survey (Sloane and Siebert 1980) suggests that females are not unduly concentrated in low-paying occupations, excluded from high-paying male occupations or concentrated in occupations where the male earnings differential is particularly high.

37. For a fuller discussion of this see Jain and Sloane (1980, 1981). In one US study (Newman 1978), 207 companies were sent two résumés, one from a fictitious black and one from a fictitious white applicant with similar personal characteristics, with the pictures being swapped round 50 per cent of the time. Applicant's race did not appear to influence the response rate, though in line with earlier suggestions companies with fewer than 8,000 employees showed a slight tendency to favour white applicants, while larger companies showed a slight preference for black applicants. Newman's methodology has been criticised by McIntyre et al. (1980).

38. In the UK registered unemployment rates for women are lower than for men, but this reflects the fact that many women choose not to register as unemployed, rather than a lower tendency to become unemployed than men. However, a more accurate measure of female unemployment is published in the General Household Survey. Further, female unemployment has in recent years been rising faster than that of men, and this is only in part a consequence of an increasing propensity on the part of women to register as unemployed.

39. As Turnbull and Williams (1974) note, taking the log of earnings has the advantage of reducing any bias arising from the fact that the dispersion of earnings is likely to increase with age or that the distribution of earnings may be skewed. The log quadratic form also appears to produce the best fit for a surprising number of data sets.

40. The residual or measure of discrimination (D) is defined as

$$D = \frac{(W_F/W_M)^0 - (W_F/W_M)}{(W_F/W_M)^0}$$

where $(W_F/W_M)^0$ = the wage ratio that would prevail in the absence of discrimination;

$W_F/W_M$ = the actual ratio.

41. This is essentially an index-number problem. Assigning the female characteristics to the male equation can be regarded as equivalent to the use of a Laspeyres price index, and assigning male characteristics to the female equation is equivalent to the use of a Paasche price index. The extent of the difference accounted for by differences in the quantities of characteristics is conversely evaluated in terms of a Paasche quantity index in the former case and Laspeyres quantity index in the latter case. Indeed, this procedure is often referred to in the literature as the index method or approach.

42. For a demonstration of this see Chiplin (1979b) and Siebert and Sloane (1981).

43. See for instance Brown *et al.* (1980a, 1980b), and Shaffer and Wilson (1980).

44. Other studies have, however, found diminishing returns to education and it would be useful to have comparable figures for later years.

45. A reverse argument has been put forward in relation to academic posts, where it has been suggested that faculty wives receive preferential treatment in order to attract their husbands. However, on one large research-orientated campus, Ferber *et al.* (1978) found that although no fewer than 38.6 per cent of academic women were married to men working in the same institution, faculty wives in their sample were not apparently inferior in terms of performance to other faculty women.

46. These results are consistent with those of Gwartney and Long (1978) who found that for all males other than Cubans average earnings in 1969 were 24–35 per cent higher when married with spouse present than otherwise. Again, the marital status variable was generally insignificant in the case of women.

47. The question also arises as to what is the appropriate treatment of widowed, separated and divorced persons. Greenhalgh (1980) points out that the (possibly) unanticipated change of life-style may force non-participating women back into the labour market, and for men either add to or diminish the incentive to work more productively according to the effect of the changed circumstances on their financial responsibilities. Hence, it seems better to exclude this group from any analysis of discrimination in order to avoid possible bias in relation to comparisons between single (never married) and married groups.

48. Recent longitudinal data suggest that women fall into three groups of roughly equal size – those working continuously, those working intermittently and those who never work. See Heckman and Willis (1977).

49. This view finds support in Osterman (1979).

50. One should not neglect the potential impact of unions on non-wage aspects of employment. Leigh (1979) found, however, that union-established institutional rules with respect to redundancy and promotion did not appear to be more discriminatory than those established in unorganised markets; Kahn and Morimune (1979) found that an increase in unionisation substantially increased the expected unemployment spells of non-union non-white males and non-white females: and Kalachek and Raines (1980) found that there was a tendency for unionised, but not non-unionised, firms to raise their hiring standards over time, which would appear to have implications for minority workers.

51. The effects of this particular programme were examined by Simeral (1978: 517). She concludes that such policies

     could potentially be an effective part of a public policy to alleviate sexual inequalities in the labour market. It seems clear that the wage determination process (but not the allocation of jobs) was less beneficial to men than to women in PEP compared with unsubsidised employment. However, the fact that such jobs may not be transferred to the post policy period casts serious doubt on the ability of a temporary public service programme to improve the status of women over the long run.

52. Also as Jackson (1973) notes, quotas will be politically difficult to enact as they will generally make the employer worse off, require high costs of administration and enforcement, and yield uncertain results in terms of the actual employment of minority workers. The advantage of a tax/subsidy system is that it is in the employers' interests to take on additional minority workers.

53. Thus Glazer (1975) points to a number of 'absurdities' in the US affirmative action programme. For example, the requirement to validate any test which blacks and whites pass at different rates might well increase the costs of testing to such a degree that testing programmes have to be abandoned.

54. Presumably a similar argument applies in the case of race. Posner (1973: 306) notes in relation to racial quotas that

> to comply, the employer must lay off workers or, what amounts to the same thing, favour black over white job applicants for as long a period of time as is necessary to attain the quota. In either case white employees untainted by discrimination are made to bear a high cost in order to improve the conditions of black workers. The result is a capricious and regressive tax on the white working class.

55. In the USA firms which tender for government contracts are required to implement affirmative action policies, which require the setting of goals and timetables for minority employment in job categories where such workers have been under-utilised in the past. This involves an annual report to the Equal Employment Opportunities Commission (EEOC) of the number of employees classified by race, sex, occupation and location.

56. Similarly in the case of sex discrimination, Medoff (1980a) finds that women in states that have ratified the Equal Rights Amendment are more likely to work in jobs commensurate with their abilities, but to receive less pay than their male equivalents in comparison with women in non-ratified states.

57. Arguing that affirmative action programmes should reduce quitting if they are at all effective in improving opportunities within the establishment, Osterman (1982) finds that women employed in industries which receive greater attention from the Office of Federal Contract Compliance (OFCC) and which are greater beneficiaries of federal expenditure exhibit lower quit rates, controlling for other variables. Thus it is possible that OFCC activities have been more effective than is often supposed.

# References

**Addison, J. T. and Siebert, W. S.** (1979) *The Market for Labour: An Analytical Treatment*, Goodyear: Santa Monica, California.

**Aigner, D. J. and Cain, G. G.** (1977) Statistical theories of discrimination in labour markets, *Industrial and Labor Relations Review*, **30**, 175–87.

**Akin, J. S. and Garfinkel, I.** (1980) The quality of education and cohort variation in black–white earnings differentials: comment, *American Economic Review*, **70**, 186–91.

**Alexis, M.** (1973) A theory of labour market discrimination with interdependent utilities, *American Economic Review, Proceedings*, **63**, 296–302.

**Allison, E. and Allen, P.** (1978) Male–female professionals: a model of career choice, *Industrial Relations*, **17**, 333–7.

**Amsden, A. M. and Moser, C.** (1975) Job search and affirmative action, *American Economic Review*, **65**, 83–91.

**Anderson, B. E.** (1970) *The Negro in the Public Utilities Industry*, University of Philadelphia Press.

**Andresani, P. J.** (1976) Discrimination, segmentation and upward mobility: a longitudinal approach to the dual labour market theory, Temple University, Philadelphia, mimeo.

**Andresani, P. J.** (1977) Internal–external attitudes, personal initiative and the labour market experience of black and white men, *The Journal of Human Resources*, 12, 308–27.

**Antos, J. R., Chandler, M. and Mellow, W.** (1980) Sex differences in union membership, *Industrial and Labor Relations Review*, 33, 162–9.

**Arrow, K. J.** (1972) Some mathematical models of race in the labour market, in Pascal, A. H. (ed.), *Racial Discrimination in Economic Life*, Lexington Books, D. C. Heath and Company: Lexington, Mass., Toronto and London.

**Arrow, K. J.** (1973) The theory of discrimination, in Ashenfelter, O. and Rees, A. (eds), *Discrimination in Labor Markets*, Princeton University Press: Princeton, New Jersey.

**Ashenfelter, O.** (1972) Racial discrimination and trade unions, *Journal of Political Economy*, 80, 435–64.

**Ashenfelter, O.** (1973) Discrimination in trade unions, in Ashenfelter, O. and Rees, A. (eds), *Discrimination in Labor Markets*, Princeton University Press, New Jersey, 88–112.

**Ashenfelter, O.** (1976) Union relative wage effects: new evidence and a survey of their implications for wage inflation, Industrial Relations Section, *Princeton University Working Paper 89*.

**Ashenfelter, O. and Godwin, L. I.** (1972) Some evidence on the effects of unionism on the average wage of black workers relative to white workers, 1900–1967, in Somers, G. G. (ed.), *Proceedings of the 24th Annual Winter Meeting, 1971, New Orleans*, Industrial Relations Research Association Series, Madison, Wisconsin.

**Barnes, W. F. and Jones, R. G.** (1974) Differences in male and female quitting, *The Journal of Human Resources*, 9, 439–51.

**Battallio, R. C., Kagel, J. H. and Reynolds, M. O.** (1978) A note on the distribution of earnings and output per hour in an experimental economy, *Economic Journal*, 88 (352), 822–9.

**Becker, G.** (1957) *The Economics of Discrimination*, University of Chicago Press: Chicago.

**Bell, D.** (1971) Bonuses, quotas and the employment of black workers, *The Journal of Human Resources*, 6, 309–20.

**Beller, A. H.** (1978) The economics of enforcement of an anti-discrimination law, Title VII of the Civil Rights Act of 1964, *Journal of Law and Economics*, 21, 359–80.

**Beller, A. H.** (1979) The impact of equal employment opportunity laws on the male/female earnings differential, in Lloyd, C. B., Andrews, E. S. and Gilroy, C. C. (eds), *Women in the Labour Market*, Columbia University Press: New York and Guildford, Surrey.

**Beller, A. H.** (1980) The effect of economic conditions on the success of equal opportunities laws: an application to the sex differential in earnings, *Review of Economics and Statistics*, 62, 379–87.

**Beller, A. H.** (1982) Occupational segregation by sex: determinants and changes, *The Journal of Human Resources*, 17, 371–92.

**Bergmann, B. R.** (1971) The effect of white incomes on discrimination in employment, *Journal of Political Economy*, 79, 294–313.

**Bergmann, B. R.** (1974) Occupational segregation, wages and profits when employers discriminate by race or sex, *Eastern Economic Journal*, 1, 103–10.

**Blau, F. D.** (1977) *Equal Pay in the Office*, Lexington Books: Lexington, Mass.

**Blau, F. D. and Hendricks, W. E.** (1979) Occupational segregation by sex: trends and prospects, *The Journal of Human Resources*, **14**, 197–210.

**Blinder, A.** (1973) Wage discrimination: reduced form and structural estimates, *Journal of Human Resources*, **8**, 436–55.

**Borjas, G. J.** (1982) The politics of employment discrimination in the federal bureaucracy, *The Journal of Law and Economics*, **25**, 271–300.

**Bosanquet, N. and Doeringer, P.** (1973) Is there a dual labour market in Great Britain?, *Economic Journal*, **83**, 421–35.

**Boulding, A.** (ed.) (1976) *Equal Employment Opportunity and the AT & T Case*, The MIT Press: Cambridge, Mass. and London.

**Boulet, J. A. and Rowley, J. C. R.** (1977) Measurement of discrimination in the labour market: a comment, *Canadian Journal of Economics*, **10**, 149–54.

**Brown, R. S., Moon, M. and Zoloth, B. S.** (1980a) Incorporating occupational attainment in studies of male/female earnings differentials, *The Journal of Human Resources*, **15**, 3–28.

**Brown, R. S., Moon, M. and Zoloth, B. S.** (1980b) Occupational attainment and segregation by sex, *Industrial and Labor Relations Review*, **33**, 506–17.

**Burnim, M. L.** (1980) The earnings effects of black matriculation in predominantly white colleges, *Industrial and Labor Relations Review*, **33**, 518–24.

**Cain, G. G.** (1976) The challenge of segmented labour market theories to orthodox theories: a review, *Journal of Economic Literature*, **14**, 1215–57.

**Cardwell, L. A. and Rosenweig, M. R.** (1980) Economic mobility, monopsonistic discrimination and sex differences in wages, *Southern Economic Journal*, **46**, 1102–17.

**Chiplin, B.** (1976) Non-convexity of indifference surfaces in the case of labour market discrimination, *American Economic Review*, **66**, 921–4.

**Chiplin, B.** (1979a) An evaluation of sex discrimination: some problems and a suggested re-orientation, in Lloyd, C. B., Andrews, E. S. and Gilroy, C. L. (eds), *Women in the Labour Market*, Columbia University Press: New York and Guildford, Surrey.

**Chiplin, B.** (1979b) The effect of omitted variables on the measurement of discrimination: a note, *University of Nottingham Discussion Papers in Industrial Economics*, **69**, 1–7.

**Chiplin, B.** (1981) An alternative approach to the measurement of sex discrimination: an illustration from university entrance, *Economic Journal*, **91**, 988–97.

**Chiplin, B., Curran, M. M. and Parsley, C. J.** (1980) Relative female earnings in Great Britain and the impact of legislation, in Sloane, P. J. (ed.), *Women and Low Pay*, Macmillan Press: London.

**Chiplin, B. and Sloane, P. J.** (1976a) *Sex Discrimination in the Labour Market*, Macmillan: London.

**Chiplin, B. and Sloane, P. J.** (1976b) Personal characteristics and sex differences in professional employment, *Economic Journal*, **86**, 729–45.

**Chiplin, B. and Sloane, P. J.** (1982) *Tackling Discrimination at the Workplace*, Cambridge University Press.

**Chiswick, B. R.** (1973) Racial discrimination and the labour market: a test of alternative hypotheses, *Journal of Political Economy*, **81**, 1330–52.

**Chiswick, B. R.** (1978) The effect of Americanization on the earnings of foreign born men, *Journal of Political Economy*, **86**, 897–921.

**Chiswick, B. R.** (1979) The economic progress of immigrants: some apparently universal patterns, in Fellner, W. (ed.), *Contemporary Economic Problems*, American Enterprise Institute.

Chiswick, B. R. (1980) The earnings of white and coloured male immigrants in Britain, *Economica*, **47**, 81–7.

Comanor, W. S. (1973) Racial discrimination in American industry, *Economica*, **40**, 363–78.

Corcoran, M. (1979) Work experience, labour force withdrawals and women's wages. Empirical results using the 1976 panel of income dynamics, in Lloyd, C. B., Andrews, E. S. and Gilroy, C. L. (eds), *Women in the Labour Market*, Columbia University Press: New York and Guildford, Surrey.

Corcoran, M. and Duncan, G. J. (1979) Work history, labour force attachment and earnings differences between races and sexes, *The Journal of Human Resources*, **14**, 3–20.

De Tray, D. N. and Greenberg, D. H. (1977) On estimating sex differences in earnings, *Southern Economic Journal*, **44**, 348–53.

Dex, S. (1979) 'Economists' theories of the economics of discrimination, *Ethnic and Racial Studies*, **2**, 90–108.

Dex, S. (1980) Discrimination and job search theories for black British male youths, *University of Keele, Department of Economics Discussion Paper 27*.

Dillingham, A. E. (1981) Sex differences in labour market injury risk, *Industrial Relations*, **20**, 117–22.

Director, S. M. and Doctors, S. I. (1976) Racial differences in blue-collar turnover rates, *Industrial Relations*, **15**, 338–42.

Doeringer, P. and Piore, M. (1971) *Internal Labour Markets and Manpower Analysis*, Lexington Books: Lexington, Mass.

Duncan, G. J. and Hoffman, S. (1979) On-the-job training and earnings differences by race and sex, *Review of Economics and Statistics*, **61**, 594–603.

Ekelund, R. E., Higgins, R. S. and Smithson, C. W. (1981) Can discrimination increase employment: a neo-classical perspective, *Southern Economic Journal*, **47**, 664–73.

England, P. (1982) The failure of human capital theory to explain occupational sex segregation, *The Journal of Human Resources*, **17**, 356–70.

Ferber, M. A. and Green, C. A. (1982) Traditional or reverse sex discrimination? A case study of a large public university, *Industrial and Labour Relations Review*, **35**, 550–65.

Ferber, M. A. and Kordick, B. (1978) Sex differentials in the earnings of Ph.D.'s, *Industrial and Labor Relations Review*, **31**, 227–38.

Ferber, M. A., Loeb, J. W. and Lowry, H. M. (1978) The economic status of women faculty: a re-appraisal, *The Journal of Human Resources*, **13**, 385–401.

Ferber, M. A. and Lowry, H. M. (1976) The sex differential in earnings: a re-appraisal, *Industrial and Labor Relations Review*, **29**, 377–87.

Festinger, L. (1957) *A Theory of Cognitive Dissonance*, Stanford University Press: Palo Alto, California.

Flanagan, R. J. (1973) Racial wage discrimination and employment segregation, *The Journal of Human Resources*, **3**, 456–71.

Formby, J. L. (1968) The extent of wage and salary discrimination against non-white labour, *Southern Economic Journal*, **35**, 140–50.

Frank, R. H. (1978) Why women earn less: the theory and estimation of differential overqualification, *American Economic Review*, **68**, 360–73.

Franklin, R. and Tanzer, M. (1968) A framework for the analysis of interurban negro–

white economic differentials, *Industrial and Labor Relations Review*, **21**, 367–74.

Franklin, R. and Tanzer, M. (1968) Traditional micro-economic analysis of racial discrimination: a critical view and alternative approach, *Industrial and Labor Relations Review*, **21**, 367–78.

Freeman, R. B. (1973a) Changes in the labour market for black Americans, *Brookings Papers on Economic Activity*, **1973: 1**, 67–120.

Freeman, R. B. (1973b) Decline of labour market discrimination and economic analysis, *American Economic Review*, **63**, 280–6.

Fuchs, V. R. (1971) Differences in hourly earnings between men and women, *Monthly Labor Review*, **94**, 9–15.

Fujii, E. T. and Trapani, J. M. (1978) On estimating the relationship between discrimination and market structure, *Southern Economic Journal*, **45**, 556–67.

Gaumer, G. L. (1975) Sex discrimination and job tenure, *Industrial Relations*, **14**, 121–9.

Gilman, H. J. (1965) Economic discrimination and unemployment, *American Economic Review*, **55**, 1077–96.

Gintis, H. (1971) Education, technology and the characteristics of worker productivity, *American Economic Review*, **61**, 266–79.

Glazer, N. (1975) *Affirmative Discrimination: Ethnic Inequality and Public Policy*, Basic Books: New York.

Goldfarb, R. S. and Hosek, J. R. (1976) Explaining male–female wage differentials for the same job, *The Journal of Human Resources*, **11**, 98–108.

Gordon, N. M. and Morton, T. E. (1974) A low mobility model of wage discrimination with special reference to sex differentials, *Journal of Economic Theory*, **7**, 241–53.

Grant, J. H. and Hamermesh, D. S. (1981) Labour market competition among youths, white women and others, *Review of Economics and Statistics*, **63**, 354–60.

Greenhalgh, C. (1980) Male–female wage differentials in Great Britain: is marriage an equal opportunity?, *Economic Journal*, **90**, 751–75.

Griliches, Z. and Mason, L. (1972) Education, income and ability, *Journal of Political Economy*, **80**, S74–S103.

Gunderson, M. (1975) Male–female wage differentials and the impact of equal pay legislation, *Review of Economics and Statistics*, **62**, 462–9.

Gurin, P. (1977) The role of worker expectancies in the study of employment discrimination, in Wallace, P. A. and La Mond, A. M., *Women, Minorities and Employment Discrimination*, Lexington Books: Lexington, Mass.

Gwartney, J. D. (1970) Discrimination and income differentials, *American Economic Review*, **60**, 396–408.

Gwartney, J. D. and Long, J. E. (1978) The relative earnings of blacks and other minorities, *Industrial and Labor Relations Review*, **31**, 336–46.

Haessel, W. and Palmer, J. (1978) Market power and employment discrimination, *The Journal of Human Resources*, **13**, 545–60.

Hakim, C. (1979) Occupational segregation: a comparative study of the degree and pattern of the differentiation between men's and women's work in Britain, the United States and other countries, *Department of Employment Research Paper, No. 9*.

Hansen, W. L., Burton, Weisbrod, B. A. and Scanlon, W. J. (1970) Schooling and earnings of low achievers, *American Economic Review*, **60**, 409–18.

Haworth, J., Gwartney, J. and Haworth, C. (1975) Earnings, productivity and changes in employment discrimination during the 1960s, *American Economic Review*, **65**, 258–68.

**Heckman, J. J. and Willis, R.** (1977) A beta-logistic model for the analysis of segmented labor force participation by married women, *Journal of Political Economy*, **85**, 27–58.

**Higgs, R.** (1971) Race skills and earnings; American immigrants in 1909, *Journal of Economic History*, **31**, 420–8.

**Hildebrand, G. H.** *et al.* (1976) A symposium: evaluating the impact of affirmative action: a look at the federal contract compliance programme, *Industrial and Labour Relations Review*, **29**, 485–584.

**Hill, M.** (1979) The wage effects of marital status and children, *The Journal of Human Resources*, **14**, 579–94.

**Hoffman, S. D.** (1979) Black–white life cycle earnings differences and the vintage hypothesis: a longitudinal analysis, *American Economic Review*, **69**, 855–67.

**Jackson, R.** (1973) Job discrimination and the use of bonuses, *The American Journal of Economics and Sociology*, **32**, 351–66.

**Jain, H. C. and Sloane, P. J.** (1980) The structure of labour markets, minority workers and equal employment opportunities legislation, *International Journal of Social Economics*, **7**, 95–121.

**Jain, H. C. and Sloane, P. J.** (1981) *Equal Employment Issues*, Praeger: New York.

**Jencks, C.** *et al.* (1979) *Who Gets Ahead? The Determinants of Economic Success in America*, Basic Books: New York.

**Johnson, W. R.** (1978) Racial wage discrimination and industrial structure, *The Bell Journal of Economics*, **9**, 70–81.

**Jones, E. B. and Long, J. E.** (1979a) Human capital and labour market employment: additional evidence for women, *The Journal of Human Resources*, **14**, 270–9.

**Jones, E. B. and Long, J. E.** (1979b) Part week work and human capital investment by married women, *The Journal of Human Resources*, **14**, 563–76.

**Kahn, L. M.** (1981) Sex discrimination in professional employment – a case study: comment, *Industrial and Labor Relations Review*, **34**, 273–5.

**Kahn, L. M. and Morimune, K.** (1979) Unions and employment stability: a sequential logit approach, *International Economic Review*, **20**, 217–36.

**Kalachek, E. and Raines, F.** (1980) Trade unions and hiring standards, *Journal of Labor Research*, **1**, 63–76.

**Kamalich, R. E. and Polachek, S. W.** (1982) Discrimination: fact or fiction? an examination using an alternative approach, *Southern Economic Journal*, **49**, 450–61.

**Katz, D. A.** (1973) Faculty salaries, rates of promotion and productivity at a large university, *American Economic Review*, **63**, 469–77.

**Kiefer, N. M. and Smith, S. P.** (1977) Union impact and wage discrimination by region, *The Journal of Human Resources*, **12**, 519–34.

**Kiker, B. F. and Liles, W. P.** (1974) Earnings, employment and racial discrimination: additional evidence, *American Economic Review*, **64**, 492–501.

**King, A. G.** (1977) Is occupational segregation the cause of the flatter experience earnings profile of women?, *The Journal of Human Resources*, **12**, 541–9.

**King, A. G. and Knapp, C. B.** (1978) Race and the determinants of lifetime earnings, *Industrial and Labor Relations Review*, **31**, 347–55.

**Koch, J. V. and Chizmar, J. F. Jnr.** (1976) *The Economics of Affirmative Action*, Lexington Books, D. C. Heath & Company; Lexington, Mass., Toronto, London.

**Krueger, A. O.** (1963) The economics of discrimination, *Journal of Political Economy*, **71**, 481–6.

**Kruse, W. J.** (1977) An empirical study of labour market segmentation: a comment, *Industrial and Labor Relations Review*, **30**, 219–20.

**Landes, W.** (1968) The economics of fair employment laws, *Journal of Political Economy*, **76**, 507–52.

**Landon, J. and Peirce, W.** (1971) Discrimination, monopsony and union power in the building trades: a cross sectional analysis, *Proceedings of the Annual Meeting*, **24**, Industrial Relations Research Association, Madison.

**Langley, P. C.** (1978) An empirical study of labour market segmentation, *Industrial and Labor Relations Review*, **32**, 86–94.

**Lazear, E.** (1979a) The narrowing of black–white wage differentials is illusory, *American Economic Review*, **69**, 553–64.

**Lazear, E.** (1979b) Male–female wage differentials: has the government had any effect? in Lloyd, C. B., Andrews, E. S. and Gilroy, C. L. (eds), *Women in the Labour Market*, Columbia University Press: New York and Guildford, Surrey.

**Lee, L.-F.** (1978) Unionism and wage rates: simultaneous equations model with qualitative and limited dependent variables, *International Economic Review*, **19**, 415–34.

**Leigh, D. E.** (1978a) Racial discrimination and labour unions: evidence from the N.L.S. sample of middle aged men, *The Journal of Human Resources*, **14**, 568–77.

**Leigh, D. E.** (1978b) *An Analysis of the Determinants of Occupational Upgrading*, Academic Press: New York, San Francisco, London.

**Leigh, D. E.** (1979) Unions and non-wage racial discrimination, *Industrial and Labour Relations Review*, **32**, 439–50.

**Leigh, D. E.** (1980) Racial differentials in union relative wage effects: a simultaneous equations approach, *Journal of Labor Research*, **1**, 95–114.

**Leigh, J. P.** (1981) Racial differences in compensating wages for job risks, *Industrial Relations*, **20**, 318–21.

**Levy, F.** (1980) Changes in employment prospects for black males, *Brookings Papers on Economic Activity*, **1980: 2**, 513–38.

**Lewis, D. E.** (1979) Comparative quit rates of men and women, *The Journal of Industrial Relations*, **21**, 331–50.

**Link, C., Rutledge, E. and Lewis, K.** (1976) Black–white differences in returns to schooling: some new evidence, *American Economic Review*, **66**, 221–3.

**Link, C., Rutledge, E. and Lewis, K.** (1980) The quality of education and cohort variation in black–white earnings differentials: a reply, *American Economic Review*, **70**, 196–203.

**Lloyd, C. B. and Niemi, B. T.** (1979) *The Economics of Sex Differentials*, Columbia University Press: New York.

**Lloyd, C. B., Andrews, E. S. and Gilroy, C. L.** (1979) *Women in the Labor Market*, Columbia University Press: New York.

**Long, J. E.** (1976) Employment discrimination in the federal sector, *The Journal of Human Resources*, **11**, 86–97.

**Lord, S. J.** (1979) Neoclassical theories of discrimination: a critique, in Green, F. and Nore, P. (eds), *Issues in Political Economy: A Critical Approach*, Macmillan: London.

**Luksetich, W. A.** (1979) Market power and sex discrimination in white-collar employment, *Review of Social Economy*, **37**, 211–24.

**McCall, J. J.** (1973) *Income Mobility, Racial Discrimination and Economic Growth*, Lexington Books: Lexington, Mass.

**McIntyre, S. J., Moberg, D. J. and Posner, B. Z.** (1980) Discrimination in recruitment: an empirical analysis – comment, *Industrial and Labor Relations Review*, **33**, 543–7.

**McNabb, R. and Psacharopoulos, G.** (1981a) Racial earnings differentials in the UK, *Oxford Economic Papers*, **33**, 413–25.

**McNabb, K. and Psacharopoulos, G.** (1981b) Further evidence on the relevance of the dual labour market hypothesis for the UK, *The Journal of Human Resources*, **16**, 442–8.

**Madden, J. F.** (1973) *The Economics of Sex Discrimination*, Lexington Books: Lexington, Mass.

**Malkiel, B. and Malkiel, J.** (1973) Male–female pay differentials in professional employment, *American Economic Review*, **63**, 693–705.

**Mallan, L. B.** (1982) Labour force participation, work experience and the pay gap between men and women, *The Journal of Human Resources*, **18**, 437–48.

**Marshall, R.** (1974) The economics of racial discrimination: a survey, *Journal of Economic Literature*, **12**, 849–71.

**Masters, S. H.** (1975) *Black–White Income Differences: Empirical Studies and Policy Implications*, Academic Press: New York, San Francisco, London.

**Masters, S. H.** (1977) Measurement of discrimination in the labour market: a reply, *Canadian Journal of Economics*, **10**, 154–5.

**Mayhew, K. and Rosewell, B.** (1978) Immigrants and occupational crowding in Great Britain, *Oxford Bulletin of Economics and Statistics*, **40**, 223–48.

**Mayhew, K. and Rosewell, B.** (1979) Labour market segmentation in Britain, *Oxford Bulletin of Economics and Statistics*, **41**, 81–116.

**Medoff, J. L. and Abraham, K. G.** (1980) Experience, performance and earnings, *Quarterly Journal of Economics*, **95**, 703–36.

**Medoff, J. L. and Abraham, K. G.** (1981) Are those paid more really more productive? The case of experience, *The Journal of Human Resources*, **16**, 186–216.

**Medoff, M. H.** (1980a) On estimating the relationship between discrimination and market structure: a comment, *Southern Economic Journal*, **46**, 1227–34.

**Medoff, M. H.** (1980b) Market power and employment discrimination: a comment, *The Journal of Human Resources*, **15**, 293–4.

**Medoff, M. H.** (1980c) The equal rights amendment: an empirical analysis of sexual discrimination, *Economic Inquiry*, **18**, 367–79.

**Medoff, M. H. and Dick, P. T.** (1978) A test for relative demand functions in American manufacturing, *Applied Economics*, **10**, 61–73.

**Mermelstein, D.** (ed.) (1970) *Economics: Mainstream Readings and Radical Critiques*, Random House: New York (1st edn).

**Mincer, J.** (1979) A comment on sex discrimination, in Lloyd, C. B., Andrews, E. S. and Gilroy, C. L. (eds), *Women in the Labour Market*, Columbia University Press: New York and Guildford, Surrey.

**Mincer, J. and Polachek, S.** (1974) Family investments in human capital: earnings of women, *Journal of Political Economy*, **82**, S76–S108.

**Mincer, J. and Polachek, S.** (1978) Women's earnings re-examined, *The Journal of Human Resources*, **12**, 118–34.

**Moore, W. J. and Raisian, J.** (1980) Cyclical sensitivity of union/non-union relative wage effects, *Journal of Labor Research*, **1**, 115–32.

**Moroney, J. R.** (1979) Do women earn less under capitalism?, *Economic Journal*, **89**, 601–13.

**Newman, J. N.** (1978) Discrimination in recruitment: an empirical analysis, *Industrial and Labor Relations Review*, **82**, 15–23.

**Nickell, S. J.** (1977) Trade unions and the position of women in the wage structure, *British Journal of Industrial Relations*, **15**, 192–210.

Oaxaca, R. L. (1973) Sex discrimination in wages, in Ashenfelter, O. and Rees, A. (eds), *Discrimination in Labour Markets*, Princeton University Press: Princeton, New Jersey.

Oaxaca, R. L. (1975) Estimates of union/non-union wage differentials within occupational regional sub-groups, *The Journal of Human Resources*, **10**, 527–37.

O'Kelly, C. G. (1979) The impact of equal employment legislation on women's earnings, *American Journal of Economics and Sociology*, **88**, 419–30.

Oster, S. M. (1975) Industry differences in the level of discrimination against women, *Quarterly Journal of Economics*, **79**, 215–29.

Osterman, P. (1975) An empirical study of labour market segmentation, *Industrial and Labor Relations Review*, **28**, 508–23.

Osterman, P. (1979) Sex discrimination in professional employment: a case study, *Industrial and Labor Relations Review*, **32**, 451–64.

Osterman, P. (1982) Affirmative action and opportunities: a study of female quit rates, *Review of Economics and Statistics*, **64**, 604–12.

Papps, I. (1980) *For Love or Money?*, Hobart Paper No. 86, Institute of Economic Affairs: London.

Pascal, A. H. and Rapping, L. A. (1972) The economics of racial discrimination in organised baseball, in Pascal, A. H. (ed.) *Racial Discrimination in Economic Life*, Lexington Books: Lexington, Mass.

Phelps, E. S. (1972) The statistical theory of racism and sexism, *American Economic Review*, **62**, 659–61.

Pike, M. (1982) Segregation by sex, earnings differentials and equal pay: an application of a job crowding model to UK data, *Applied Economics*, **14**, 503–14.

Polachek, S. W. (1978) Sex differences in college major, *Industrial and Labor Relations Review*, **31**, 498–508.

Polachek, S. W. (1981) Occupational self selection: a human capital approach to sex differences in occupational structure, *Review of Economics and Statistics*, **63**, 60–9.

Posner, R. W. (1973) *Economic Analysis of Law*, Little, Brown & Co.: Boston, Toronto.

Psacharopoulos, G. (1978) Labour market duality and income distribution: the case of the UK, in Shorrocks, A. and Krelle, W. (eds), *The Economics of Income Distribution*, North-Holland: Amsterdam, Holland.

Ragan, J. F. Jr. and Smith, S. P. (1981) The impact of differences in turnover rates on male/female pay differentials, *The Journal of Human Resources*, **16**, 343–65.

Rapping, L. A. (1970) Union induced racial entry barriers, *Journal of Human Resources*, **5**, 447–74.

Rasmussen, D. (1970) A note on the relative income of non-white men, 1948–1964, *Quarterly Journal of Economics*, **84**, 168–72.

Reagan, B. B. (1975) Two supply curves for economists? Implications of mobility and career attachment of women, *American Economic Review*, **65**, 100–7.

Reich, M. (1970) The economics of racism, in Gordon, D. M. (ed.), *Problems in Political Economy: An Urban Perspective*, Lexington Books, D. C. Heath & Co.: Lexington, Mass.

Reich, M. (1980) The persistence of racial inequality in urban areas and industries, 1950–70, *American Economic Review, Papers and Proceedings,* **70**.

Robb, R. E. (1978) Earnings differentials between males and females in Ontario, 1971, *Canadian Journal of Economics*, **11**, 350–9.

Roemer, J. E. (1979) Divide and conquer: microfoundation of a Marxian theory of wage discrimination, *The Bell Journal of Economics*, **10**, 695–705.

**Rosenbaum, J. E.** (1980) Hierarchical and individual effects on earnings, *Industrial Relations*, **19**, 1–4.

**Rosenberg, S.** (1980) Male occupational standing and the dual labour market, *Industrial Relations*, **19**, 34–49.

**Rumberger, R. W. and Carnoy, M.** (1980) Segmentation in the US labour market: its effects on the mobility and earnings of whites and blacks, *Cambridge Journal of Economics*, **4**, 117–32.

**Sandell, S. H. and Shapiro, D.** (1978) An exchange: the theory of human capital and the earnings of women, *The Journal of Human Resources*, **13**, 103–17.

**Scully, G. W.** (1974) Discrimination: the case of organised baseball, in Noll, R. G. (ed.), *Government and the Sports Business*, Brookings Institution: Washington, DC.

**Shaffer, L. J. and Wilson, R. M.** (1980) Racial discrimination in occupational choice, *Industrial Relations*, **19**, 199–205.

**Shapiro, D.** (1978) Relative wage effects of unions in the public and private sectors, *Industrial and Labor Relations Review*, **31**, 193–203.

**Shepherd, W. G.** (1970) *Market Power and Economic Welfare*, Random House: New York.

**Shepherd, W. G. and Levin, S. G.** (1973) Managerial discrimination in large firms, *Review of Economics and Statistics*, **55**, 412–22.

**Siebert, W. S. and Addison, J. T.** (1977) Discrimination within the labour market: theory with evidence from Britain and the United States, *International Journal of Social Economics*, **4**, 159–91.

**Siebert, W. S. and Sloane, P. J.** (1981) The measurement of sex and marital status discrimination at the workplace, *Economica*, **48**, 125–41.

**Siebert, W. S. and Young, A.** (1983) Sex and family status differentials in professional earnings: the case of librarians, *Scottish Journal of Political Economy*, **30**, 18–41.

**Silver, M.** (1968) Employee tastes for discrimination, wages and profits, *Review of Social Economy*, **26**, 183–5.

**Simeral, M. H.** (1978) The impact of the public employment programme on sex-related wage differentials, *Industrial and Labor Relations Review*, **31**, 509–19.

**Sloane, P. J. and Siebert, W. S.** (1980) Low pay amongst women – the facts, in Sloane, P. J. (ed.), *Women and Low Pay*, The Macmillan Press: London.

**Smith, D. A.** (1980) Government employment and relative black/white relative wages, *The Journal of Human Resources*, **15**, 77–86.

**Smith, J. P. and Welch, F.** (1979) Inequality: race differences in the distribution of earnings, *International Economic Review*, **20**, 515–26.

**Smith, M. M.** (1979) Industrial racial wage discrimination in the US, *Industrial Relations*, **18**, 110–16.

**Smith, S.** (1976) Pay differentials between federal government and private sector workers, *Industrial and Labor Relations Review*, **29**, 179–97.

**Sowell, T.** (1975) *Race and Economics*, David McKay Co.: New York.

**Stiglitz, J.** (1973) Approaches to the economics of discrimination, *American Economic Review, Papers and Proceedings*, **63**, 287–95.

**Strauss, R. P. and Horvath, F. W.** (1976) Wage rate differences by race and sex in the US labour market, 1960–1970, *Economica*, **43**, 287–98.

**Strober, M. H. and Quester, A. O.** (1977) The earnings and promotions of women faculty: a comment, *American Economic Review*, **67**, 207–13.

**Swinton, D. H.** (1975) Factors affecting the future economic prospects of minorities, *American Economic Review*, **65**, 53–6.

**Thurow, L. C.** (1969) *Poverty and Discrimination*, Brookings Institution: Washington, DC.

**Thurrow, L. C.** (1976) *Generating Inequality*, Basic Books and Macmillan Press: London.

**Toikka, R. S.** (1976) The welfare implications of Becker's discrimination coefficient, *Journal of Economic Theory*, **13**, 472–7.

**Tsuchigane, R. and Dodge, N.** (1974) *Economic Discrimination Against Women in the United States: Measures and Changes*, Lexington Books: Lexington, Mass.

**Turnbull, P. and Williams, G.** (1974) Sex differentials in teachers' pay, *Journal of the Royal Statistical Society*, Series A, **37**, 245–58.

**Viscusi, W. K.** (1980) Sex differences in worker quitting, *Review of Economics and Statistics*, **62**, 388–98.

**Vrooman, J. L. and Greenfield, S. J.** (1978) A missing link in the heroic schooling model, *The Journal of Human Resources*, **13**, 422–8.

**Wallace, P. A. and LaMond, A. M.** (1977) *Women, Minorities and Employment Discrimination*, Lexington Books: Lexington, Mass.

**Watts, M.** (1978) Screening, inter-firm exploitation and job search, *Scottish Journal of Political Economy*, **5**, 187–200.

**Weiss, Y. and Gronau, R.** (1981) Expected interruptions in labour force participation and sex related differences in earnings growth, *The Review of Economic Studies*, **48**, 607–20.

**Welch, F.** (1973) Black–white wage differences in the returns to schooling, *American Economic Review*, **63**, 893–907.

**Welch, F.** (1975) Human capital theory: education, discrimination and life cycles, *American Economic Review*, **65**, 63–73.

**Welch, F.** (1980) The quality of education and cohort variation in black–white earnings differentials: a reply, *American Economic Review*, **70**, 192–5.

**Williams, W. E.** (1978) Race and economics, *The Public Interest*, **53**, 147–54.

**Wolff, E. N.** (1976) Occupational earnings behaviour and the inequality of earnings by sex and race in the United States, *Review of Income and Wealth*, **22**, 151–66.

**Zellner, H.** (1972) Discrimination against women, occupational segregation and the relative wage, *American Economic Review*, **62**, 157–60.

**Zincone, L. H. and Close, F. A.** (1978) Sex discrimination in the paramedical profession, *Industrial and Labor Relations Review*, **32**, 74–85.

# CHAPTER FOUR

# Job search and the functioning of labour markets

Christopher A. Pissarides

## 1. Introduction and scope

The model of job search deals with the operation of labour markets characterised by imperfect information about job opportunities and the availability of labour. There is no central agency which can convey information about these matters and supervise the drawing up of contracts between firms and workers; the collection of information about vacancies and wage offers, and the drawing up of employment contracts, is left to individual market participants. Thus, exchange in the labour market is a costly economic activity, and the decision about how much to spend before agreeing to an exchange is taken according to economic optimisation principles. As a result of this, the movement of labour between firms is a slow process, employment contracts may be of long duration, and their terms (in particular wage rates) may not be the same for all firms.

This type of market is clearly closer to reality than the perfect market of Walrasian economics, so collections of facts about individual and aggregate behaviour in such markets, and attempts to explain them intuitively or by *ad hoc* theorising, abound in the early literature of economics. By the 1930s, when the most conspicuous characteristic of the labour market was its slow adjustment to new conditions, a systematic exposition of the problems of imperfect information and search began to appear in the literature. Most notable of these were Hicks's (1932) description of entrepreneurial behaviour under the 'two general circumstances which do not receive much attention in equilibrium theory − the time and trouble required in making economic adjustments, and the fact of foresight' (p. 58), and Hutt's (1939) theory of the 'pseudo-idleness of labour'. Hicks recognised that general changes in firms' wage offers depend 'upon the action of workmen, on their moving from one employer to another, or on their consideration of the possibility of such movement ... so the equalising forces do not act quickly and easily, but nevertheless they do act' (pp. 74−6). But he did not describe *how* workmen behave and why the process is slow when they act as rational economic men. The absence of a good supply model is even more conspicuous in Keynes's *General Theory*, where frictions and slow adjustment are also emphasised. By contrast Hutt, writing in response to Keynes's neglect of labour supply, developed a fairly detailed supply model, emphasising very much the same issues as emphasised by the 'pioneering' papers on job search in the 1960s. Hutt's model was meant to show that imperfect knowledge about alternative job opportunities may lead a worker to reject immediately available work, in the hope of finding a better job somewhere else. In his own words, when an individual is *'actively* searching, the situation is that he is really investing in himself by working on his own account without immediate remuneration. He is prospecting ... He judges that the search for a better opening is worth the risk of immediately foregone income' (Hutt 1939: 60).

So it was realised quite early by economists that the problem of search is a problem in the theory of capital and investment, and that the crucial role in search markets is played by workers, 'on their moving from one employer to another, or on their consideration of the possibility of such movement'. Yet, the models of Hicks and Hutt were ignored. Formal treatment of the model of search did not materialise, until the developments in the theory of human capital on the one hand, and in the theory of choice under uncertainty on the other, enabled Stigler (1962) and Alchian (1970) to formulate the issues precisely, and so prepare the ground for formal analysis. However, the success of the theory of search in the early 1970s is not due so much to methodological advances within the area, as to the fact that the search model was thought capable of offering a satisfactory answer to an independently exposed defect of Walrasian economics: the theory of adjustment and disequilibrium exchange. It became evident in the 1960s that Walrasian adjustment theory (*tâtonnement* or *non-tâtonnement*) could not provide a satisfactory theoretical framework for the analysis of either Keynesian employment dynamics (Clower 1965; Leijonhufvud 1968), or Phillips-curve unemployment and inflation dynamics (Phelps 1967; Friedman 1968). Thus, most of the stimulus to research in models of job search came from two sources. On the one hand, Alchian (1970) and Leijonhufvud (1968: 75−81) asserted that search theory could provide a rationale for price inflexibility and quantity dynamics, and this was thought to be a possible microfoundation for Keynesian theory. On the other hand, Phelps (1970) and Mortensen (1970a) built search-theoretic models that offered a reconciliation of the observed short-run trade-off between inflation and unemployment, and Friedman's (1968) and Phelps's (1967) assertions that in the absence of money illusion the trade-off cannot persist in the long run. Thus the search model appeared to provide at one and the same time a rationale for Keynesian multiplier processes, Phillips-curve dynamics, and long-run quantity theory predictions.

A lot of the early optimism was, of course, misdirected. In the decade that followed it became evident that the dynamics of the search model were not of the same nature as the Keynesian multiplier; the short-run trade-off between inflation and unemployment was not the one discovered by Phillips, and it was probably not consistent with the data; and even in the long run, search theory with adaptive expectations of the kind assumed by Phelps, Mortensen and Friedman could not produce the equilibrium natural rate of unemployment.

The employment dynamics which characterise Keynesian models result from wage (or price) rigidities and 'multiply' over time; that is, when a person cannot sell his labour services because there is insufficient demand for them at the going wage rate, he cuts back his consumption of goods. If many workers experience difficulties selling their labour, the resulting decrease in consumption demand would lead to further reductions in the demand for labour, and the multiplier process would gather momentum. By contrast, in the search model, the unemployed *choose* to be unemployed, because by doing so they increase their lifetime income prospects. Although a job searcher is obviously better off when he accepts a job than when he rejects it to remain unemployed, unemployment in his case is not likely to reduce his expected income by very much. So his consumption is not likely to suffer by very much either. Moreover, in the search model wages are flexible; more precisely, there is nothing in the structure of the model of job search that makes wage rigidity a more likely outcome than wage flexibility. Thus the model of job search is as far removed from the Keynesian multiplier model as the earlier neo-classical model with full employment (Grossman 1973).

It is more controversial to argue that the short-run trade-off between inflation and unemployment studied by Phelps (1970) and Mortensen (1970a) was not the one discovered by Phillips. Phillips presented simply broad empirical facts, which are certainly consistent with the Phelps – Mortensen model. But in Lipsey's (1960) early rationalisation of Phillips's facts, inflation is *caused* by labour-market disequilibrium. Unemployment responds to changes in the demand for labour and becomes the driving force in the inflation – unemployment plane. Thus, an increase in aggregate demand raises the demand for labour; firms take on more workers, and this reduces unemployment; 'excess demand' in the labour market rises, giving rise to inflationary pressures. By contrast, in the search model the driving force in the inflation – unemployment plane is inflation, and the reason for a negatively sloped trade-off is the existence of errors in the formation of expectation (Pissarides 1976b:Ch.14). An increase in aggregate demand leads, in the first instance, to more wage inflation; job searchers are offered higher wages, which they mistakenly think are due more to good luck than to general wage inflation; they are therefore more likely to accept them, leading to a reduction in unemployment.

These broad empirical predictions are consistent with the data. But there are some finer points to these predictions which do not seem to be consistent with the data (Tobin 1972). Foremost among these is the prediction that most cyclical fluctuations in unemployment result from changes in job-acceptance behaviour (and also job quitting, which is even more difficult to sustain empirically).

Finally, even the early optimism that search theory could provide a model of inflation and unemployment which would be characterised by the equilibrium natural rate of unemployment in the long run was misdirected, though more recent developments in this area have rectified the inadequacies of the early models (Lucas 1971, 1973). Thus, although the early models with adaptive expectations could not produce a natural rate, because of the persistence of expectational errors, the change-over to rational expectations has led to models with natural-rate properties.

More recently, the model of search has been used for the investigation of other questions, which although anticipated by the earlier models, are far removed from the macroeconomic questions investigated by them. Although work in these areas is still very active, so it may be premature to evaluate the contribution of search theory in their development, two applications in particular seem to be promising: the investigation of unemployment flows and the efficiency analysis of unemployment, with and without unemployment insurance programmes and other kinds of taxation.

We shall not discuss these developments here. However, it seems to be the case that search theory has provided a new stimulus to the analysis of data about the labour market, and in some cases it has even led to the collection of new data sets. The main stimulus here came from the general way of looking at labour markets, which search theory has popularised, rather than from the finer details of search models. This general way of looking at labour markets will occupy us a great deal in this survey (Kiefer and Neuman, 1981; Lancaster 1979; Nickell 1979a).

The efficiency analysis of unemployment asks whether the optimising decisions taken by firms and workers during search lead to a socially efficient rate of unemployment. Most authors who looked at this question concluded that there are some externalities in labour markets (and also various taxes and subsidies) which are likely to make private decisions inefficient (Phelps 1972; Tobin 1972; Diamond and Maskin 1979; Diamond 1981, 1982; Mortensen 1982; Pissarides 1984a). The analysis of the welfare implications of unemployment insurance programmes also falls into this category, and it has been formalised recently using the equilibrium model of job search (Baily 1978; Flemming 1978; Shavell and Weiss 1979; Pissarides 1983).

Given the diversity of the questions investigated by models of search, a short survey must, necessarily, be limited in scope. For this reason, in this paper I will restrict the discussion to the less controversial (positive) questions of job acceptance and job termination, and to questions of job offers.[1] The behaviour of the labour market implied by the micro models will be discussed in some detail, but first the paper will set out the basic models of workers' and firms' behaviour analysed by the theory.

Section 2 considers the basic question of job acceptance. Section 3 moves on to the study of job offers by firms, and section 4 completes the investigation of the exchange between individual firms and workers by discussing job separations. Section 5 uses the results of the previous sections to investigate the behaviour of wages and unemployment when there are exogenous changes in the demand for output, and section 6 concludes with some brief remarks on the previous discussion.

## 2.   The supply of labour: job acceptance

An unemployed worker looking for a job has to decide, first, the method which he will use to search firms, and second, when to accept an offer and terminate his search. Stigler (1962), whose model is the first formal attempt to derive an optimal search policy, assumed that the worker chooses at random $n$ firms and searches them. He then stops searching and takes the highest offer observed. Thus for

Stigler the task of a search model is to determine the optimal $n$. However, as is well known from the theory of optimal stopping (see, for instance, DeGroot 1970), the Stigler-type fixed-sample rule is inferior to the sequential optimal-stopping rule when the searcher knows the distribution of job offers.[2] In the sequential rule the individual is assumed to search one firm per period, and decide whether to take its job offer (if one is made), before he searches any more firms. Partly because information in labour markets is not totally absent, and partly because the sequential rule is more convenient for the analysis of market processes than the fixed-sample rule, almost all search models which followed Stigler's adopted the sequential assumption.

In the sequential model, every time the searcher observes a job offer he works out the returns from taking it, and the expected returns from rejecting it and continuing the search. He then takes the offer if the former exceed the latter, and does not take it otherwise. Under certain conditions, the strongest of which is the requirement that the individual knows the distribution of wage offers in the market, an optimal sequential searching policy satisfies the *reservation wage property*. The acceptance or rejection of a wage offer is determined by a reservation wage, which is chosen by the individual at the beginning of the period in such a way as to maximise his expected returns from search. If the observed wage offer is less than the reservation wage the offer is rejected; otherwise it is accepted. Given the abundance of formal models of reservation wages we shall not derive an optimal reservation wage formally, but simply state the main question investigated and the main results obtained. (See McCall 1970, Mortensen 1970b, Lippman and McCall 1976a, and Pissarides 1976a, for formal derivations and summaries of results.)

We begin by assuming that firms offer different wages to individuals of the same skill, and that the individual knows the true probability that he will be offered a given wage rate. We also assume that not all firms that are searched have vacancies, and that the individual knows the probability of receiving a job offer from a randomly chosen firm. In a general model the offer probability should depend on the firm's wage rate, since high-wage firms are less likely to make offers, but this extension does not influence any of the results that we shall describe. Also, since in the model of search we are interested mainly in whether the individual observes a job offer within a given period of time, and not in whether a randomly chosen firm makes an offer, the offer probability should depend on the intensity of search. Models with variable intensity have been considered by Whipple (1973), Mortensen (1978), Burdett (1979), Pissarides (1983) and others. Their results indicate that the reservation wage satisfies the same properties, regardless of whether search intensity is variable or fixed. The advantage of a variable search intensity is that search-related considerations might influence market outcomes even in markets where there is no wage variability for workers of the same skill. In such markets, the concept of the reservation wage loses its significance, since each worker faces a unique wage which he has to accept (or drop out of the market). But if not all firms have job vacancies, search intensity remains a choice variable for workers looking for jobs, and through it workers might influence the workings of the market.

In what follows we shall discuss the properties of reservation wages for a given search intensity. Most of what we shall have to say can also be said about search intensity, when it is explicitly assumed to be a choice variable. We shall therefore have only brief remarks to add about the choice of search intensity.

When a firm makes a job offer the individual accepts it if the wage rate exceeds his reservation wage. The probability that the individual *leaves* unemployment during the period is then obtained as the product of the offer and acceptance probabilities. For a given offer probability, an increase in the reservation wage reduces the probability of leaving unemployment. At the end of search the individual expects to earn a wage that is at least as high as his reservation wage, so his expected post-unemployment wage is the conditional mean of all wage offers that exceed the reservation wage. If, as is usually the case, there are some jobs that the individual is not willing to accept, the expected post-unemployment wage exceeds the mean wage offer. Since rejected wage offers are not observed by anyone other than the individual rejecting them, the mean wage offer is unobservable, but the mean *acceptable* wage (or the expected post-unemployment wage) is observable, and corresponds to the average market wage. An increase in the reservation wage increases the expected post-unemployment wage, and hence the average market wage, even if the distribution of wage offers is unchanged.

The basic trade-off faced by the worker in his choice of an optimal reservation wage may be described as follows. By raising his reservation wage by a small amount, the individual raises his expected wage after the termination of search; but he also raises his expected duration of unemployment, since a higher reservation wage implies a lower acceptance probability. The optimal reservation wage is the value that equates the marginal return from a small rise (higher expected wage received over the expected duration of the job) with the marginal cost (forgone wage income for the additional period of unemployment). The main task taken up by the sequential models is the investigation of the properties of this trade-off.

There are two questions that are raised, in general, in relation to the behaviour of reservation wages. First, the question of the dynamic path of reservation wages during search, and second, the effects of changes in various parameters on the whole sequence of reservation wages. The pioneering papers on sequential search, in particular McCall (1970) and Mortensen (1970b), introduced assumptions which ensured that reservation wages remained unchanged over time if the environment did not change, so their models dealt with the second question; their models have been formalised and extended (but at the same time taken out of the labour-market context) by Kohn and Shavell (1974). However, that reservation wages change over time was noted by Kasper (1967) and Holt (1970) in their empirically oriented work, and subsequently analysed by Gronau (1971), Salop (1973b) and Pissarides (1976a).

The main assumptions required for unchanging (or stationary) reservation wages are an infinite planning horizon and a stationary environment (including the distribution of wage offers). Although in practice a completely stationary environment can only be an approximation to a long-run situation, the results of the search models which make these assumptions have been used to describe the cyclical behaviour of the economy (Phelps *et al.* 1970). This, however, does not seem to have produced any serious inconsistencies. When the results of search theory are applied to the economy as a whole, only some broad generalisations of these results are used; for instance, two critical results which are often used are the dependence of reservation wages (or search intensities) on the *expected* mean wage offer, and their dependence on the number of job offers. These results hold in models where workers have an infinite horizon and the market environment is unchanging, as well as in models where workers have finite horizons and some changes are taking place in the market environment. Of course, the detailed predictions of the stationary model do not hold in a changing economy (Lippman and McCall 1976b). But in many applications of the search model these detailed predictions seem to be a small price to pay for the far greater simplicity of the stationary model (but see Lippman and McCall 1976a: 357–61, for a different view).

The conclusion reached by the authors who considered the path of reservation wages during search is that the optimal path will almost certainly decline during search. This is consistent with empirical findings by Kasper (1967) and Kiefer and Neuman (1979) (see also Holt 1970). In general, reservation wages fall during search if the attractiveness of future search declines with time. Factors that may induce a decline in the attractiveness of future search include the availability of only a finite number of searching opportunities, the possibility of non-random search, rising costs of search, and the deteriorating wealth/leisure ratio during search.[3]

The number of searching opportunities during search is an important determinant of its attractiveness, because the higher the number of potential employers that can be searched, the higher the maximum wage the individual can expect to be offered. If a searching opportunity is lost without success and the total number of these opportunities is finite, the returns from future search fall, so the individual reduces his reservation wage (Karlin 1962; Gronau 1971). Non-random search implies that the individual will search his better prospects before the less promising ones, so when an opportunity is lost the average attractiveness of the remaining opportunities declines (Holt 1970; Salop 1973a). Costs may rise during search either because easily accessible firms are searched first, or because capital market imperfections and diminishing marginal utility induce a rising marginal cost (monetary or psychic) as wealth declines during search. When the declining wealth position during search is considered alongside the accumulated leisure, than at the margin, the individual becomes more willing to substitute a unit of money for leisure (Kasper 1967).

The effects of changes in the environment on the whole path of reservation wages may be obtained simply by considering the effects on the initial value of the reservation wage (or, following most of the literature, by assuming a stationary environment). In general we may distinguish two sets of parameters that influence the reservation wage; those related to the *market* environment and those related to the *individual's* environment. In the usual utility-maximising model subject to a sequence of wage-offer distributions, the market parameters define mainly the sequence of distributions, whereas the individual parameters define the utility function and the horizon. Thus market parameters are likely to affect all individuals in a similar way, whereas individual parameters are likely to vary between individuals. We consider first changes in the main market parameters and then changes in the individual parameters.

First, an increase in some or all wage offers, for example a rightward shift in the distribution of wage offers, increases the expected returns from search, so it raises the reservation wage. Of course, an individual observing a rise in a single wage may not know if this is a result of a movement along an unchanging distribution, or if it is the result of a shift in the whole distribution. Sorting out movements along a distribution from shifts in the distribution plays a crucial role in the application of the search model to the analysis of aggregate inflation and unemployment. We shall take up this question in a later section. Here, we may simply note that if the individual thinks that the whole distribution of wage offers has changed, he will change his reservation wage much more than if he thinks that only a few firms are now offering higher wages. The optimal reservation wage depends primarily on (expected) market conditions, not on the wage offers of particular firms.

Second, an increase in the dispersion of wage offers increases the expected returns from search if the individual is not 'very' risk averse, so it also raises the reservation wage. (If the increase in dispersion is about the mean utility level, and not about the mean wage offer, the expected returns from search rise for all individuals.) The best way of seeing the reason for this result is to imagine a risk-neutral individual, who is not interested in changes in the variability of wage offers *per se*. This individual will have a reservation wage, and so he will reject low wage offers. An increase in the dispersion of wage offers corresponds, broadly, to an increase in the high wage offers, and a decrease in the low wage offers, which the individual can expect to observe with given probabilities. Since the individual rejects low wage offers in any case, the fact that these wage offers are now even lower does not make him worse off, but the fact that the acceptable high wage offers are now higher makes him better off. So he will raise his reservation wage rate in response to this change. If the individual is risk averse he has a dislike for variability *per se*. The increased variability then, has two effects − the positive effect described above and the negative effect resulting from risk aversion. Which effect dominates depends on how risk averse the individual is.

Third, an increase in the vacancy/unemployment ratio, or more generally in the number of vacancies per searcher, increases the probability of being offered a job, and so it increases the reservation wage.

The most important parameters which are related to the individual's environment include the cost of search, his attitude towards risk, his rate of time preference and the length of his horizon (age). First, a fall in the cost of search, for example because the searcher's current income receipts (in particular his unemployment compensation) have risen, or because any out-of-pocket costs of search have fallen, increases the reservation wage. Second, more risk-averse individuals are likely to have a lower reservation wage, since for the more risk averse the uncertainty attached to the outcome of search will be more costly than for the more risk tolerant. Third, a fall in the rate of discount will make the individual less impatient for results, so he will increase his reservation wage. Finally, individuals who are likely to benefit more from search than other individuals because they expect to spend more time holding a job, will have higher reservation wages. Prime-age males normally fall into this category of individuals who expect to spend more time holding a job.

If, instead of assuming that the searcher knows the parameters of the distribution of wage offers with complete certainty we assume that he has partial information about it, then his optimal policy would be influenced not by the *objective* distribution of offers but by his *subjective* estimate of it. Thus differences in subjective estimates would also give rise to differences in reservation wages, and different experience during search would result in further differences through the revision of subjective estimates. The formal treatment of learning in models of search is difficult, not least because the reservation wage property may no longer hold (Kohn and Shavell 1974; Rothschild 1974). But as Rothschild (1974) noted, most of the main results of the model without learning carry over for some 'important' cases. In the sequel we shall ignore the problems introduced by learning, assuming that the reservation wage property holds at all times.

Empirical work on the model of search has concentrated mainly on cross-sectional differences in reservation wages. Thus, various authors have used observations on the duration of unemployment and the post-unemployment wage of a sample of individuals to draw inferences about the determinants of the reservation wage (Ehrenberg and Oaxaca 1976; Classen 1979; Kiefer and Neumann 1979, 1981; Lancaster 1979; Nickell 1979a; Lynch 1983). Both the *expected* duration of unemployment and the *expected* post-unemployment wage depend on the reservation wage, since when the reservation wage is higher the individual is less likely to accept a job, but he will, on average, earn a higher wage when he ends his search. By investigating the relation between the characteristics of unemployed workers and systematic variations in the duration of unemployment and the post-unemployment wage of the same workers, these empirical studies were able, in general, to confirm the predictions of the model of job search. In particular, a number of household characteristics have been identified as influences on reservation wages, and it has been established that a rise in unemployment benefits reduces the probability of leaving unemployment by raising the reservation wage. Moreover, a lower job-offer probability reduces the reservation wage. In theory, this could cause either a rise or a fall in the probability of leaving unemployment. The rise in the reservation wage reduces the probability of accepting a job, and this could offset the positive effect of the rise of the probability of being offered a job. However, the results of empirical studies appear to indicate that a rise in the job-offer probability increases the probability of leaving unemployment (see also Lancaster and Cheshire 1983).

Applications of the model of search to the study of the labour market as a whole have aggregated over all individuals, and so they simplified the model by assuming that the typical worker's probability of receiving a job offer depends only on the vacancy/unemployment ratio; his probability of accepting the offer and his expected post-unemployment wage depend only on the mean wage offer and his reservation wage; and the reservation wage depends mainly on the *perceived* mean wage offer. We shall turn to a discussion of the results of these models in later sections of this paper.

We consider finally the choice of search intensity by a job searcher. In general, this may be defined as the choice of contact probability with a potential employer during a short period of time. Workers looking for jobs could influence this probability by spending more resources (including time) on job search – for example by scanning more advertising boards, asking more friends about potential job offers, and so on. The more a worker spends on job search, the more likely he is to locate an employer within a given period of time.

The determinants of the optimal search intensity are essentially the same as the determinants of the optimal reservation wage. Thus, a rise in the mean wage offer raises the intensity of search, whereas a rise in unemployment benefits reduces it. Also, an exogenous increase in the ratio of vacancies to unemployment reduces the intensity of search, but the overall effect on the probability of leaving unemployment is likely to be positive. It is worth mentioning that the choice of search intensity remains a non-trivial choice problem even when there is no wage variability in the market for workers of a given skill. The search then is over vacancies, not over a wage distribution for high wage offers, but the probability of leaving unemployment would still depend on all the supply variables that we have discussed in this section if search intensity is variable. So although it is true that the concept of the reservation wage is non-trivial only when there is wage variability, it is not necessary to have wage variability in order to apply the results of the model of search to the functioning of labour markets.

## 3.   The demand for labour: job offers

Most of the new results about the behaviour of the labour market obtained by search models owe their derivation to in-depth analysis of the supply side of the market. Yet, the early models have utilised the concept of the reservation wage, and a critical assumption made by them is that there is an exogenous distribution of wage offers for individuals of the same skill. Since wages are usually fixed by firms, the results of these models are valid only if optimising behaviour on the part of firms in a search environment can be shown to lead to wage variability across firms (Rothschild 1973).

Early work in this direction (Fisher 1970; Diamond 1971; Hey 1974) produced negative results, in that the Phelps – Mortensen assumptions about job search did not seem capable of supporting wage variability. These papers found that if all firms maximised profits given a supply of labour flow similar to that generated by the model of search, the most likely outcome in the long run was the monopsony wage. Mortensen (1970a) was the first economist to note explicitly that firms in this environment have some monopsony power, but he did not consider the convergence of wages in the absence of exogenous shocks. Instead he analysed the implications of this monopsony power for aggregate behaviour, conditional on the existence of wage variability.

Mortensen's argument is that if individuals have different reservation wages, a firm can raise the probability that a randomly selected job searcher will accept its offer by raising the offered wage. It follows that in a large market the fraction of searchers willing to accept the firm's offer is an increasing function of the firm's wage, i.e. the firm has some monopsony power over the supply of labour to itself. Mortensen argued that this monopsony power is temporary, in that in the long run a firm that does not pay the market average will lose all its employees to other firms. However, this requires that employees continue looking for a job after they accept the firm's offer, a condition that need not be satisfied if search is costly. The process by which monopsony power is eroded in labour markets has not been set out, and if the results of the related literature on commodity markets is anything to go by, erosion will probably not take place: convergence, if it happens, will probably be to the monopsony wage.

In Mortensen's model (and also in the related model of Phelps 1970) the firm can influence the *flow* of labour to itself by varying its wage offer. This contrasts sharply with traditional monopsony theory, where the firm controls the *stock* of labour directly, and where it maximises profit by moving along a labour-supply curve with wage on one axis and the stock of employment on the other. In the search model, a slightly higher wage implies a slightly higher rate of growth in the stock of employment; in other words, if the firm wants to adjust faster it will have to pay its employees more. In this sense the search model is similar to the models of costs of adjustment in investment (Eisner and Strotz 1963) so the results of that literature carry over to the labour market. In particular, if there is a rise in the desired stock of labour, for example because the demand for output has risen, the firm will raise its wage rate to attract more labour, but the target adjustment rate will be slow and full adjustment will take place only in the long run. But if there is a decrease in the desired stock of labour there is no reason why the firm should not adjust immediately through a wage reduction. This implication of asymmetric adjustment in employment has not been explored fully in the literature, nor has it been tested empirically.

Returning now to the question of wage variability across firms, there seem to be two factors which can give rise to it. The first relates to stochastic shocks in the demand for output, which cancel out in aggregate, and indeed take place independently of any aggregate shocks. If firms change their wages every time the demand for their output changes, even if they know it to be temporary, then it is possible to derive a stationary long-run distribution of wages with firms moving up and down this distribution depending on whether demand is buoyant or slack (Lucas and Prescott 1974). If we ignore these shocks, or assume that firms do not respond instantly to temporary changes in demand (e.g. they may smooth fluctuations by holding inventories), then non-trivial wage variability can arise only if there are firm-specific variations in productivity. Similar workers must have different productivities when employed by different firms. This requirement does not appear to be too difficult to fulfil: productivity may vary because some firms may choose to offer firm-specific training whereas others may not offer it (Salop 1973b); because capital intensity, or more generally the technique of production, may vary; or simply because of idiosyncratic characteristics of firms and workers (Mortensen 1978; Jovanovic 1979).

Now if there are substantial differences in firm-specific productivities, firms will realise that the reason a searcher is willing to accept their offer is due mainly to a better-than-average job match between their vacancy and the searcher. Firms may try to exploit this advantage by reducing the wage offer, but since they also realise that other searchers may not be so well matched to their vacancies, they will not want to reduce wages by so much as to discourage the well-matched workers from accepting their offer. This has important implications for the equilibrium wage rate in a model of search that have not yet been explored in the literature.[4] In this environment, the wage offered to a person depends not only on his own productivity, but also on the productivity of other workers who may search the firm. In a very long-run situation the firm may open up a sufficient number of vacancies to accomodate all workers who are willing to work for it, but in the short run the profit-maximising wage of poorly matched workers may be well below their productivity, and may even be negative. Thus the firm may refuse to offer a job to poorly matched workers, in the hope that better-matched workers will be found in the future (Pissarides 1976b: Ch. 3; Akerlof 1981). The firm's policy in this connection is formally identical to that of the job searcher investigated in the last section: it chooses an optimal reservation profit level and makes appropriate job offers to all searchers who, at a positive profit-maximising wage, yield as much profit as the reservation level. The trade-off faced by the firm is that a higher reservation profit level (or lower wage offer) ensures higher expected profits when production starts, but it also reduces the probability that a worker willing to accept the firm's offer will be found. As with reservation wages, we may expect reservation profit levels to fall over time when vacancies stand idle. Also, it can be shown that the *real* value of reservation profit falls when the price of output rises, so the firm becomes more willing to make job offers when the demand for its output rises (Pissarides 1976b: Chs 3–4).

Thus, although there is nothing in the search model to suggest that wages may be slow to respond to changes in the demand for output, in the model with stochastic job matchings firms may refuse to offer jobs to some workers even with complete wage flexibility. Another element of the search model may explain asymmetric wage adjustment. Since by assumption workers observe their own wage first, and the wage of other firms after time-consuming search, wage reductions by a firm bring forth an immediate response from its workforce, but wage rises bring forth only a slow response from job searchers. Thus a firm anticipating a change in demand may be inclined to raise its wage offer well before the date of an anticipated increase, but wait until a decrease occurs before reducing wages. A generalisation of Mortensen's (1970a) model in this direction seems worth while, but has not yet been undertaken.

If there is no wage variability the choice facing the firm is a lot more straightforward, and the results of traditional labour-demand models hold. Firms which want to expand employment open up more vacancies if they are wage takers, and they raise, in addition, their wage offer if they are monopsonists. It is not unreasonable to assume, in general, that there is a level of 'desired employment', which the firm chooses along conventional marginal productivity lines. The level of vacancies is then the difference between this desired employment and the actual employment level of the firm. Search theory has very little to add to this choice problem, so we shall not dwell on it here.[5]

## 4.  Job separations

In the original models of search (e.g. those in Phelps *et al.* 1970) job separations were always initiated by workers. A worker quits either to join another firm, or to become unemployed to look for another job. The arguments put forward by the early search theorists (most notably Alchian 1970) to justify quitting to search for another job while unemployed proved both unconvincing and inconsistent with the data (Tobin 1972; Parsons 1973; Mattila 1974), and the most effective criticism of the original models of search came from this quarter. Empirically, we observe that not many searchers accept jobs on a temporary basis until they find a better offer, but we also observe that quitting accounts for a small fraction of the total flow into unemployment. Most quitting takes place because workers have found better jobs with other firms.

Thus, as far as voluntary movements between employment and unemployment are concerned, we observe a certain unwillingness of workers to change status frequently; most unemployed and most employed (on-the-job) searchers appear to be looking for a permanent job. A number of extensions of the early models of search attempted to reconcile these observations. The upshot of these models is that although search theory can offer some explanation for job separations when no unemployment is involved, it has not offered a convincing explanation for the bulk of the inflow into unemployment.

There are two types of transaction costs that account for the fact that unemployed workers search mainly for permanent jobs, and yet dissatisfied employees do not quit before finding a job. First, the cost of on-the-job search may be higher than the cost of off-the-job search, and second there may be substantial moving costs (especially high set-up costs for new jobs). Differential search costs were invoked by Alchian (1970) to explain why workers prefer to search while unemployed. His model was formalised by Burdett (1978), who showed that if the cost of on-the-job search is higher, unemployed workers will adopt two reservation wages during search. Jobs offering less than both reservation wages will be rejected; jobs offering more than the low reservation wage but not as much as the high reservation wage will be accepted, but the worker will continue searching on the job after acceptance; and finally, jobs offering more than both reservation wages will be accepted and search given up altogether. The difference between the two reservation wages depends on the cost differential. If the differential is zero then the job searcher is likely to accept the first job that he is offered, and continue searching on the job if the wage is not high enough. But since, as we saw, it is reasonable to assume that during unsuccessful search reservation wages fall, if on-the-job search does not lead to a high wage offer before the reservation wage falls down to the level of his own wage rate, it is given up altogether. Thus declining reservation wages may be one reason for the well-known observation of an inverse relation between tenure and job quitting.

Although difficult to test directly, differential search costs have not been very convincing in explaining off-the-job search. Employed searchers, after all, receive higher income during search, and may have better access to information channels about jobs. A more convincing explanation for the unwillingness of workers to accept jobs on a temporary basis is the existence of substantial job-changing costs. Jobs have set-up costs of various kinds, for example learning the new environment, moving physically to a new location, bearing part of the initial training cost, and if the worker anticipates these he will raise his reservation wage to compensate (Hey and McKenna 1979). Even if the cost of search is lower on the job, unemployed workers will be reluctant to accept jobs temporarily in order to avoid paying unnecessary set-up costs. Indeed, firms which anticipate the possibility of quitting may shift more of the set-up cost towards the worker, in order to discourage temporary job acceptance (Salop and Salop 1976).

The existence of moving costs may also explain why on-the-job searchers are reluctant to quit before finding a new job. If, for some reason, an employed worker decides to look for another job, it will obviously not be to his advantage to become unemployed to search, unless off-the-job search is less costly than on the job search, and his dissatisfaction with his current job outweighs the advantage of the higher income during search. The existence of moving costs, like transaction costs in the theory of portfolio selection, does not push job searchers to any state in particular (e.g. unemployment), but simply tends to encourage the searcher to remain in his initial state until he finds a permanent job.

Moving costs, of course, are not infinite, and differential search costs may indeed exist. Thus some temporary job-taking does take place, and some searchers quit to search off-the-job. There is, however, another explanation for quitting within this model, especially as it relates to employees with short tenure on the job. The basic model of search assumes that the searcher can obtain full information about the job offer immediately upon inspection. If, instead, we assume that there are some characteristics of the job that cannot be observed except by actually taking the offer and experiencing them for a short period of time, then searchers may take jobs conditionally, intending to search again if their experience is not as good as a preassigned level (Wilde 1979; McKenna 1983). In a general model where there are both 'inspection' and 'experience' characteristics (e.g. the wage rate is an 'inspection' characteristic, the agreeableness of the boss an 'experience' characteristic; see Nelson 1970), and also differential search costs and moving costs, we may observe the following: searchers take jobs if the inspection characteristics exceed a reservation level; they settle at the job if the experience characteristics are revealed to be above a reservation level; they search on the job if experience characteristics are below a 'high' reservation level but above a 'low' one; and leave the job to search off the job if experience characteristics are below a low reservation level. Thus quitting is inversely related to tenure, and some quitting to search while unemployed may take place.

Most job separations, as we remarked above, take place because workers leave their firms to take better-paying jobs elsewhere. A condition for this within the simple model of search is that employed workers search continuously on the job. Although this is usually assumed away by the model, there are several low-intensity search methods that may lead to job offers at no cost to the employee. For instance, a firm or a person's friends may provide information about jobs. Thus, professional jobs in particular, are advertised regularly in trade journals and national newspapers that the employed person is likely to read, even if he is not an active job seeker; friends may talk about suitable vacancies that they know on social occasions; and a manual worker may come across vacancy notices outside factories in the vicinity of his job or home. The search model has not concerned itself with this process, largely because it is not very interesting in the study of unemployment. In particular, this contributes little to our understanding of the flows in and out of unemployment, which was the primary concern of the original models, except perhaps to the extent that inter-firm information flows about jobs and job-changing create externalities to unemployed searchers.

But even if we choose to ignore these externalities in the study of unemployment, it is clearly the case that it is these low-cost information flows that lead to most job separations. The firm is likely to take a greater interest in this form of labour turnover than in the worker who quits a few months after accepting a job to search off the job. The question then arises as to whether the existence of these information flows can explain the inverse relation between tenure and the probability of quitting.

There are two reasons for this inverse relation within this framework, in addition to the ones already examined. The first utilises the distinction between 'specific' and 'general' skills, and the second breaks away from the human capital framework, postulating that within any short period of time wages need not bear a close relation to the marginal product of labour. In the first case workers are assumed to receive offers from outside which correspond to their general skills, whereas their own wage rises in accordance with their specific skills. If specific skills on the job rise faster than general skills, the probability that an outside offer exceeds the worker's own wage, adjusted for the cost of movement, declines with tenure (Mortensen 1978; Jovanovic 1979). In the second case the firm and the worker are assumed to recognise explicitly that a job is likely to last more than a few periods. The firm is then concerned about the present value of wage costs, and the worker about the present value of his income; and as long as the present value of a worker's marginal product is equal to the present value of wages (adjusted for the supply elasticity if it is not infinite), the wage need not be equal to the value of marginal product within any single period. Under these conditions the firm may find it optimal to start paying the worker a wage below the value of his marginal product, and compensate him by letting his wage rate rise faster with tenure than the value of his marginal product. Two reasons that may induce firms to behave in this way are, firstly, that the firm may want to hold part of the worker's product as 'deposit', in case he defaults (e.g. steals output, or takes more leisure on the job). The deposit is accumulated by paying wages below the marginal product at first, and if the worker does not default it is returned as a pension, or as payment of wages above marginal products when the worker gains 'seniority' (Lazear 1981). Secondly, by letting wages rise faster than marginal products the firm raises the probability that the worker will stay with it until the end of his career, since future wage offers from other firms will correspond to the worker's marginal product for the rest of his working life. For a given present value of earnings the worker is made better off by this arrangement if he is risk averse, because he is likely to have more information about lifetime wages at his own firm, than at other firms that may make him an offer (Ioannides and Pissarides 1983).

Empirically it is very difficult to distinguish between the human capital view and the long-term contract view of quitting. In both cases wages received from one's own firm rise faster with tenure than wage offers received from other firms. But the existence of arrangements like mandatory retirement (Lazear 1979) and some recent direct evidence from firms (Medoff and Abraham 1980) supports the view that senior workers are paid wages in excess of the value of their marginal product.[6]

We may summarise the theory of supply-initiated job separations by saying that although some separations may lead to entry into unemployment, especially of short-tenure employees who are still learning the job, most supply-initiated separations take place only after the worker has secured another job. It follows then that most entrants into unemployment are either new labour-force entrants (and re-entrants), or people who lost their job 'involuntarily'. New entrants and re-entrants, however, are not a big fraction of the inflow, so most of the entry into unemployment is the result of lay-offs and redundancies.[7]

In the model of search, as we saw, there is nothing which may make a firm choose to lay off workers, rather than reduce their wages until they quit, when the demand for its output falls. When there are skill differentials (or firm-specific variations in the productivity of job matchings) some lay-offs may take place when demand drops, because the optimal wage offer of poorly matched employees may fall below a minimum constraint (e.g. it may become negative, even if their productivity remains positive). These lay-offs are likely to become more important when external constraints, like union rules or 'fairness' considerations, force the firm to fix a wage rate for a job before ascertaining the productivity of job applicants. Under this constraint, the firm chooses a wage rate suited to the 'average' productivity of potential employees, and refuses to take on low-productivity workers (Ehrenberg 1973; Pissarides 1976b). Alternatively, if workers' productivity is an 'experience' good, in the sense that the firm finds out about a worker's productivity only after employing the worker for a number of 'probationary' periods, low-productivity workers may be taken on but laid off quickly when the opportunity arises (McKenna 1980). When demand falls the firm may reduce its wage offer slightly, but it may also raise its hiring standards and lay off marginal employees. By behaving in this way the firm ensures that good employees do not leave, so the brunt of the adjustment is born by poorly matched employees who were not very profitable, and are easily replaceable (Hicks 1932; Pissarides 1976b).

Another kind of lay-off explored in the literature stimulated by search theory, but not related directly to the main assumptions of the search model, is the 'temporary' lay-off (Feldstein 1975, 1976; Baily 1977; Medoff 1979; Pissarides 1982). Here the firm is viewed as laying off workers temporarily during a depression, with the intention of recalling the workers to their former job either when demand recovers or even earlier.[8] This phenomenon is more prevalent in the USA than in the UK, but even there its importance seems to have been exaggerated by the early models. A critical condition for the optimality of temporary lay-offs (rather than wage reductions) is that laid-off workers enjoy an extra income (e.g. unemployment benefits) or leisure during lay-off. The related literature on risk shifting (Baily 1974; Azariadis 1975) has argued that if workers are more averse to income fluctuations than firms, wage rigidity in the face of firm-specific demand shocks is optimal, but zero lay-offs in the presence of unemployment insurance may not be optimal. However, it is doubtful whether these models explain a sizeable fraction of the inflow into unemployment (Akerlof and Miyazaki 1980; Pissarides 1981); and, of course, the models investigate temporary, not permanent, job separations.

How much of the total inflow into unemployment these models explain is a question that needs investigation. In the UK in particular we know very little about the causes of unemployment: we do not even know if old-fashioned wage rigidity is responsible for extensive lay-offs in recessions, although some economists have argued that it may have a lot to do with the industrial recession of the 1970s.[9]

## 5.  Cyclical fluctuations in unemployment and wages

Like other economic models, the model of search derives its main results by simplifying the structure of the market and the rules of behaviour in several directions. As such, it is suitable for the analysis of some labour-market phenomena, but it is not suitable for the analysis of others. The previous section suggested that search may contribute significantly to our understanding of the determinants of the probability of leaving unemployment and it may add to our knowledge of inter-firm labour movements, but it probably does not contribute very much to our understanding of the determinants of the flow into unemployment.[10]

In this section I use a simplified search model with an exogenous (and constant) flow into unemployment and no inter-firm labour movements, to investigate the original question posed by Phelps (1970), Mortensen (1970a) and others, which did so much to stimulate interest in these models: how does the labour market respond to exogenous changes in the demand for output? In particular, if the demand for output is subject to cyclical fluctuations, do unemployment and wages also fluctuate cyclically? There are no precise rigorous answers to these questions in the literature, but various possibilities may be investigated within the framework of the model with a fair degree of confidence.

Three possibilities immediately suggest themselves about the response of the labour market to (say) a decrease in the demand for output. First, firms may reduce their wage offers but keep the number of offers constant; workers may mistakenly think that the reason they now observe lower offers is 'bad luck'. Second, firms may continue offering the same wages, but reduce the number of offers; workers may realise there has been a decrease in the number of vacancies, and respond accordingly. Finally, firms may reduce their wage offers, as in the first case; workers may correctly realise that when a firm reduces its wage offer sometimes other firms follow and sometimes they do not, because sometimes the shocks are 'macro' and sometimes 'micro'. Their behaviour will depend on whether they have any information on the nature of the shock.

The first case is the one investigated by the original models of search, especially those in Phelps et al. (1970), and it is this case that has come to be known as the search view of the business cycle. According to this view, a worker collects information about the market by observing the offers of individual firms. If his expectations about the market are inelastic (e.g. if they are adaptive), when he observes a wage cut by a single firm he thinks that other firms have cut their wages by less, i.e. he believes that the firm that he has searched has moved down the wage-offer distribution. His reservation wage is revised downwards according to his view of the movement of the entire wage distribution, so it does not fall by as much as the observed wage rate. It follows that the probabililty that the worker will accept the offer is now less than what is was before the wage cut, and given the assumed constant flow of workers into unemployment, this implies that the stock of unemployment will rise. Also, since firms respond to the decrease in the demand for output mainly by reducing their wage offers, the number of job offers probably does not fall by very much; though as in frictionless neo-classical models with some monopsonistic elements, the number of jobs may fall a little even with full wage flexibility. But since unemployment rises through job rejection, vacancies probably rise − or at least do not fall by very much. So unlike unemployment, vacancies should not show a strong countercyclical movement.

The inflexibility of reservation wages in this environment also has implications for the behaviour of observed wage rates. Even if all firms in the market cut their wage offers by the same percentage, the fact that reservation wages fall by a smaller percentage implies that previously acceptable jobs that lie near the bottom of the wage distribution will now be rejected. Observed wage rates in the market are inevitably those accepted by workers, so the mean observed wage falls by a percentage that lies somewhere between the percentages by which the mean offer on the one hand, and the mean reservation wage on the other, fall.

Observationally then, and despite the assumption of complete wage flexibility in the downward direction, the model gives the impression of sticky wages and rising unemployment. But in fact, it is the rising unemployment that causes the wage stickiness: by staying unemployed longer, workers find better-paying jobs, and so they do not have to suffer the effects of the full reduction in wage offers.

It is noteworthy that if we move to the other extreme and assume complete rigidity of wage offers we shall also observe a small decrease in wages and a rise in unemployment. For suppose firms do not cut their wages when the demand for output falls, but reduce instead their hiring rates. Unemployed workers who realise this will adjust their reservation wages downwards, because the probability of receiving a job offer by a firm that they search falls. 'Reasonable' behaviour, and some empirical evidence (Nickell 1979a; Lancaster and Chesher 1983), suggest that reservation wages do not overreact: the probability of leaving unemployment falls when firms reduce their hiring rates, but the probability that a given vacancy is taken rises. With a constant inflow rate, unemployment rises because the outflow falls, and observed wage rates fall because workers are now willing to accept lower-paying jobs. But unlike the previous case of reduced wage offers, now wages are sticky not because unemployment is higher but vice versa: unemployment is higher because wage offers are sticky and jobs are withdrawn, and observed wage rates are lower because workers are willing to accept them in the face of reduced job offers.

Thus the two extremes, reduced wage offers with constant hiring rates on the one hand, and constant wage offers with reduced hiring rates on the other, have similar implications for the behaviour of aggregate unemployment and average wage rates. It follows that all combinations of these two extremes (which is probably where the truth lies) are also observationally equivalent, at least as far as unemployment and wages are concerned. Both extremes have some attractive features, but they also have some that are not attractive. The major disadvantage of the 'fixwage' extreme (fixed wage offers, variable hiring rates) is, of course, the old problem that post-war Keynesian macroeconomics faced, and has not yet been able to solve: why do firms not reduce their wage offers in the face of economy-wide reductions in demand?[11] If we ignore this problem, the other predictions of the fixwage model seem to be consistent with experience during depressions – vacancies fall, unemployment rises, wages do not fall by very much, and workers become more willing to accept and keep jobs.

The 'flexwage' extreme (fully flexible wage offers) has the advantage that it is consistent with profit-maximising behaviour by firms, at least in the market environment postulated by the model of search. But its other assumptions and predictions are not so satisfactory. First, it relies heavily on mistakes in the formation of expectations. These cannot persist for very long, and some economists argue that they should not be assumed in the first place (Muth 1961; Lucas 1972; Sargent 1973). If the depression lasts longer than the time it takes workers to learn about the rest of the market, unemployment should fall to pre-depression levels before the recovery of demand, something not observed. The recent work of Lucas, Sargent and others has done a lot to correct this deficiency in the expectational assumptions of these models, but as we shall argue below, the problem is far from solved.

Second, the predictions of the flexwage model about the behaviour of vacancies and job acceptance are contrary to experience. Although the model may be defended by arguing that neither vacancies nor job rejections can be observed accurately, most available measures of vacancies vary procyclically. In Britain vacancies notified to employment exchanges and the CBI index of labour shortages in manufacturing fall in recessions. If the flexwage view of recessions is correct, vacancies and labour shortages should not fluctuate very much over the cycle. Also, although we do not have accurate data on job rejections, the related data on job quits show a strong procyclical movement. It is the prediction of the (flexwage) theory that quits should vary countercyclically that led (in this paper) to the rejection of the theory as one capable of explaining flows into unemployment over the cycle; a similar criticism, though less forceful, may be made of its prediction about job rejection.

At the time of Friedman's (1968) presidential address and of the publication of Phelps *et al.* the received theory of expectations was 'adaptive' expectations: slow response of the expected to the actual, even in the face of other evidence that changes in the actual are general and permanent. The work on rational expectations (Lucas 1972, 1973, 1975; Sargent 1973; Sargent and Wallace 1975) criticised adaptive expectations for their sub-optimality, and established rational expectations, efficient utilisation of all available information in the formation of expectations, as the received doctrine. The crucial question now is what is the 'available' information; Muth (1961) argued that it is reasonable to assume that it is the information contained in the 'relevant' economic model used to explain the relevant variable. More recent theorists have taken a more liberal view, and have relied more on intuition, empirical evidence, or on trying out various possibilities and comparing results (Barro 1976, 1977; Fama 1976; Fischer 1980). The discussion that follows draws mainly on Lucas's (1973) model of the behaviour of firms in a related context.

We generalise the Phelps – Mortensen flexwage model by assuming that the demand for a firm's output is subject to two types of shocks. Shocks that are specific to the firm or to its immediate micro market (henceforth referred to as micro shocks), and shocks that are experienced by all firms in the economy (macro shocks). If a firm knows exactly whether a shock is macro or micro it may respond differently in each case; for example, it may reduce wage offers if there is a macro decline in demand, but not if there is a micro decline. Similarly, the worker may respond differently in each case when he is confronted with a cut in wage offers. Suppose, however, that firms' wage offers respond in the same way to the two types of shocks, for example because wage setters are unable to distinguish between them. Workers who observe a wage reduction know that sometimes this is due to a micro shock, and sometimes to a macro shock. If the worker does not know which shock is applicable in a particular case, he will revise his expectations about the market average wage according to the relative frequency of macro and micro shocks in the past: if macro shocks are relatively more frequent, expectations will be adjusted rapidly in response to the observation, if micro shocks are relatively more frequent expectations will be more sticky. Since reservation wages are adjusted according to expected wages in the market as a whole, the increase in unemployment and the apparent stickiness of wage rates in response to a macro reduction in demand will be greatest when the predominant shocks in the market are micro. Loosely speaking, if the predominant shocks are micro, the job searcher confuses the macro shock for micro. If the predominant shock is macro, the degree of the confusion is less, so reservation wages are adjusted more fully, leading to stable unemployment rates.

This 'rational' expectations view of reservation wages meets the criticism that in the original Phelps – Mortensen models workers are consistently wrong. But it is subject to another criticism – the only relevant information seachers and firms have is their own experience. If either read newspapers, or know something about a 'relevant' macro model, they will soon be able to distinguish between micro and macro shocks, and behave accordingly. If they do distinguish correctly between these shocks, and firms always follow flexwage policies, there will be no room for unemployment fluctuations in this model.[12] Also, even if we accept that the expectations problem has been solved, the other criticisms made of the 'flexwage' view of recessions still hold.

## 6.   Concluding remarks

The model of search addresses a question to which most labour economists paid lip-service in the 1950s and 1960s: the process by which firms and workers trade labour services. It has given satisfactory answers to some questions, but not to others. One of the themes of the discussion in this paper is that it would be a mistake to treat the search model as a complete model of unemployment. Its treatment of the supply side, job acceptance and quitting, is the most satisfactory part of the model, and it is likely to become the standard model of labour supply for empirical work and policy applications; to a large extent it already is. But flows into and out of unemployment are also influenced by the demand side, and in particular by the response of wages to fluctuations in the demand for output. The behaviour of wages within the search framework is still the main problem confronting the model. The empirical analysis of wages is made more difficult by the fact that neither wage offers nor reservation wages are observable. We argued that quite diverse hypotheses about the behaviour of wage offers can have similar predictions about the behaviour of *accepted* wages, which is the only wage variable that can be observed. The problems of search theory in this connection are not very different from those of fixprice Keynesianism: the predictions that we derive about the behaviour of wages and unemployment are more 'reasonable' when we assume that the brunt of fluctuations in the demand for output is borne by the number of job offers (vacancies), and not by wage offers; but the theoretical model elaborated so far suggests that profit-maximising firms will choose to adjust wage offers when demand fluctuates. The theory of wage adjustment appears to be in need of elements not at present incorporated into search models, and this is an area that needs to attract more empirical and theoretical work in the future.

## Notes

1. See Pissarides (1984b) for a discussion of some of the externalities that are likely to be associated with job acceptance.
2. The fixed-sample rule might be preferable to the sequential rule in cases where the searcher is ignorant of the distribution of wage offers, and so he is likely to work out a prior distribution which bears no resemblance to the true one. But even in these cases the Stigler rule is not optimal; a mixed rule, where the searcher searches *at most n* firms sequentially, is preferable.

3. A finite horizon may also induce a decline in the attractiveness of search, since during unsuccessful search the individual moves closer to the date of retirement. However, with non-trivial discounting this is likely to be a significant influence on older workers only. See Pissarides (1976a, 1976b) for further discussion of declining reservation wages.

4. The parallel with Becker's (1975) distinction between specific and general human capital is obvious.

5. In some situations firms may open up vacancies speculatively, in order to attract more workers quickly. We do not discuss this possibility because there is no formal analysis of this problem in the literature yet.

6. The direct evidence concerns mainly the 'regret' which some firms record in employees' files when they quit. Other things equal, firms seem to regret more the departure of junior employees than the departure of senior employees, indicating that the former are more profitable from the firm's point of view than the latter.

7. In the UK detailed figures on the cause of job separations are not normally published; for the USA see Hall (1972, 1980).

8. Early recall of some workers would normally be followed by laying-off of other workers. This ensures that the expected duration of unemployment is short, and so workers remain attached to the firm by giving up the search for an alternative job, which they may not find worth while (see Pissarides 1982 for a formal model).

9. For instance, Sachs (1979) and Grubb et al. (1982) offer explanations of the recession that are not very different from old-fashioned views about wage inflexibility.

10. It should be stressed that this is a personal view, and other search theorists may disagree; some may agree with Alchian (1970) that the model contributes to our understanding of flows into unemployment; others may argue that it does not say much of interest about outflows because most workers search for vacancies and never reject jobs. On the latter point, it should be noted that there is no evidence that workers never reject jobs, and, in any case, the model may account for supply influences during the search for vacancies by endogenising the intensity of search. See Barron (1975) for some evidence that workers search mainly for vacancies.

11. Barro and Grossman (1976) acknowledge this problem; see also Barro (1979).

12. But fluctuations may come from 'intertemporal substitution' of leisure – workers buying more leisure when wage offers are abnormally low; on this see Lucas and Rapping (1970) and Altonji and Ashenfelter (1980).

## References

**Akerlof, G. A.** (1981) Jobs as dam sites, *Review of Economic Studies,* **48**, 37–49.

**Akerlof, G. A. and Miyazaki, H.** (1980) The implicit contract theory of unemployment meets the wage bill argument, *Review of Economic Studies,* **47**, 321–38.

**Alchian, A. A.** (1970) Information costs, pricing and resource unemployment, in Phelps E. S. *et al., Microeconomic Foundations of Employment and Inflation Theory,* Norton: New York.

**Altonji, J. and Ashenfelter, O.** (1980) Wage movements and the labour market equilibrium hypothesis, *Economica,* **47**, 217–45.

**Azariadis, C.** (1975) Implicit contracts and unemployment equilibria, *Journal of Political Economy,* **83,** 1183–202.

**Baily, M. N.** (1974) Wages and employment under uncertain demand, *Review of Economic Studies,* **42,** 37–50.

**Baily, M. N.** (1977) On the theory of layoffs and unemployment, *Econometrica,* **45,** 1043–63.

**Baily, M. N.** (1978) Some aspects of optimal unemployment insurance, *Journal of Public Economics,* **10,** 379–402.

**Barro, R. J.** (1976) Rational expectations and the role of monetary policy, *Journal of Monetary Economics,* **2,** 1–32.

**Barro, R. J.** (1977) Unanticipated money growth and unemployment in the United States, *American Economic Review,* **67,** 101–15.

**Barro, R. J.** (1979) Second thoughts on Keynesian economics, *American Economic Review,* Papers and Proceedings, **69,** 54–9.

**Barro, R. J. and Grossman, H.** (1976) *Money, Employment and Inflation,* Cambridge University Press: Cambridge.

**Barron, J. M.** (1975) Search in the labor market and the duration of unemployment: some empirical evidence, *American Economic Review,* **65,** 934–42.

**Becker, G. S.** (1975) *Human Capital,* Columbia University Press: New York (2nd edn).

**Burdett, K.** (1978) A theory of employee job search and quit rates, *American Economic Review,* **68,** 212–20.

**Burdett, K.** (1979) Search, leisure, and individual labour supply, in Lippman, S. A. and McCall, J. J. (eds), *Studies in the Economics of Search,* North-Holland: Amsterdam.

**Classen, K. P.** (1979) Unemployment insurance and job search, in Lippman, S. A. and McCall, J. J. (eds), *Studies in the Economics of Search,* North-Holland: Amsterdam.

**Clower, R. W.** (1965) The Keynesian counter-revolution: a theoretical appraisal, in Hahn, F. H. and Brechling, F. P. R. (eds), *The Theory of Interest Rates,* Macmillan: London.

**DeGroot, M. H.** (1970) *Optimal Statistical Decisions,* McGraw-Hill: New York.

**Diamond, P. A.** (1971) A model of price adjustment, *Journal of Economic Theory,* **3,** 156–68.

**Diamond, P. A.** (1981) Mobility costs, frictional unemployment, and efficiency, *Journal of Political Economy,* **89,** 789–812.

**Diamond, P. A.** (1982) Wage determination and efficiency in search equilibrium, *Review of Economic Studies,* **49,** 217–27.

**Diamond, P. A. and Maskin, E.** (1979) An equilibrium analysis of search and breach of contract, I: steady states, *The Bell Journal of Economics,* **10,** Spring, 282–316.

**Ehrenberg, R. G.** (1973) Heterogeneous labour, minimum hiring standards, and job vacancies in public employment, *Journal of Political Economy,* **81,** 1442–50.

**Ehrenberg, R. G. and Oaxaca, R. L.** (1976) Unemployment insurance, duration of unemployment, and subsequent wage gain, *American Economic Review,* **66,** 756–66.

**Eisner, R. and Strotz, R. H.** (1963) Determinants of business investment: the theoretical framework, in Commission on Money and Credit, *Impacts of Monetary Policy,* Prentice-Hall: Englewood Cliffs.

**Fama, E. F.** (1976) *Foundations of Finance,* Basil Blackwell: Oxford.

**Feldstein, M. S.** (1975) The importance of temporary layoffs: an empirical analysis, *Brookings Papers on Economic Activity,* **1975:3,** 725–44.

**Feldstein, M. S.** (1976) Temporary layoffs in the theory of unemployment, *Journal of Political Economy,* **84,** 937–57.

**Fischer, S.** (1980) (ed.) *Rational Expectations and Economic Policy,* University of Chicago Press: Chicago.

**Fisher, F. M.** (1970) Quasi-competitive price adjustment by individual firms: a preliminary paper, *Journal of Economic Theory,* **2,** 195–206.

**Flemming, J. S.** (1978) Aspects of optimal unemployment insurance: search, leisure, savings and capital market imperfections, *Journal of Public Economics,* **10,** 403–25.

**Friedman, M.** (1968) The role of monetary policy, *American Economic Review,* **58,** 1–17.

**Gronau, G.** (1971) Information and frictional unemployment, *American Economic Review,* **61,** 290–301.

**Grossman, H. I.** (1973) Aggregate demand, job search, and employment, *Journal of Political Economy,* **81,** 1353–69.

**Grubb, D., Jackman, R. and Layard, R.** (1982) Causes of the current stagflation, *Review of Economic Studies,* **49,** 707–30.

**Hall, R. E.** (1972) Turnover in the labour force, *Brookings Papers on Economic Activity,* 1972: 3, 709–56.

**Hall, R. E.** (1980) Employment fluctuations and wage rigidity, *Brookings Papers on Economic Activity,* 1980: 1, 91–124.

**Hey, J. D.** (1974) Price adjustment in an atomistic market, *Journal of Economic Theory,* **8,** 483–99.

**Hey, J. and McKenna, C. J.** (1979) To move or not to move?, *Economica,* **46,** 175–85.

**Hicks, J. R.** (1932) *The Theory of Wages,* Macmillan: London.

**Holt, C. C.** (1970) Job search, Phillips' wage relation, and union influence, in Phelps, E. S. *et al., Microeconomic Foundations of Employment and Inflation Theory,* Norton: New York.

**Hutt, W. H.** (1939) *The Theory of Idle Resources,* Jonathan Cape: London.

**Ioannides, Y. and Pissarides, C. A.** (1983) Wages and employment with firm-specific seniority, *Bell Journal of Economics,* **14,** Autumn, 573–80.

**Jovanovic, B.** (1979) Firm-specific capital and turnover, *Journal of Political Economy,* **87,** 1246–60.

**Karlin, S.** (1962) Stochastic models and optimal policy for selling an asset, in Arrow, K. J., Karlin, S. and Scarf, H. (eds), *Studies in Applied Probability and Management Science,* Stanford University Press.

**Kasper, H.** (1967) The asking price of labor and the duration of unemployment, *Review of Economic Statistics,* **49,** 165–72.

**Kiefer, N. M. and Neuman, G. R.** (1979) An empirical job-search model with a test of the constant reservation-wage hypothesis, *Journal of Political Economy,* **87,** 89–108.

**Kiefer, N. M. and Neuman, G. R.** (1981) Individual effects in a non-linear model: explicit treatment of heterogeneity in the empirical job-search model, *Econometrica,* **49,** 965–79.

**Kohn, M. G. and Shavell, S.** (1974) The theory of search, *Journal of Economic Theory,* **9,** 93–123.

**Lancaster, T.** (1979) Econometric methods for the duration of unemployment, *Econometrica,* **47,** 939–56.

**Lancaster, T. and Chesher, A.** (1983) An econometric analysis of reservation wages, *Econometrica,* **51,** 166–76.

**Lazear, E. P.** (1979) Why is there mandatory retirement?, *Journal of Political Economy,* 87, 1261–84.

**Lazear, E. P.** (1981) Agency, earnings profiles, productivity, and hours restriction, *American Economic Review,* 71, 606–20.

**Leijonhufvud, A.** (1968) *On Keynesian Economics and the Economics of Keynes,* Oxford University Press: New York.

**Lippman, S. A. and McCall, J. J.** (1976a) The economics of job search: a survey, Parts I and II, *Economic Inquiry,* 14, 155–89 and 347–68.

**Lippman, S. A. and McCall, J. J.** (1976b) Job search in a dynamic economy, *Journal of Economic Theory,* 12, 365–90.

**Lipsey, R. G.** (1960) The relation between unemployment and the rate of change of money wages in the United Kingdom, 1862–1957: a further analysis, *Economica,* 27, 1–31.

**Lucas, R. E.** (1971) Econometric testing of the natural rate hypothesis, in Eckstein, O. (ed.), *The Econometrics of Price Determination Conference,* Federal Reserve Board; Washington, D.C.

**Lucas, R. E.** (1972) Expectations and the neutrality of money, *Journal of Economic Theory,* 4, 103–24.

**Lucas, R. E.** (1973) Some international evidence on output – inflation tradeoffs, *American Economic Review,* 63, 326–34.

**Lucas, R. E.** (1975) An equilibrium model of the business cycle, *Journal of Political Economy,* 83, 1113–44.

**Lucas, R. E. and Prescott, E. C.** (1974) Equilibrium search and unemployment, *Journal of Economic Theory,* 7, 188–209.

**Lucas, R. E. and Rapping, L. A.** (1970) Real wages, employment and inflation, *Journal of Political Economy,* 77, 721–54; reprinted in Phelps, E. S., *et al., Microeconomic Foundations of Employment and Inflation Theory,* Norton: New York.

**Lynch, L.** (1983) Job search and youth unemployment, *Oxford Economic Papers,* 35, supplement, 271–82.

**McCall, J. J.** (1970) Economics of information and job search, *Quarterly Journal of Economics,* 84, 113–26.

**McKenna, C.** (1980) Wage offers, layoffs and the firm in an uncertain labour market, *Manchester School,* 48, 255–64.

**McKenna, C.** (1983) A study in the theory of the labour market under uncertainty, D. Phil. Thesis, York University.

**Mattila, J. P.** (1974) Job quitting and frictional unemployment, *American Economic Review,* 64, 235–9.

**Medoff, J.** (1979) Layoffs and alternatives under trade unions in U.S. manufacturing, *American Economic Review,* 69, 380–95.

**Medoff, J. and Abraham, K.** (1980) Involuntary terminations under explicit, implicit and no employment contracts, mimeo.

**Mortensen, D. T.** (1970a) A theory of wage and employment dynamics, in Phelps, E. S. *et al., Microeconomic Foundations of Employment and Inflation Theory,* Norton: New York.

**Mortensen, D. T.** (1970b) Job search, the duration of unemployment, and the Phillips curve, *American Economic Review,* 60, 847–62.

**Mortensen, D. T.** (1978) Specific capital and labor turnover, *Bell Journal of Economics,* 9, 572–86.

**Mortensen, D. T.** (1982) The matching process as a non-cooperative/bargaining game, in McCall, J. J. (ed.), *The Economics of Information and Uncertainty,* University of Chicago Press.

**Muth, J. F.** (1961) Rational expectations and the theory of price movements, *Econometrica,* 29, 315–35.

**Nelson, P.** (1970) Information and consumer behavior, *Journal of Political Economy,* 78, 311–29.

**Nickell, S. J.** (1979a) Estimating the probability of leaving unemployment, *Econometrica,* 47, 1249–66.

**Nickell, S. J.** (1979b) The effect of unemployment and related benefits on the duration of unemployment, *Economic Journal,* 89, 34–49.

**Parsons, D. O.** (1973) Quit rates over time: a search and information approach, *American Economic Review,* 63, 390–401.

**Phelps, E. S.** (1967) Phillips curves, expectations of inflation and optimal unemployment over time, *Economica,* 34, 254–81.

**Phelps, E. S.** (1970) Money wage dynamics and labor market equilibrium in Phelps, E. S. *et al., Microeconomic Foundations of Employment and Inflation Theory,* Norton: New York.

**Phelps, E. S.** (1972) *Inflation Policy and Unemployment Theory,* Macmillan: London.

**Phelps, E. S.** *et al.* (1970) *Microeconomic Foundations of Employment and Inflation Theory,* Norton: New York.

**Pissarides, C. A.** (1976a) Job search and participation, *Economica,* 43, 33–49.

**Pissarides, C. A.** (1976b) *Labour Market Adjustment: Microeconomic Foundations of Short-Run Neoclassical and Keynesian Dynamics,* Cambridge University Press: Cambridge.

**Pissarides, C. A.** (1981) Contract theory, temporary layoffs, and unemployment: a critical assessment, in Currie, D., Nobay, A.R. and Peel, D. (eds), *Microeconomic Analysis* (AUTE 1979), Croom Helm: London.

**Pissarides, C. A.** (1982) Job search and the duration of layoff unemployment, *Quarterly Journal of Economics,* 97, 595–612.

**Pissarides, C. A.** (1983) Efficiency aspects of the financing of unemployment insurance and other government expenditure, *Review of Economic Studies,* 50, 57–69.

**Pissarides, C. A.** (1984a) Search intensity, job advertising, and efficiency, *Journal of Labor Economics,* 2, 128–43.

**Pissarides, C. A.** (1984b) Efficient job rejection, *Economic Journal Conference Papers* (AUTE 1983), 94, 97–108.

**Rothschild, M.** (1973) Models of market organization with imperfect information: a survey, *Journal of Political Economics,* 81, 1283–308.

**Rothschild, M.** (1974) Searching for the lowest price when the distribution of prices is unknown, *Journal of Political Economy,* 82, 689–711.

**Sachs, J. D.** (1979) Wages, profits and macroeconomic adjustment: a comparative study, *Brookings Papers on Economic Activity,* 1979: 2, 269–319.

**Salop, J. and Salop, S.** (1976) Self-selection and turnover in the labor market, *Quarterly Journal of Economics,* 90, 619–27.

**Salop, S. C.** (1973a) Systematic job search and unemployment, *Review of Economic Studies,* 40, 191–201.

**Salop, S. C.** (1973b) Wage differentials in a dynamic theory of the firm, *Journal of Economic Theory,* 6, 321–44.

**Sargent, T. J.** (1973) Rational expectations, the real rate of interest, and the natural rate of unemployment, *Brookings Papers on Economic Activity,* 1973: 2, 429–80.

**Sargent, T. J. and Wallace, N.** (1975) 'Rational' expectations, the optimal monetary instrument, and the optimal money supply rule, *Journal of Political Economy,* **83**, 241–54.

**Shavell, S. and Weiss, L.** (1979) The optimal payment of unemployment insurance benefits over time, *Journal of Political Economy,* **87**, 1347–62.

**Stigler, G. J.** (1962) Information in the labour market, *Journal of Political Economy,* **70**, 94–105.

**Tobin, J.** (1972) Inflation and unemployment, *American Economic Review,* **62**, 1–18.

**Whipple, D.** (1973) A generalized theory of job search, *Journal of Political Economy,* **8**, 1170–83.

**Wilde, L. L.** (1979) An information – theoretic approach to job quits, in Lippman, S. A. and McCall, J. J. (eds), *Studies in the Economics of Search,* North-Holland: Amsterdam.

# CHAPTER FIVE

# Trade unions and wages

Derek Carline

## 1. Introduction

In 1980 there were almost 13 million trade unionists in the UK, representing over half the total number of employees. Throughout the post-war years this proportion has never fallen below 40 per cent (Price and Bain 1976, Department of Employment and Productivity Gazette February 1982). With this membership it is not surprising that the economic implications of union activity have figured large in discussions of UK economic performance. This survey considers that part of the debate dealing with the effects of unions upon wages. Two issues are examined: firstly, their impact upon wage differentials, or the relative wage effect of unions; secondly, whether unions generate inflationary pressures in the economy by causing the general level of wages to rise at a faster rate than productivity. The latter has received continuing academic attention since the Second World War, but it is only in recent years that sufficient UK data have become available to enable economists to estimate the union influence upon the wage structure.

A large membership is not necessarily a sign that unions have had an important effect upon UK wages. In conventional economic analysis unions are institutions which use their monopoly power to improve wages and working conditions but, with the possible exception of monopsonistic labour markets, at the cost of reducing the demand for their members' services. This cost is presumed to influence union wage bargaining so that, *cet. par.*, union success in raising wages will be inversely related to the elasticity of demand for union labour. Thus for Friedman (1976:160) '... the power of unions, as of any other monopoly, is ultimately limited by the elasticity of the demand curve for the monopolised services. Unions have significant potential power only if this demand curve is fairly inelastic at what otherwise would be the competitive price.' An implication is that unions operating in product markets where there is non-union competition will have only a modest effect on wages, because of the high elasticity of demand for their members' services. Phelps Brown (1966) suggests that this is likely to be so in the internationally exposed manufacturing sector of British industry.

However, there are writers who question the degree to which the exercise of union power is constrained by the threat of unemployment. Thus Mitchell (1980) notes that union-induced wage increases are just one of a number of possible causes of unemployment, and that union members may attribute unemployment to these factors rather than to collective bargaining. Similarly, Ross (1948, 1957), on the basis of US experience, stresses the importance to trade unionists of obtaining wage increases similar to those received by comparable groups of workers, and argues that union leaders must take account of the comparability factor in their bargaining; concern with unemployment is subsidiary to achieving satisfactory settlements. It is also argued that trade unionists are less affected by unemployment than unorganised workers, and that unemployment has to reach high levels before union wage policy is affected. Turner (1959) notes that unemployment in the early post-war recessions was most severe among the less organised sections of the labour force, married women and young workers for example; while Bowers (1979) points to the heavy incidence of unemployment among the young and suggests that they are likely to have little influence upon union wage policy. Government subsidisation of unprofitable activities also weakens the link between higher wages and lower labour demand, and this is likely to be particularly important in the heavily unionised public sector of the economy.

Disagreement over such a fundamental issue as the importance of unemployment for union policy-making illustrates the limited progress economists have made in the analysis of trade unions. In particular, understanding of their economic role has not reached the point at which a generally acceptable model of unions can be developed. As Johnson (1975: 23) remarks, '... the problem of modelling trade union behaviour has proved to be virtually intractable'. The best-known attempt is that of Dunlop (1950:4) who argues that, like the theory of the firm, an '... economic theory of a trade union requires that the organisation be assumed to maximise (or minimise) something', but the various maximands he proposes have attracted many objections and his formal models are widely regarded as unsatisfactory (Rees 1962). Given this weak theoretical base, there is inevitably much controversy about the importance of unions in wage determination. This survey discusses the major issues underlying the debate and in the first section it examines the evidence of union effects on relative wages.

## 2.   Unions and relative wages

Economists' interest in this topic springs largely from their concern with the effects of unions upon the allocation of resources. If unions do alter the wage structure, they are likely to change the allocation of labour and, like any other monopolistic distortion, reduce the value of total output by causing employment to be lower in the unionised sector and higher in the residual 'competitive' sector. Estimates of the union relative wage effect are, therefore, a step towards measurement of the output loss caused by wage bargaining, as illustrated in the following analysis derived from Rees (1979). He assumes an economy in which a fixed supply of homogeneous labour is employed in two sectors which are initially non-unionised. Figure 5.1 shows this situation where $S$ represents the total supply of labour, $D_u$ and $D_n$ the demand for labour in the two sectors and $D_t$ the total labour demand. As the sector demand curves are marginal value product schedules, the area under each up to the respective employment levels measures the total output of each sector. The competitive wage is $W_c$ and is the same in both sectors. Of total employment, $(E_0 + N_0)$, $E_0$ and $N_0$ workers are employed in sectors $U$ and $N$ respectively. If sector $U$ is then organised by a union which raises the wage to $W_u$, the numbers employed in the sector fall to $E_1$ and, assuming that the displaced workers wish to work at a lower wage rather than be unemployed, they can obtain work at a wage of $W_n$. Employment in the non-union sector increases to $N_1$. Total output falls because the value of the product of these workers is less than it was in their previous employment. The fall in output in the unionised sector is given by $aE_1E_0b$ and output increases by $cN_0N_1d$ in the competitive sector. When, as in the diagram, the sector demand schedules are parallel, the net output loss is the shaded area under $D_u$ and it can be seen that this is equal to half the product of the wage differential and employment change:

$$\text{Output loss} = \tfrac{1}{2} (W_n - W_u)(E_0 - E_1)$$

This framework of analysis can be used as a basis for empirical investigation into the output loss caused by union wage bargaining. Rees (1963), using Lewis's (1963) estimates of American unions' effect on relative wages and employment, has made a rough estimate that it was a mere 0.14 per cent of GNP in 1957, though the actual loss may be higher than this if some of the displaced workers become unemployed. Subsequent work by Johnson and Mieszkowski (1970) also showed the loss to be of the same order of magnitude. The assumption that the pre-union labour markets are competitive is an important one. If they are in fact monopsonistic, unions may do no more than raise wages to their competitive level without affecting employment and output. Ideally, therefore, information about the extent of monopsony in an economy is needed to supplement that about union relative wage and employment effects when measuring the output loss. In the UK, however, this knowledge of monopsony is lacking and all that presently exist are a number of estimates of the relative wage effect. Before examining these it is important to be clear about what is being measured. In terms of Fig. 5.1 the estimates are of $W_u - W_n$: the wage difference between unionised and non-unionised workers. This is not the same as the change in workers' wages brought about by unionisation which is $W_u - W_c$. In this example, therefore, the size of the union relative wage effect exceeds the wage gain from union membership because it incorporates the wage reduction in the non-unionised sector. Estimates of the relative wage effect can themselves be complicated, however, by the response of non-union employers who may pay the union rate in the hope of dissuading their workers from becoming trade unionists. Wage comparisons between unionists and non-unionists, with the latter including some of these workers, will then show a smaller union impact on relative wages than has actually occurred. As the question at issue is the impact of unions on relative wages it becomes important to include these workers in the calculation of the union wage. This can be compared with the wage of non-union workers whose pay is not so determined.

One final caveat is that any output loss from this source is only one way in which unions can affect economic welfare. Rees (1963) suggests that his estimate of lost American production is less than that caused by the restrictive

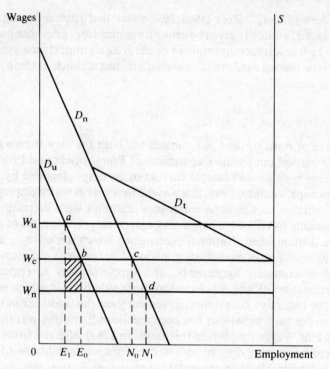

FIG. 5.1   Economic welfare and union wage bargaining

working practices of unions, and this may be also true of the UK. Changes in the wage structure will also affect economic welfare through their impact upon income distribution. Johnson and Mieszkowski (1970) analyse the consequences of union wage gains for the wages of non-union labour and profits. Because of the fall in wages in the non-union sector they conclude that most of the gains of union labour are at the expense of unorganised workers rather than profits. This rather doleful picture of union activity is not a complete one of course; unions may also help to raise output in a variety of ways. For example, by providing their members with labour-market information they can improve labour mobility, and their wage gains may also induce employers to become more efficient. Unions may also provide management with the least cost method of obtaining information about workers' preferences on issues such as the times for starting and finishing work. As Freeman (1976) has pointed out, unions are institutions through which workers can express their discontent over wages and working conditions. This may be a cheaper source of information for firms than the alternative of workers finding employment elsewhere. Unions may therefore reduce the cost of labour turnover for employers.

They may also increase employee welfare in other ways. Thus Flanders (1970) emphasises their role in protecting workers against the arbitrary actions of employers. Collective bargaining is not only concerned with workers' wages but 'equally their security, status and self-respect – in short, their dignity as human beings' (Flanders 1970:42). Rees (1962:195) states that 'protection against the abuse of managerial authority given by seniority systems and grievance procedures seems to be to be a union accomplishment of the greatest importance. Any overall appraisal of trade unions needs to take account of factors such as these as well as their economic impact.'

## RELATIVE WAGE ESTIMATES

The data source of most of the UK estimates has been the New Earnings Survey (NES) of 1973 carried out by the Department of Employment and Productivity. While there have been annual sample surveys of earnings classified by age, sex, industry and occupation since 1968, this was the first year in which employers were asked to say whether or not their employees' earnings were determined either directly or indirectly by collective bargaining agreements. Three types of collective coverage were distinguished. National agreements, which settle wages and other working conditions across an industry; national agreements supplemented by district, local or company agreements, and supplementary agreements only. Indirect determination of wages referred to those situations in which employers not party to the collective bargaining agreement paid the trade union rate. One possible reason for such behaviour has been mentioned; another was the need to adhere to the Fair Wages Resolution (rescinded in 1983) whereby firms awarded government contracts were obliged to observe terms and conditions of employment not less favourable than those laid down in collective agreements. The importance of this indirect coverage is shown by the fact that in manufacturing industry in 1973 some 80 per cent of the adult male workforce was covered by a collective agreement but only 55 per cent were union members (Mulvey and Foster 1976).

    The unrefined NES data shows that in 1973 the average earnings of most workers covered directly or indirectly by collective bargaining agreements were higher than those not covered. Table 5.1 taken from Thomson *et al.* (1977) and derived from the NES demonstrates this.

    Thus there is a positive differential for all covered manual males and females in all sectors of the economy, though this is not the case for non-manuals. Of course, the differentials may be due to many influences other than union bargaining: the higher wage of manual males may be the result of higher-quality labour being employed in firms where collective bargaining prevails, and the lower wage of women in manufacturing be caused by the greater incidence of collective bargaining among the less skilled. Such differences in labour quality between covered and uncovered workers, together with differences in other earnings-determining variables, need to be eliminated before the association between collective agreement coverage and earnings can be measured. The aim is to establish the proportionate union – non-union differential for otherwise homogeneous labour, and the estimating technique employed utilises the fact that the average wage in an industry or occupation is a weighted average of the union wage and the non-union wage, using as weights the proportions of workers paid the union and non-union wage respectively. Thus

TABLE 5.1    Average gross hourly earnings by all agreements and no agreement for adults in Great Britain in April 1973

| Sample group | Agreement coverage | | |
|---|---|---|---|
| | All agreements | Differential | No agreement |
| Manual males | (£) | (%) | (£) |
| Manufacturing | 0.87 | +8.8 | 0.80 |
| Non-manufacturing | 0.79 | +16.2 | 0.68 |
| Public sector | 0.81 | +12.5 | 0.72 |
| Private sector | 0.84 | +12.0 | 0.75 |
| All | 0.83 | +12.2 | 0.74 |
| Manual females | | | |
| Manufacturing | 0.52 | +13.0 | 0.46 |
| Non-manufacturing | 0.49 | +28.9 | 0.38 |
| Public sector | 0.50 | +31.6 | 0.38 |
| Private sector | 0.51 | +18.6 | 0.43 |
| All | 0.51 | +18.6 | 0.43 |
| Non-manual males | | | |
| Manufacturing | 1.13 | −14.4 | 1.32 |
| Non-manufacturing | 1.25 | 0.0 | 1.25 |
| Public sector | 1.28 | +6.7 | 1.20 |
| Private sector | 1.13 | −11.7 | 1.28 |
| All | 1.21 | −4.7 | 1.27 |
| Non-manual females | | | |
| Manufacturing | 0.57 | −1.7 | 0.58 |
| Non-manufacturing | 0.76 | +33.3 | 0.57 |
| Public sector | 0.83 | +36.1 | 0.61 |
| Private sector | 0.58 | +3.6 | 0.56 |
| All | 0.73 | +28.1 | 0.57 |

Source: Thomson et al. (1977).

$$W_i \equiv W_i^u T_i + W_i^n(1 - T_i) \qquad [1a]$$

where $W_i$ = the average industry or occupation wage;

$W_i^u$ = the union wage in the industry or occupation weighted by $T_i$ the proportion of workers covered by the union agreement;

$W_i^n$ = the non-union wage weighted by the uncovered proportion.

This becomes

$$W_i \equiv W_i^n + (W_i^u - W_i^n) T_i \qquad [1b]$$

so that the average industry or occupation wage is the sum of the non-union wage and the absolute union/non-union differential weighted by the covered proportion. The NES 1973 provides $W_i$ and $T_i$ for occupations and industries, and if we assume that all factors that influence relative wages other than the unions are identical across industries and occupations, i.e. labour is homogeneous, then the relationship between collective agreement coverage and wage levels could be obtained by regressing earnings in the industry or occupation on the coverage rate. This not being so, it is necessary to estimate the non-union mean wage by replacing this term in the identity by a number of variables which will, it is hypothesised, determine it. Some variables which research indicates do affect the industrial wage structure, for example, are the level of education and training across industries, the degree of product market competition in the various industries and their geographical location, the relative level of demand for the industry's products, and the age structure of the labour force. The estimates are in practice done in logarithmic form which produces a proportionate rather than an absolute differential, and this is more useful in making comparisons over time or across skill groups. Equation [1b] becomes:

$$\log W_i \equiv \log W_i^n + \log(1 + \lambda_i)T_i$$

where $\lambda_i$ is the proportionate coverage differential and the means are geometric ones. After $W_i^n$ is replaced by its determinants, $\lambda_i$ is estimated by regression analysis. A problem with this method is that it is likely to produce a biased estimate. Creedy (1979) notes that since the differential will not be constant across occupations, equation [1b] does not satisfy the conditions necessary for regression analysis and is likely, therefore, to result in an overestimate of the differential.

One further note of caution is called for in interpreting the estimated differential. Establishing a significant relationship between agreement coverage and wages does not necessarily mean that unions have caused the higher wages. It is possible that high wages may encourage people to join unions so that the causal relationship runs in the opposite direction, or that union membership and high wages may be simultaneously determined by some other variable. While most investigators have interpreted their results as evidence of union influence on relative wages there are sceptics and their views will be discussed later.

Apart from Pencavel (1974), the British studies by Mulvey (1976), Mulvey and Foster (1976), Stewart (1976), Metcalf (1977), Nickell (1977) and Layard *et al.* (1978) use NES data on collective agreement coverage, but they differ in the type of worker covered, in the variables used to estimate wages in the absence of unions, and in the use of hourly or weekly earnings. Despite these disparities they all find that unions have a marked effect on wages, though Pencavel's estimates are much lower than the others. Table 5.2 summarises them.

Pencavel's (1974) study of the union relative wage effect differed from subsequent work in that it used union membership rather than collective agreement coverage as a basis for the work and, as noted earlier, this will produce an underestimate of the relative wage effect. Using data on union membership by industry for 1964, Pencavel employed the standard technique to estimate the average effect of unions on the hourly earnings of manual workers in twenty-nine industries. The variables used to determine the non-union wage and designed to catch the effect of human capital on earnings, were the fractions of females, young workers and unskilled workers in manual employment in each industry. The

TABLE 5.2   Estimates of trade union effect on relative wages

| Author | Year covered | Scope of study | Estimates (%) | |
|---|---|---|---|---|
| Pencavel (1974) | 1964 | *Industrial manual workers' hourly earnings* | | |
| | | All types of collective agreement | 0–10 | |
| | | Local agreements | 14 | |
| | | National agreements | 0 | |
| Mulvey and Foster (1976) | 1973 | *Adult males' weekly earnings* | | |
| | | All types of agreement | 22–31 | |
| Mulvey (1976) | 1973 | *Adult males' in manufacturing hourly earnings* | | |
| | | All types of agreement | 26–35 | |
| | | National agreements only | 0 | |
| | | National and supplementary or supplementary only | 41–48 | |
| Stewart (1976) | 1971 | *Manual males' in manufacturing weekly earnings* | 40–47 | |
| Nickell (1977) | 1972 | *Male/female manuals' in manufacturing industry hourly earnings* | | |
| | | | Males | Females |
| | | All types of agreement | 18–21 | 19–26 |
| | | National only | 10.5–14 | 19.5–23 |
| | | National and supplementary or supplementary only | 20–28 | 44–49 |
| Layard et al. (1978) | 1973 | *Male manual and non-manual workers' hourly earnings* | | |
| | | All types of agreement, manual | 25 | |
| | | All types of agreement, non-manual | 0 | |

results indicated that for manual workers in the early 1960s the average differential associated with union membership ranged from 0 to 10 per cent. Where wages were determined predominantly by national collective bargaining there was no evidence of any significant wage effect, but in industries where factory bargaining was important the wage difference was about 14 per cent. Pencavel noted that these figures were not dissimilar to Lewis's (1963) estimate that in the late 1950s American unions had affected relative wages by 10–15 per cent on average.

Mulvey and Foster's (1976) study examined the union wage effect for adult male workers by broad occupational classifications, using data indicating the proportion of workers in each occupation whose wages were subject to collective agreements in 1973. Average weekly rather than hourly earnings were chosen as the variable to be estimated. Two samples were examined; one of ninety-nine occupations which included professional and managerial workers not normally affected by union activity, and another of eighty-three occupations which excluded these so that the sample was confined to a more relevant group of workers. The variables used to estimate the non-union wage reflected the generally accepted view that differences in individual earnings are in part a return to investment in education and training, and that the relative strength of demand for labour in the various occupations is also likely to affect relative wages. As the NES did not contain data on human capital characteristics, these had to be obtained from other sources; thus for educational levels the percentage of male workers in each occupation who remained at school beyond 15 years of age was culled from the 1961 Census of Population. As a proxy variable for changes in occupational labour demand, the proportionate change in employment in each occupation between 1961 and 1971 was used; the authors note that the validity of this variable as an indication of demand pressure on relative wages depends upon the assumptions that the short-run elasticities of supply are similar for each occupation and are less than perfect. These assumptions are described as heroic by the authors. The occupational classifications also vary between different sources and in order to match the NES data to that from other sources adjustments of an *ad hoc* nature were made. The deficiencies of all but the NES data together with the rather arbitrary nature of some of the occupational classifications means that the estimates of the union mark-up 'must be very approximate indeed and treated with due caution' (Mulvey and Foster 1976:270).

As will be seen later, one of the authors has already suggested a substantial adjustment to them (Mulvey and Abowd 1980). For the larger sample the range of estimates from various regression equations is of a union mark-up of from 22 to 31 per cent, and for the smaller and more relevant sample the estimates range from 36 to 60 per cent. Mulvey and Foster considered that the most plausible figures from these ranges were 22 and 36 per cent for the two samples respectively. These are estimates for weekly earnings, and it has been argued by Metcalf (1977) that this is likely to produce an underestimate of the union effect. The use of weekly earnings as the dependent variable was justified on the grounds that workers are mainly concerned with the weekly wage packet, and this involves negotiating both hourly earnings and hours of work. However, if union members work fewer hours than non-unionists, and there is some evidence that they do (Metcalf *et al.* 1976), then hourly earnings data produce a more accurate estimate. Stewart (1976) also uses weekly earnings as the dependent variable. To estimate the non-union wage he uses data on the educational and training characteristics of some 2,000 individuals derived from the General Household Survey, as well as measures of industrial concentration, plant size and changes in employment. For manual males in manufacturing industry in 1971 his estimates range from 40 to 47 per cent.

A further article, Mulvey (1976) also found large union wage effects. He investigated the impact of collective agreement coverage across manufacturing industry for adult males, though on this occasion he estimated average hourly earnings. In addition to the proportion of skilled workers in each industry, and changes in employment, other variables used to estimate the non-union wage were: plant size, degree of concentration in each industry, sex mix of an industry and output per man, all of which have been used to explain the industrial wage structure (Reder 1962). The estimates of the average differential for workers covered by a collective agreement in 1973 ranged from 26 to 35 per cent. However, the mark-up for workers whose wages were settled by a national collective agreement only was nil, but for workers covered by national and supplementary agreements or supplementary agreements only it was between 41 and 48 per cent. These results, together with those of Pencavel, suggest that local bargaining is the significant mode for trade unionists.

One of the features of post-war British industrial relations has been the growth of such bargaining as documented by the Royal Commission on Trade Unions and Employers Associations (1968) and more recently in Brown (1980). Thus Brown notes that while multi-employer bargaining was the principal method of collective bargaining for manual workers in the 1930s, this is now the case for only some 27 per cent of these workers in private manufacturing industry. Casual observation suggests, however, that national bargaining is not always ineffective, as the National Union of Mineworkers has shown in recent years. The relative advantage to unions of local over national bargaining may also vary with the level of aggregate demand. National wage agreements are often seen as a bulwark against sectional wage cutting in times of high unemployment. In local bargaining, competition from one wage-cutting employer may force others to follow, but in national bargaining employers join to present a single wage offer to unions and competitive wage cutting may be prevented. Turner (1970) suggests that national wage agreements were important in the inter-war depression years in slowing down the general trend of falling wages.

The preceding studies have been either of male workers or have not distinguished between males and females. Nickell's (1977) article estimates the union effect on hourly earnings for both male and female manual workers in manufacturing industry. To estimate the non-union wage he includes some variables not used in the other studies. Thus the proportion of an industry's labour force working in conurbations is included to reflect the higher wages needed to compensate for the urban cost of living. The proportion of employees in each industry working shifts is also used on the grounds that such workers require compensation for irregular working hours, and the proportion covered by payment by result schemes because of the increased earnings that such schemes can produce. Using the NES data, he concludes for 1972 that there were strong union effects for males and females; female wages were increased by betwen 19 and 26 per cent and male wages by 18 and 21 per cent when all collective agreements were included in the estimates. When categorised by type of collective agreement, he also found that those with a local bargaining component showed larger wage differences than those without, though in this study workers covered only by national agreements receive a substantial premium over non-covered workers, ranging from 10.5 to 14 per cent for males and 19.5 to 23 per cent for females. The greater female mark-up, shown in all the results, is surprising, as the generally lower skill levels of women compared to men suggests greater short-run substitutability of non-union for union women, and theory postulates that this will tend to weaken a union's ability to raise wages. It has also been argued that women are less committed trade unionists than men (Blackburn 1967), though this has been contested by

Lockwood (1958) and Bain (1970), and that they have little say in union policy-making. These circumstances may have changed in recent years, but it is also possible that the Equal Pay Act of 1970 is partly responsible for these results.

The most recent estimate is that of Layard *et al.* (1978). They remark on the importance of making adequate adjustments to ensure that workers of equal quality in the union and non-union sectors are being compared when estimating the union wage effect. They point to the limited number of variables indicative of differing labour quality in the group data used in some of the previous studies, and turn to the General Household Survey of 1973 as a data source for a large number of quality variables for a large number of individuals. The variables include educational qualifications, marital status, industrial training, plant size, concentration ratio and father's occupation. The NES coverage data is then used in conjunction with that of the Household Survey to estimate the union mark-up for broad occupational groups of male workers: all manual workers, manual workers in manufacturing, and all manual workers excluding those working in primary industries. They find that average hourly earnings of male manual workers covered by a collective agreement are 25 per cent more than for workers not covered by an agreement. For non-manual workers they found no reliable evidence that collective bargaining affected relative wages.

If these various estimates are a sound indication of the order of magnitude of the union wage effect then it would be generally agreed that the union mark-up is a substantial one. It might prove to be even greater if the non-wage income of workers was included in the comparison. Examples of non-wage pecuniary benefits are employers' contributions to pension funds and subsidised meals; such income has been increasing as a proportion of total labour income (DEP Gazette, September 1980). A similar growth has occurred in the USA where unions have shown a strong interest in their improvement. Mitchell (1980) believes that their inclusion would increase the difference between American union and non-union wages. The estimates are averages, of course, based on broad classifications of workers, and American work has shown that there are considerable differences in the mark-up between groups of workers. Thus Ashenfelter (1976) finds for 1975 that craftsmen producing durable goods had a mark-up of 6 per cent compared with 22 per cent for labourers, while Rees (1962) believes that a union such as the Amalgamated Clothing Workers (of America) has had little or no effect upon earnings in the post-war years, even though much of the industry is organised by trade unions. Faced with declining product demand and low profits, the union has been unwilling to risk jobs by pursuing an aggressive policy. In a similar vein, Stigler (1966) believes that some unions may reduce slightly the wages of the members in return for receiving other benefits. 'An example is the American Association of University Professors. To the extent that the A.A.U.P. has persuaded professors of the need for appointments on indefinite tenure (for life), which have certain costs to the employing institution, they have substituted this security for larger money income' (Stigler 1966:267). A number of US studies showing the variation in the union wage effect are reviewed by Parsley (1980) who notes that manual occupations have higher differentials than non-manuals. One would conjecture that this would also be the case for the UK, for white-collar unionism in this country has until recently been much less militant than its blue-collar counterpart. The one UK study that does identify non-manuals shows no effect (Layard *et al.* 1978).

It is also probable that the union wage effect varies considerably over time and these early 1970s estimates for the UK may not be typical. Thus Lewis (1963) found the peak union wage effect in the USA occurred about 1932–33, near the bottom of the Great Depression, and that by 1947–48, a period of rapid inflation, the effect was close to zero. This latter experience has been explained by referring to the slow response of union wages to changed economic conditions because of long collective bargaining contracts, and also by the reluctance of employers of union labour to agree to large wage increases in periods of rapid inflation, in case unions resist wage decreases in subsequent deflations. As employers of non-union labour are not inhibited by these factors, the union/non-union differential narrows. Conversely, the contract period helps maintain union wages during recession and unions oppose wage cuts during deflations, for fear that the trend of prices may be reversed. The argument invoking contract length may be less applicable to the UK, however, as collective agreements are not normally legal contracts and thus there is no legal obstacle to revising an agreement if, for example, inflation proves to be greater than originally anticipated. A different explanation has been proposed by Holt (1970) who argues that in periods of low unemployment, union bargaining power declines relative to that of individuals, even though both are more powerful *vis-à-vis* employers than in depression conditions. The individual worker is in a stronger position because if he leaves the firm the cost of replacing him will be higher when there is less rather than more unemployment. It is possible, therefore, that employers become even more responsive to the quit threats of individuals than to the threats of collective action by unions; hence the relative wage advantage of unions falls. The result is reversed when unemployment is high.

Evidence for the UK about variation in the wage effect is sparse. Demery and McNabb (1978) re-estimated the Pencavel model and introduced into it overtime hours to represent demand conditions in the labour market. They found that the union wage effect was inversely related to this measure of labour demand. Layard *et al.* (1978) also produced estimates for 1961–75, using for each year the collective agreement coverage data for 1973, the only such information available. The accuracy of the findings is, therefore, dependent on the assumption that agreement coverage was reasonably constant over this period. They also found that the higher the level of unemployment the greater the wage differential for male manual workers in manufacturing: in the early 1970s it was higher than in the 1960s when unemployment was lower. However, they interpret the larger differential and higher unemployment as evidence of increased union militancy, with monetary policy only partially validating the higher wages.

## SOME RESERVATIONS

The overall message of most of these studies is that union wage bargaining does make a substantial difference to the structure of wages in the UK. The average wage differential attributable to collective bargaining is estimated to exceed 20 per cent, possibly by a large margin. Such a differential might imply a considerable union impact upon resource allocation. However, the results may overestimate the actual differential and there are a number of possible reasons for this in addition to that mentioned earlier (Creedy 1979). Metcalf (1977) notes that it is difficult to control adequately for quality differences between workers and, therefore, wage effects may be attributed to unions when they are in fact caused by union firms employing higher-quality labour than non-union firms. This may be one explanation of the high union wage effect associated with local collective bargaining, in that firms which have company agreements, such as ICI and Ford, tend to employ quality labour and operate a high wage and low turnover policy. Another link between trade unionism and labour quality noted by Lewis (1963) is that created when employers react to union-induced wage increases by replacing lower-quality labour with better workers who are now attracted to these firms. Higher wages are thus offset to some degree by higher productivity. Prior to this substitution, the statistical association between union density and wages represents the effect of unions but, subsequently, part of the higher wage reflects the greater output of the abler workers. The danger, therefore, is that this will not be adequately controlled for in empirical work. Nickell (1977) acknowledges this possibility, but points out that as the union mark-up changes from year to year unlike, we may suppose, labour quality, the wage differential is not purely a quality effect. Moreover there will continue to be welfare effects as the allocation of workers of differing quality between industries and occupations is altered by these developments.

A further possibility is that the wage differential may be the result of the type of training workers receive rather than trade union bargaining. In Becker's (1964) theory of industrial training, firms try to protect their investment in specific training by paying workers higher wages than they could receive elsewhere. But as Johnson (1975) suggests, the inability of these workers to increase their wages by changing jobs may incline them to trade unionism, and unions themselves will be more willing to organise firms where low labour turnover reduces organising costs. The danger is that unions may be wrongly credited with wage levels which are in fact the result of specific labour training. In this situation specific training jointly contributes to high wages and unionisation. Working conditions may have a similar effect. Stafford and Duncan (1980), using a small sample of American workers and regressing union status on various measures of working conditions, found that unions were more common in onerous work environments. One explanation is that union organisation is stimulated by such conditions, and they note that even without unions these would cause a compensating rise in wages. Measurements of the union wage effect which omit working conditions from the analysis may therefore overestimate its magnitude. An alternative explanation is that union bargaining causes wages to rise, and employers respond to their increased costs by introducing more demanding work practices. In time, therefore, some part of a union wage gain becomes a compensating payment and this may not be picked up in empirical work.

High wages may also directly stimulate union membership. Reder (1965) suggests that the greater the union relative wage effect the greater the numbers wishing to become members, and Dunlop (1950), in formulating one model of union behaviour, treats union membership as a positive function of the union wage rate. Historians of British trade unionism, Clegg *et al.* (1964:482) writing of the years 1889–1910 note 'that there is a clear association between high earnings and trade union density. Coalmining, shipbuilding, printing, cotton spinning and tinplate manufacture all provide evidence of this. ... The association may, however, prove either that trade unionism provides higher earnings or that high earnings encourage trade unionism, and this period offers little evidence to settle the question.'

There have been a number of American studies which attempt to take account of the effect of wages on union membership. A set of simultaneous equations is used to estimate the union wage effect, rather than the single equation approach of the articles discussed earlier. Unionisation thus becomes an endogenous rather than an exogenous variable as assumed in the single equation method. The general, though not universal, conclusion from the limited number of such studies, for example Ashenfelter and Johnson (1972), Schmidt and Strauss (1976), is that the wage effect of unions is smaller than indicated by the single equation method and that wages have a positive effect on union membership. Nevertheless, the authors of these studies suggest caution in the evaluation of these findings. Thus Ashenfelter and Johnson (1972:505) state that 'given the qualitative and quantitative limitations of the data, we are prepared to say only that we are uncertain of the magnitude of the effect of unions on inter-industry wage differences', while Schmidt and Strauss (1976:211) conclude that their findings 'may suggest that the common statement that unions raise wages may suffer from an incomplete notion of causation'. There have been no UK studies which use this methodology, but the American ones do at least raise the possibility of an upward bias in the existing estimates.

Given the difficulties of correcting for non-union influences on wages, the possibility of simultaneous determination of union membership and high wages, and of union membership being directly influenced by high wages, it is not surprising that there is scepticism about the results of many of these studies. Mulvey and Abowd (1980) have in fact suggested that Mulvey's earlier work and that of others may have seriously overestimated the union wage effect. The authors note that in the USA, data about the wages of large numbers of individual workers have become available in recent years together with information about union status, education, training and other wage-determining variables. Estimates of the union mark-up derived from this information have tended to be lower than those using more aggregate data, such as the proportion of union members by industry or occupation. While detailed individual information is not available for the UK, Mulvey and Abowd conclude from their use of data contained in the NES 1974 that the error in British estimates of the differential may be as large as 50 per cent or more.

The problems of statistical work in this area are also emphasised by Wabe and Leech (1978). Their investigation is concerned with explaining variations in male hourly earnings, excluding overtime pay, across manufacturing industry in 1968. One of their dependent variables is collective agreement coverage and, using the 1973 data, they find this to have no influence on hourly earnings. They contrast this result with the substantial influence shown by Mulvey (1976) and suggest that a number of variables omitted by him but used in their estimating equation are responsible for the difference. Thus they use the percentage of semi- and unskilled as well as skilled workers by industry. The numbers of employees involved in shift work and payment by result schemes are also included. Their main conclusion is that the factors that influence relative wages are so many and complex that empirical work using cross-section data is unlikely to be very successful in unravelling them, and that a disaggregated approach might achieve better results. A similar conclusion is reached by Richardson and Catlin (1979). In an article mainly concerned with the growth of union membership in the UK, they express doubts about studies showing high wages to be the result of union bargaining: 'The reality probably is that relative wages, union density, workforce characteristics and the industrial structure are all interrelated in a highly complex causal pattern' (Richardson and Catlin 1979: 384).

The reader will realise by now that firm conclusions are difficult to reach in this area of economics. The British estimates support the findings of many American studies that unions do affect the relative wage structure. The American studies indicate that this varies over time, and one of the British studies does suggest that the early 1970s estimates were higher than they had been in the previous decade. The average differential for manual workers in the UK was in excess of 20 per cent in and around 1973, and was very marked for local collective agreements. It is possible, however, that the true union differential was below this. Most of the British studies cited in this survey emphasise the tentative nature of their conclusions, and Metcalf (1977) says that the union mark-up may be small after properly controlling for labour quality. Until data become available which will enable this to be done and until more is known about the effect of high wages on union growth, it seems wise to regard the current results with considerable caution. This also applies to studies which make use of the estimates. Thus Minford and Peel (1981:15) write: 'Union power probably raises real labour costs in union sectors by 12–25%,' and they quote Mulvey and Foster (1976), Metcalf (1977) and Parsley (1980). Then they proceed: 'If we assume that this represents 50% of the labour force the Liverpool model suggests that this raises permanent unemployment by 0.4–0.8 millions.' The Liverpool model referred to is a model of the UK economy. In the light of so many reservations, one might question whether the estimates can bear the weight of such a statement.

## 3.   Unions and inflation

Although there is a measure of agreement that unions do change the structure of relative wages, there is no such consensus about their influence upon the general wage level. Many economists believe that they have a considerable effect, and that because they have caused aggregate wages to rise more rapidly than aggregate productivity they have been a major cause of UK inflation. Others consider that they have had little if any such role, and that inflation has been the result of excess aggregate demand together with expectations of continuing price increases. The different policy implications of these views are well known. If unions do cause inflation the appropriate policy seems to be to persuade or coerce them to moderate their wage demands through the mechanism of an incomes policy. The cure for an inflation originating with excess demand is to eliminate this by pursuing a restrictive monetary policy, which may also influence price expectations. However, if monetary policy is used to check an inflation caused by trade unions it may require substantial unemployment to restrain union wage settlements, while, on the other hand, incomes policies are not designed to deal with the problem of excessive monetary expansion though they may conceivably serve to depress expectations of future price rises. Correct diagnosis of the cause of inflation is important therefore.

The evidence that unions affect relative wages does not, of course, necessarily imply that they also raise the general level of wages. It has been seen that workers who lose their jobs because of union wage increases may cause wages to fall in non-union firms, and this may be sufficient to prevent a general rise. However, minimum wage laws may act as a brake on wage reductions, the levels of unemployment compensation and social security benefits can encourage unemployment rather than job search, and some of those seeking work may lack the necessary skill or live too far from employment for them to be suitable job candidates. In circumstances such as these, the necessary fall in wages may not occur and a union effect on relative wages will also raise the general wage level.

Another consequence will be more unemployment, as a higher real wage in the union sector and wage rigidity elsewhere reduces the quantity of labour demanded. The assumption here is that the government refrains from increasing the money supply so that prices cannot rise sufficiently to offset the higher wage level. Now if unions are concerned with the unemployment effects of their behaviour, and as noted earlier opinions differ about its importance, it seems likely that they will reach an optimum situation at which they will be unwilling to sacrifice jobs for further wage increases. For wages to go on rising beyond this optimum requires the highly improbable condition of a continuous rise in union monopoly power or, alternatively, an ever-increasing willingness to use that power. Secular inflation is thought to be an unlikely consequence of the union relative wage effect, therefore, although it may cause the price level to be higher than otherwise. As an example of this, Friedman and Schwartz (1963) suggest that the 150 per cent rise in American union membership in the period 1933–37 can help to explain the inflation of those years. A number of British studies have also used union membership to proxy union power while others have used strike trends to represent union militancy, and these will be examined later. However, the original UK concern with union-push inflation did not emanate from this type of 'once and for all' rise in prices, but with the possibility of unions causing a continuous inflation.

The problem arises if governments try to prevent union wage bargaining causing unemployment. Thus if unions do raise real wages, governments may respond by increasing the money supply so that prices rise sufficiently to maintain employment at its previous level. Unions are, therefore, thwarted in their attempts to gain particular increases in real wages, and may try to recoup their gains by obtaining further increases in money wages and governments may again respond by increasing the money supply. A government commitment to maintain employment becomes a recipe for a continuing inflation. Monetary expansion becomes dependent upon the rise in union wages; correlation between changes in the money supply and prices becomes evidence of inflation caused by cost push rather than excess demand. An increase in union membership is not a necessary condition for this sequence; what is suggested is that the unemployment constraint is removed from unions so that their existing bargaining power is more fully utilised. It can be maintained, of course, that the inflation is the result of an accommodating government monetary policy rather than union pressure. However, it seems useful to argue, as Machlup (1960) has done, that the money-creating power of the authorities would be exercised to a smaller extent in the absence of union pressure to raise wages. Also by focusing upon the role of unions it becomes possible to envisage a cure for such inflations through a reform of the collective bargaining system, for example an incomes policy, rather than by manipulating the money supply.

The origin of this approach to inflation can be traced to the policy implication of Keynes's *General Theory* that government macroeconomic policy could ensure the maintenance of high levels of employment. Soon after its publication, it was argued by Robinson (1937) that a government commitment to full employment combined with the normal practice of collective bargaining would cause chronic inflation. Others expressed similar opinions: Beveridge (1944) and Kalecki (1944) thought it possible that, with the threat of unemployment removed, unions would use their bargaining power to gain higher wages, that the resulting higher prices would provoke further inflationary wage settlements, and so on. It was noted by Worswick (1944) that if workers were organised in only one union which bargained simultaneously for all its members, the self-defeating effects of such settlements upon real wages would be obvious and might result in non-inflationary money wage agreements; but, as in practice unions bargained separately and at different times, it was not in the interests of individual unions to moderate their wage demands, for there was no guarantee that others would do likewise. It was rational for unions, therefore, to continue to press for higher money wages which might in total exceed the aggregate rise in productivity.

Another writer who pointed to the inflationary potential of unco-ordinated wage bargaining was Reder (1948), who developed a model in which it was assumed that each union aimed to achieve a certain real wage rate for its members and bargained for money wage rates on the basis of product prices existing at the time of the bargain. He further assumed that each union gained its money wage demands but employers responded by raising their product prices. At the end of the wage agreements enough prices had risen to propel a new round of demands for inflationary money wage increases. Reder suggested that unions might learn to bargain in terms of expected price increases and so produce an increasing rate of inflation. The implication of these ideas was that by committing themselves to full employment, governments relinquished control over the price level. Other economists writing subsequently have expressed similar views. Thus Hayek (1959:47) asserted that: 'Since it has become the generally accepted doctrine that it is the duty of the monetary authorities to provide enough credit to secure full employment, whatever the wage level ... the power of the unions cannot but lead to continuous progressive inflation.' Haberler (1959) also envisaged a continuing inflation if governments accommodate union wage awards by increasing the supply of money. Reference to such writings is not, of course, in itself proof that part of the post-war inflation has been of the type suggested, and readers will know that there is an alternative explanation which points to excessive monetary expansion, together with the development of inflationary expectations, as the cause rather than the effect of inflation. Nevertheless, it is worth bearing in mind that many reputable economists did predict that inflation would result from the enhanced position of the trade unions in conditions of high employment.

These two approaches to wage-push inflation are largely relevant to different periods of post-war inflation. In the years of high employment, roughly from the Second World War to the late 1960s, it was the interaction between union bargaining power and government monetary policy which led many economists to regard unions as the major cause of the UK inflation. Union power may have fluctuated during these years and the price level may have changed because of this, but the predominant wage-push view was that based on the government's full employment commitment. However, the higher levels of unemployment of recent years make this an untenable theory of subsequent inflation. Unions are now aware that governments cannot or will not maintain high employment levels. In its place is the belief that inflation has been caused by increased union power or a greater willingness to use their power. In one view inflation can be a continuous process and in the other it will be ended eventually by rising unemployment; the distinction is between the behaviour of unions in different economic environments.

The early writings on the full employment approach left many questions unresolved. What would determine the level of inflation? Would it accelerate as suggested by Reder (1948)? Could the role of employers be as passive as was seemingly implied, particularly in an open economy with governments committed to fixed exchange rates? Inflationary wage claims would then face employers in the traded goods sector of the economy with the prospect of lower profits. Governments themselves would be unable to maintain the pound's parity if UK prices rose more rapidly than those of its competitors, and they might therefore choose to let unemployment rise in the face of excessive wage settlements. If so, how much unemployment would be needed for unions to moderate their wage demands? Finally, how could students distinguish between cost push and the more traditional excess demand theories? Both required high levels of employment to explain inflation, and given the imprecision of the term 'full employment' and the difficulty of identifying excess aggregate demand, distinguishing one from the other was likely to prove difficult. The 'unemployment' approach also needed to deal with some of these issues, and in particular what degree of unemployment would be needed to check inflation. Subsequent work has attempted to fill these gaps but, as will be seen, it has had limited success. Wood (1978:20), in making his own theoretical contribution, notes that the cost-push models are 'far from fully developed. They are for the most part short of microeconomic behavioural under-pinnings. ...'

Two rather distinct explanations of the role of unions in initiating an inflationary process have developed in the UK. One emphasises the importance to workers of receiving a 'fair wage' in relation to some traditional reference group. It is argued that a change in wage differentials previously regarded as fair can have inflationary consequences, because the workers whose wages are now relatively lower than before will seek compensating wage increases through the agency of their trade unions. If such compensating wage demands are successful and such comparisons are widespread in the economy, the increase in aggregate wages may exceed the aggregate rise in productivity and cause inflation. The other approach is based on the idea that union members became accustomed to regular rises in real wages in the early post-war years and expected these increases to continue. The expected rate of increase in real wages has been called the target rate of increase, and according to this theory union money wage demands are pitched at the level required to achieve the target. Inflation will result if, in the aggregate, the money wage increase needed to do this exceeds the aggregate rise in productivity. Infla-tion will accelerate if the gap between target and actual real wage growth widens because, say, of a fall in the productivity growth rate. Unions will then, it is claimed, increase the level of their money wage demands in order to compensate for this shortfall. Each explanation uses the concept of a fair wage, with emphasis on subjective notions of equitable wage structures in one case and on equitable real wage increases in the other. Each is a partial theory of union wage policy: the level of wage increase needed to satisfy union members will rise if their relative pay falls or if real wage growth is below that expected. Higher wage claims result in higher wage awards because of the greater threat of union industrial action. Employers have to compare the effect on their profits of either conceding or rejecting the claim; the greater the cost the union appears willing to accept to further its claim the greater the probability of the employer accepting it.

The two theories will be examined in turn.

## THE RELATIVE WAGE THEORY

That workers' concern with equitable wage relativities might have an important influence on the aggregate level of wages is not a new hypothesis. Keynes (1936), explaining the slow response of money wages to high unemployment, argued that workers opposed cuts in money wages because their relative wage position might deteriorate in the process of unsynchronised money wage reductions. The same argument is now applied to increases in wages. It involves explaining individual or group behaviour partly in terms of interdependent utility functions: one person's utility depends not only upon her income, for example, but also upon the income of others. Although this is a commonplace idea, it is not normally utilised in economic theorising. Analysis of consumer behaviour usually assumes that an in-dividual's welfare depends solely upon her own consumption and is unaffected by the consumption of others. Mitchell (1980) explains this by referring to the analytical difficulties which follow from the recognition of interdependent utility functions, while Lindbeck (1977) notes how little is known about the formation of preferences and how they are influenced by interpersonal relations. However weak its theoretical development, the effect of interpersonal comparisons on wages is central to some students' explanation of some periods of post-war UK inflation. Thus Turner (1957:126) has maintained that:

> ... given a general situation of high employment, the British system and techniques of collective wage regulation permit particular groups of workers to increase their wages faster than the generality. Other workers then demand wage increases to restore 'established relativities'. The unions' tendency is to convert such sectional wage demands into general demands. General wage increases, however, are only a palliative, and may themselves – by their effect on differentials – provoke renewed discontent.

While Turner does not regard this as the sole factor in explaining wage inflation, he believes it to be a significant one. Lydall (1958) also argues that wage increases in one sector of the economy spread to other sectors as workers bargain to maintain relativities, and that this process determines the rate of increase of wages and, to a considerable degree, prices. For Hicks (1974) the wage experience of the post-war years can be divided into two periods. Up to the late 1960s inflation was largely the result of excess demand, though even then wages rose in industries where there was no labour shortage to prevent the emergence of 'unfair' wage differentials. Subsequently the dominant cause of wage inflation became wage increases that emerged from the comparisons which groups of workers made with each other. The main force behind rising wages was no longer labour scarcity but social pressure, with wages rising by a similar amount in both recessions and booms. Phelps Brown (1975) also believes that wage comparisons have been an important cause of wage inflation since the Second World War. One further source of pressure is the effect of worker comparisons upon union leaders. Ross (1948) suggests that a crucial test of a union leader's competence is his ability to match the wage increases obtained by similar groups of workers; if he fails to do this his own job may be at risk and union membership may fall. The same view is expressed by Flanders (1967), Wiles (1973) and Hahn (1982), who note that union officials compete among themselves for success which is measured by the relative wage gain achieved for their members.

The comparisons made by workers as indicated by surveys of their attitudes show that 'the choice of pay comparisons is typically unambitious and powerfully shaped by custom' (Hyman and Brough 1975:61). Thus Runciman (1966) found that manual workers tended to compare themselves with other manuals, and Daniel's (1977) study of work-place bargaining found that local comparisons with workers doing similar jobs were most frequently cited in pay negotiations. The National Board for Prices and Incomes (Report 19, 1966) acknowledged that there was widespread reference to relative wage levels in union wage claims. In the electricity supply industry the pay increases received by the manual and technical workers, to compensate for a changed pattern of working hours, prompted the clerical and administrative grades to claim similar increases, though there had been no change in their working hours. The Board also found the comparison argument used by employees of different firms in different localities but employed in the same industry. Thus, a wage settlement for London busmen was cited by provincial busmen as a basis for a claim. Comparisons were also made across industries. The London busmen had referred to the pay of London Underground motormen in their negotiations while, in turn, the motormen had compared their pay with that of British Railways engine drivers. Of course, these examples do not themselves prove that changes in relative pay affect the outcome of negotiations. Unions marshal many arguments to support their wage claims and not all need to be taken seriously. However, there are many studies which do conclude that wage settlements are affected by these comparisons.

In their investigation of a number of labour markets for engineering workers, Mackay et al. (1971) found evidence to suggest that strong non-competitive pressures exist to maintain conventional differentials between different grades of engineering worker: 'Equitable comparisons within the plant are, therefore, important, so that the employer who attempts to meet labour shortages by raising wages for particular groups of employees has to bear in mind the probability that this will give rise to wage demands from other groups' (p.127) and 'while the internal wage structure was not rigid, the earnings of different groups were interrelated so that it was difficult to modify internal wage structures in the face of coercive comparisons' (p. 130). Another study of the engineering labour market in Lerner et al. (1969) also refers to the important role of the notion of fair relative wages in workshop bargaining. Comparisons were made not only with wages of other workers in the same plant, but on occasions with the average earnings in the industry for comparable grades of worker. The effects of shop stewards' combine committees on earnings in the engineering industry have been examined by Lerner and Marquand (1963). The committees consist of shop stewards from the various plants of particular companies and they act as collectors and dispersers of wage information, passing on details of earnings increases in one plant to plants in other districts by correspondence and personal contact. The dissemination of this information did, in the authors' view, influence wage levels in engineering (Lerner and Marquand 1963:290):

> ... increases in earnings in one works of a company create pressures for increases on grounds of 'comparability' or to restore 'fair relativities' in the region where the works are, in the works of the company elsewhere, and hence in other regions. A relatively low demand for labour is not sufficient to prevent increases in earnings on grounds of comparability with earnings in other regions with a high level of demand for labour.

Within the public sector, wage comparisons have been of great importance, and the wages of the majority of employees have resulted from comparisons made between their pay and that of similar workers in privately owned industry. Elliott and Fallick (1981) note that in national government and in several of the nationalised industries, specific procedures have been adopted to ensure that the wages of public employees are linked to wages in the private sector, and that wage settlements in local government are frequently based on the wages paid for comparable work in private industry.

A final example of the importance of comparisons is provided by Brown and Sissons (1975) in their study of wage relativities in the Fleet Street newspaper and Coventry engineering industries. In Fleet Street they found that comparisons with employees of other newspapers were most important in explaining changes in pay from 1961 to 1964, but that subsequently, comparisons of wage differentials within each firm became dominant. They explained this development by noting that the simplification of pay structures had made it easier to compare occupational earnings within newspapers, and that the large differences in earnings which had developed over the years became clear to workers. Concern about these differentials meant that they became more important in wage negotiations and had a greater effect upon wage settlements. In Coventry, comparisons with earnings in other plants were important from 1964 to 1971, but subsequently comparisons with other grades within plants became increasingly significant. The replacement of fluctuating piece-rate earnings by job-evaluated plant-wide pay structures in the early 1970s made wage comparisons within plants easier, and collective bargaining subsequently caused a narrowing of differentials. The authors' interpretation of their results can be criticised; that these wage movements occurred at the same time as changes in the quality of plant information does not necessarily imply a causal relationship (Burton and Addison 1977). Nevertheless, this sample of studies indicates that relative wages appear to be important to employees, and suggests that comparisons affect actual wage levels both within firms and across industries. They provide some microeconomic basis for the theory that inflation can be propelled by comparability-based wage settlements for, if their conclusions are correct, it follows that the price of particular goods can rise because of imitative wage determination and, if this is widespread, so too can the general price level.

A number of studies have investigated this behaviour at the macro level. These studies do not test the predictions of a formal model of the comparability theory of wage determination because there is no such model. Instead, investigators have been mainly concerned with examining labour-market phenomena which seem difficult to explain in terms of competitive wage theory but which appear consistent with the comparability theory. One example of this is the claim that there is a national wage round. It has been argued that most UK workers receive annual wage increases of a similar size; as a result of collective bargaining over wage differentials and of such institutional features of the British labour market as the omnipresence of the general workers' unions and the attention paid by wage arbitrators to wage increases negotiated elsewhere. To use the wage round concept as evidence of a non-competitive explanation of inflation implies that its features would not exist in a predominantly competitive labour market. Diverse product and labour-market conditions in the industries engaged in collective bargaining would not, it is supposed, produce similarities in the timing, size and regularity of their wage settlements. However, if wage increases are partly determined by the expected rate of increase in the price level and these expectations are common to employees and employers generally, the influence of different market circumstances can be swamped by these price expectations and so produce similar wage settlements. Moreover, although the wage round is widely believed to exist, a number of authors have failed to discover it, and the one major work that claimed to have done so, OEEC (1961), has been strongly criticised.

The OEEC study examined wage-rate changes for all manual workers between 1953 and 1960 and concluded that collective bargaining had tended to become concentrated into short periods of time, and that this pattern was repeated at fairly regular intervals. The size of wage settlements was also found to be similar but, although a few key bargains determined the general level of wage agreements, there were no groups of workers who persistently settled early in the round and who might, therefore, be regarded as the regular pace-setters. Knowles and Robinson (1962) argue, however, that these conclusions were not substantiated by the evidence. In particular, they criticised the way in which wage rounds had been distinguished from each other. This had been done in terms of the number of workers affected by wage-rate changes in a particular time period rather than by the number of negotiated wage increases. Consequently, any period which included the engineering workers' national wage settlement was bound to show a high monthly concentration because of the large number of workers covered by this agreement. For their own study they examined the experience of 146 negotiating groups connected with the Transport and General Workers' Union between 1952 and 1958. They found no evidence of an annual wage round in the sense of all wage earners receiving a wage rise every 12 months. Nor did particular groups of workers receive increases at the same time each year, and nor were the increases of a similar size.

In the most recent study Elliott (1976) examined 190 nationally negotiated manual workers' agreements for 1950–73, including the larger wages councils, for evidence that the size and timing of wage settlements was markedly and repeatedly similar. Considerable differences were found, however, in the number of settlements reached by different negotiating groups. Thus in a period when all the negotiating groups in the sample had obtained at least one wage increase, some had achieved five; a national wage round was not, therefore, identifiable by this criterion. Nor was the timing of wage settlements similar for most of the period studied. In some years, such as 1971 and 1972, there was a tendency for the same number of wage awards to occur each month, but in the late 1950s there was much greater concentration of settlements in particular periods. Overall, therefore, there was no discernible cycle in the incidence of wage agreements. Elliott also found considerable differences in the size of wage increases, so that he concluded that there was no national wage round in the UK. The weight of evidence indicates, therefore, that there is considerable diversity among negotiating groups in the size, timing and frequency of wage increases so that a national wage round as popularly conceived does not exist.

There is evidence, however, of similar wage experience for some groups within the public sector, and this has been attributed to the maintenance of fair relativities rather than the operation of market forces. In an examination of wage settlements for unskilled workers from 1950 to 1965, Elliott and Fallick (1981) found that the agreements in gas, water, health and local authorities followed that reached in electricity supply, and that there was a 'remarkable degree of similarity' (p. 79) in these awards. An objective of the unions in these industries was, in fact, to achieve parity of pay for unskilled workers. In turn the electricity supply unions used the pay awards in electrical contracting, gas, building and engineering as the bench-mark for their own claims. The wages of unskilled workers in railways, railway workshops and London Transport were also found to be linked. These particular relationships were often the results of workers belonging to the same trade union or of a similar negotiating history. Thus local transport, public utilities and health were once local government services paying similar rates for unskilled workers. The links did not, however, constitute a public sector wage round, as different groups within the public sector received markedly different wage awards during the years studied and there was considerable variation in the number of agreements reached by the various negotiating groups.

The rejection of the national wage round hypothesis as defined above does not necessarily mean that wage comparisons are unimportant in the generation of inflation. As Clegg (1979) notes, there would be a regular wage round only if comparison was the sole influence on wage agreements, and as this is not so, disparate changes in the other determinants will cause dissimilar pay awards. In recent years he refers to productivity bargaining and measured day-work agreements as sources of differential wage increases. Moreover, despite his criticism of the hypothesis, Knowles (1962) believes that the institutional features of the British labour market do contribute to the generalisation of particular wage increases.

Sargan (1971) provides some evidence consistent with wage comparability. He examined UK wage settlements for eighteen industries from 1956 to 1967 and correlated each industry's annual wage change with the wage changes in each of the other industries lagged one quarter. He found a high simple correlation coefficient for all the industries and proposed that wage comparisons were responsible for these relationships, with workers in each industry taking particular notice of wage changes in specific industries when formulating their own wage claims. The transport, communication, and professional and service industries were prominent as pace-makers, possibly, he suggested, because of the diverse industrial contacts of transport workers and the publicity sometimes given to the wage settlements of professional and scientific workers. It can be argued, however, that other settlements received even greater publicity – car workers in the period covered – and there are other groups of workers who come into contact with trade unionists in many industries, for example electricians. It is not obvious why the wage increases of these workers should be less important than those indicated in the study.

Evidence of a regional wage transfer mechanism has also been produced. Thomas and Stoney (1971) found that regional unemployment differences had an important effect on the aggregate rate of increase of money wages for the periods 1925–38 and 1950–66: the greater the dispersion in unemployment rates the greater the increase in the general wage level. Wage increases in low unemployment areas such as London and the south-east of England affected wage settlements in the high unemployment areas but not vice versa. Excess demand for labour could explain the increases in the former regions but not those in the slacker labour markets, and the authors suggest an explanation in terms of successful union bargaining to maintain differentials. For 1960–65, Cowling and Metcalf (1967) also found that the rate of increase in wages in London and the South-east affected wage increases in the higher unemployment areas. On the other hand Hart and Mackay (1977), in a study of engineering wages in the inter-war and post-war years, discovered that wage increases in regions with low unemployment were themselves affected by wage increases in other regions. While they acknowledge the importance of labour mobility in explaining the transmission of earnings increases across regions, they conclude that the effect of wage comparisons is also important.

It has also been argued that imitative wage behaviour spreads from the high productivity growth industries; Streeten (1962) and Hicks (1976) argue that this often stimulates a general rise in wages. Similarly, Jackson and Turner (1972) point to international evidence indicating that wages rise most quickly in capital-intensive oligopolistic industries with high rates of productivity growth, and they argue that equitable wage comparisons as well as market forces then spread the wage increase to the low productivity growth sectors of economies. The general price level rises because the increase in prices in the low productivity growth in-dustries is not offset by price reductions in industries where productivity growth is rapid. The empirical foundation of the Jackson and Turner thesis has been ques-tioned by Knight and Mabro (1972), who criticise the appropriateness of the statistical procedures and also note that no direct measure of labour productivity growth is used in the empirical work. Jackson and Turner also use the well-known 'kinked demand curve model' to explain oligopolistic pricing: productivity growth in one firm does not lead to price reductions because of the fear of a downward spiral of competitive price cutting. The model has been criticised by Stigler (1947, 1978) on both theoretical and empirical grounds and, in view of this, Jackson and Turner's description of it as an 'empirically founded proposition' (p. 24) seems unwarranted. A subsequent study of productivity growth in fifteen industrial countries from 1958 to 1967 by Eatwell et al. (1974) found that much of the inter-national variation in wage inflation was explained by the three industries experien-cing the most rapid productivity growth. However, Burton and Addison (1977:354) note that the Netherlands was excluded from the sample which generated these results, and that once it was included, the estimating equation 'performs hardly any better than an equation in which the rate of money wage inflation is presumed to be a linear function of the average rate of labour produc-tivity growth in the economy.' Copeland (1977) points out that there is no a priori reason why the top three productivity growth industries should be selected rather than some other number, and he also found that the average rate of productivity growth provided a better explanation of wage inflation.

While all the above studies invoke wage comparisons as a wage transmission mechanism, it is possible that competitive forces provide a better explanation of wage interrelationships. The effect of common price expectations has been noted earlier, but also, if one assumes an inflation caused by monetary expansion, it is likely that some industries will experience the excess demand before others and their wages will be the first to rise. Wage increases will follow in other industries as they experience a shortage of labour. In an open economy such as the UK and assuming a fixed exchange rate, excess demand could emanate from abroad and initially raise the demand for labour in those industries. An increase in the prices of tradeable goods because of this increase in demand will cause some substitution of non-tradeable goods, so increasing labour demand in that sector. In this situation the domestic rate of wage inflation thus becomes determined by the world rate of inflation of tradeable goods. As noted by Parkin (1978), this prediction is the same as that made by the model developed by Edgren *et al.* (1969), whereby the growth rate of wages in the traded goods industries is limited by the need to remain internationally competitive. This rate of growth determines the level of wage settlements in those parts of the economy not exposed to foreign competition though, in their model, the transmission mechanism involves institutional as well as competitive channels.

There are a number of other explanations of wage linkages. Brechling (1973) in a study of American wages found that wage increases in high-wage regions influenced wage settlements in the low-wage areas but, unlike Thomas and Stoney, that the effect of low unemployment area wages upon wages elsewhere was slight. Brechling suggests that regional wage levels are linked through potential or actual migration from low- to high-wage areas. A further possibility suggested by Burton and Addison (1977) and Mitchell (1980) is that there may be wage leadership in labour markets analogous to price barometric leadership in oligopolistic product markets. Some firms may use the wage awards of a wage leader as a proxy for their own labour-market conditions; it may be more economic to use this information than to gauge labour-market conditions more directly. As a final example it has been suggested that the wages paid by firms in oligopolistic industries are related, but that neither labour-market competition nor union bargaining is the major cause. In an article based on a study of American industry, Dunlop (1957) argues that the limited degree of competition in some product markets enables firms to pay higher wages than employees could receive elsewhere, and that the wage increases received by some grades of worker across these firms are highly interrelated. Companies whose wage settlements were so linked formed 'wage contours' in Dunlop's terminology. Although unions could be partly responsible, the practice was so widespread that the main cause was thought to be the structure of the product market.

The adherents of the cost-push approach do not deny that there are competitive forces at work in labour markets, but they do believe, to varying degrees, that non-competitive factors are crucial to an explanation of UK inflation. In adopting this attitude they are part of a tradition in British labour economics which has long been critical of the neo-classical approach to the analysis of labour markets and, in particular, of the relevance of the competitive theory of wages. This doubt has been based upon such phenomena as the large differences in the wages often paid to workers of the same occupation in the same local labour market (Robinson 1970), the difficulty experienced in some studies of finding a relationship between change in relative labour demands and changes in relative wages (Mackay *et al.* 1971), and the downward inflexibility of money wages in the face of rising unemployment. One needs to emphasise that the neo-classical approach remains pertinent for many economists, and recent advances in the analysis of human capital (Becker 1964), wage contracts (Azariadis 1975) and internal labour markets (Williamson *et al.* 1975) for example, have utilised it in explaining these characteristics of the labour market. Nevertheless, it is the importance of wage comparisons that has featured in this explanation of UK inflation. As Hicks (1975:4) has written 'One is driven to the conclusion – it is, after all, a very common-sense conclusion – that there are forces at work in the determination of money wages which are non-competitive. It is just not true that money wages are determined by supply and demand.' Quoting Hicks (1955:397) again: 'In practice, differentials do tend to be acceptable if they have custom behind them – if they are in accordance with what the people who suffer from them, as well as those who gain from them have come to expect.' If this non-competitive theory is to provide a satisfactory explanation of British inflation it has to illuminate both the moderate inflation of the early post-war years and its acceleration from the mid-1960s. The average annual rate of increase of retail prices was 6.2 per cent in the period 1968–71, compared with an annual rise of only 2.8 per cent in the previous years. It also has to explain why this pattern was common to many countries. It will be seen that the theory's adherents differ considerably in their answers to these questions.

For Jackson and Turner (1972), relatively stable inflation was largely the result of stable productivity growth in the high productivity growth areas of the economy which, according to their theory of wage leadership, resulted in a generally stable rate of wage increase. The acceleration is explained by Wilkinson and Turner (1972) by two developments which increased worker militancy. One was the non-realisation of employee expectations of continuing increases in real take-home pay (the real wage target hypothesis), but the other was the decline in the relative take-home pay of significant numbers of lower-paid manual workers between 1961 and 1971. Because tax allowances were not index-linked to the rate of inflation, many low-paid workers began to pay taxes for the first time in these years and, as a result of this and other features of tax policy, after-tax pay for the lower paid fell relative to that of the higher paid. This deterioration in relative take-home pay caused increased strike activity as unions became more militant, and this helped produce the wage explosion of 1970–71.

The disturbance of established wage relativities as a possible source of wage inflation is also suggested by Baxter (1973), who argues that the reduction in the rate of growth of real wages at this time may have caused workers to become more concerned with their relative economic position and more willing to use union bargaining power to improve it. The wage explosion is explained by Clegg (1971) as partly the reaction of workers to the devaluation of 1967, but also as the result of the growth of productivity bargaining which disturbed pay differentials. Large wage increases were often achieved through these bargains and other workers sought similar ones. A different approach is that of Wood (1978) who believes that it took some years for workers to adapt to the inflation that their bargaining over differentials was causing. Eventually, however, this persistent inflation came to be anticipated, and so produced higher wage settlements not only in the UK but in other countries. Accelerated wage-push inflation had been predicted by Fellner (1959:235):

> The process starts by the effort of some groups to gain at the expense of others in real terms. Aggregate income is insufficient to satisfy all claims, but the wage and price increases in some sectors catch other sectors unawares. The gains are partly offset by a subsequent wage pull on the other sectors, that is, by price increases. In the subsequent phase, any group attempting to make gains in real terms is almost certain to claim a compensation for price increases as well as to make a bid for a relative improvement in real terms. In such circumstances, after a while one must run fast in order to stand still and in reality one wants to get ahead rather than merely stand still.

The post-war inflation for Phelps Brown (1971, 1975) is largely the result of high employment levels increasing union bargaining power, but also of a cumulative change in the attitudes and expectations of employees not only in the UK but in many western countries. Improved communications have made workers more aware of pay rises received elsewhere, including other countries. The steady improvement in real wages in the 1950s and 1960s also accustomed workers to expect an annual improvement in living standards. What initially prevented accelerating inflation was the influence of older workers, whose wage bargaining was restrained by memories of the unemployment of pre-war years. By the mid-1960s, however, a younger generation had become influential in union decision-making in many countries. This change in attitudes caused the sharp increase in the rate of inflation, possibly sparked off by the large rise in the pay of French workers in 1968. The changed attitudes of workers is also emphasised by Wiles (1973), who points to the breakdown of a deferential class structure and to the importance of improved communications in promoting imitative wage behaviour.

Each of these explanations suggests that unions became more militant towards the end of the 1960s and that higher inflation ensued. However, the considerable differences between these authors as to why this happened might be regarded as a weakness of the approach. It is also possible to account for an increase in militancy without reference to either relative wages or real wage growth. In the 1960s, higher unemployment benefits reduced the cost of unemployment, and 'one likely result has been that in pressing wage claims trade unions and similar bodies have been less sensitive than before to any given level of unemployment among the workers concerned. This may well have exerted an appreciable influence' on wages (Meade 1971:16). Another deficiency, previously noted, is that no formal 'relativities model' has been developed. Such a model would need to specify the precise form of employee wage comparisons, and while there is evidence (Behrend 1973) that they are made in absolute terms, Wood (1978) and Mayhew (1981) argue that workers are more concerned with percentage comparisons. It would also have to specify the actual comparisons made by these groups, and the factors that would determine the extent to which feelings of injustice are translated into actual wage changes. Given the number of bargaining groups in the economy and the lack of any generally accepted model of union behaviour or of union – employer bargaining, the prospects for developing such a model are remote. The lack of a model precludes econometric testing. In defending this situation Wood (1978:216) argues that the nature of wage inflation makes it resistant to macroeconometric modelling: 'Quite small changes in supply and demand conditions in particular sectors, or in the power or militancy of particular groups of employees, or in the availability of information, can in the present model cause changes in the pace of wage inflation which are both quite large and from the purely macroeconomic viewpoint incomprehensible.' Wood acknowledges that insufficient attention is often paid in discussion to the ways in which ideas of fairness actually bring about changes in wage differentials. In particular the interests of employers are often ignored and wage increases appear to be a free good.

A further weakness of this approach is its explanation of the similarity of the inflationary experience of much of the western world, and especially the common surge in inflation rates in the late 1960s. It is possible that employee attitudes have developed in a similar way and at a similar pace in many countries, and that the consequent increase in militancy has affected the rate of increase of money wages uniformly, but the articles cited do not provide any country-by-country evidence of these changes. It is also possible that events in France in 1968 affected the attitudes of British workers, but no evidence has been produced in support of this claim; the juxtaposition of events is not proof of a causal relationship. Moreover Laidler and Parkin (1975) argue that it is equally plausible to suggest that workers in a particular country follow the example of their more 'docile' neighbours rather than their more 'militant' ones. Why should British workers take more notice of French workers than of German or American ones? If one accepts the difficulty of measuring changes in attitudes one could, as Lipsey (1979) suggests, use the techniques of the historian to support the hypothesis, but with few exceptions (e.g. Phelps Brown 1975) this has not been attempted. In the light of all these problems it is not surprising that many economists have rejected the claims that wage bargaining over relativities has a significant role in explaining inflation.

Another reason for caution is that there is a model of inflation which has been econometrically tested, and which to the satisfaction of many, but clearly not all, economists can explain the inflationary experience of recent years both in the UK and elsewhere. Thus inflation is the result of excess aggregate demand together with the inflationary expectations of price and wage setters. A world in which foreign exchange rates between countries are fixed can be thought of as a closed economy in which each country is a price taker, and in which changes in the rate of increase of the world money supply determine the rate of change of aggregate world demand and thus, *cet. par.*, the rate of world inflation. An increase in the world rate of inflation would occur if the world money supply increased more quickly than hitherto, as happened in the late 1960s because of a rise in the US money supply. The subsequent substitution of flexible for fixed exchange rates has allowed countries to determine their own rates of inflation, but these continue to be determined by excess aggregate demand and inflationary expectations. The same economists also regard this explanation as superior to the 'target real wage' theory of inflation which has become prominent in recent years and to which we now turn.

## REAL WAGE TARGETS

The basis of the theory is that unions are concerned with obtaining a target growth of real wages and use their bargaining strength to gain money wage increases that will achieve this end. The target is usually, though not invariably, thought of as the post-tax wage, though in an early article Sargan (1964) used the pre-tax wage. To reach this goal in an inflationary era involves unions estimating inflation over the period of a wage agreement; an underestimate will mean that the target will not be realised. In that event, unions are assumed to compensate for the failure by raising their money wage demands when they next bargain over wages, thereby raising the rate of inflation. An unanticipated increase in personal taxes during the term of a wage settlement can similarly frustrate real wage aspirations and lead subsequently to higher rates of inflation. The unemployment rate is often regarded as an additional possible influence on the size of money wage increases; when this is included, the equation for the target real wage theory resembles that for the price expectations augmented Phillips curve, with the addition of the term relating current money wage increases to the difference between actual and target real wages.

Economists associated with the Cambridge Economic Policy Group, such as Cripps and Godley (1976) and Coutts et al. (1976), adhere to a target theory of wage determination, but in their approach unions vary the length of wage agreements rather than forecast future inflation to enable them to achieve the target real wage. It is argued that initially, unions obtain the desired real wage which is then eroded by inflation. When the real wage declines to the minimum tolerable level, new wage settlements are reached to restore real wages to the target levels. The more rapid the inflation, the shorter the period between wage settlements.

The targets set by unions are clearly of critical importance for, as Artis (1981) observes, unattainable ones will cause an accelerating inflation as unions continually increase their money wage demands in a vain attempt to achieve the impossible. However, there is no direct evidence about the size of union target rates of real wage growth. If unions have these targets they do not announce them and, therefore, in testing the theory it is usually assumed that they are determined by the previous trend in real wage growth. In the absence of such evidence it is difficult to decide whether or not this is a plausible assumption. It may be equally realistic to suggest that unions aim to improve upon the trend rate of growth.

A number of studies have examined the hypothesis. It was noted earlier that Wilkinson and Turner (1972) argue that union militancy increased in the late 1960s partly because of the slow-down in real wage growth. Sargan (1964, 1971) has estimated the rate of change of money wages for the periods 1947–60 and 1949–68 using an equation that included a 'real wage catch-up term', so that if the real wage increase is different from the union target, money wage settlements would adjust accordingly. The target real wage was assumed to be generated by the time trend of real wage increase. Other variables included in the estimating equations were the rate of unemployment and, in the second study, the inflation rate. The results of the latter study indicate a target growth rate of 1.6 per cent p.a.; the catch-up variable was significant and showed that failure to reach the target caused a larger subsequent increase in money wages. The inflation variable was insignificant and had the wrong sign; and although unemployment was insignificant, higher rates were associated with lower rates of increase of money wages.

Sargan's work has been developed by Henry *et al.* (1976) who used his estimating equation for the longer period of 1948–74. The initial results were poor, but after amending the equation by replacing the pre-tax real wage rate with post-tax earnings, the empirical results showed strong support for the hypothesis with 2–2.5 per cent being the typical target increase in take-home earnings for much of the post-war period. The unemployment term was negatively signed and significant in the years 1948–66 but subsequently it became insignificant, indicating that unemployment had no appreciable effect upon wage inflation after 1966. From 1948 to 1966 the price variable was insignificant but subsequently became significant, possibly because of the higher rates of inflation in those years. On the basis of these results, the authors conclude that unions appear to be an important cause of wage inflation. Unfortunately for this hypothesis, the equation has been unsuccessful in forecasting subsequent increases in money wages. The equation was used by Henry and Ormerod (1978) to estimate money wage change from 1974 to 1977 and they found that in 1975 it predicts greater wage increases than actually occurred. The years 1975–78 were ones in which real wages rose by less than the assumed target rate of increase, yet money wages did not increase at the rate needed to compensate for this shortfall in real wage growth.

Investigation of the target hypothesis has also been carried out by Johnston and Timbrell (1974), building upon a wage-bargaining model developed by Johnston (1972). Their central hypothesis is that union members are concerned with the growth of their net real earnings, and that adverse changes in taxes and prices will result in higher wage claims and an increased willingness to use union bargaining power to achieve them. The problem for a cost-minimising employer is to form an estimate of the union's real wage claim: the minimum wage increase that will reduce the probability of a strike to negligible proportions. If, for example, workers have to pay higher taxes, the previously acceptable wage offer will no longer suffice and the probability of a strike (or some other form of industrial action) will increase. Faced with this threat, the employer will raise his wage offer and, therefore, increases in the estimated real claim lead to higher wage settlements. A higher expected rate of inflation will similarly also lead to larger wage awards. The proportion of gross wages paid in taxes (the retention ratio) and a measure of expected inflation were, therefore, two of the variables used in the empirical analysis of the movement in manual workers' money wages. Others were the rate of profit per unit of output and a measure of the time rate of discounting used by employers. As an alternative to regressing changes in money wages on these separate variables, Johnston and Timbrell also combined them to examine the effects of the failure of net real wages to grow at the hypothesised target rates of 2 and 3 per cent. The periods studied were 1957–71 and 1952–71. For the shorter one they find that a larger tax burden was related to higher subsequent wage settlements, and that when real net wage rates grew at a slower rate than the two assumed target rates, the rate of growth of money wages increased. For the whole sample period, price expectations had affected wages but the retention ratio and the target rate variables performed less satisfactorily. The authors note that the rise in the tax burden and the fall in the growth of real income were most pronounced in the second half of the 1960s, and they suggest that this explains the greater effect of the target wage in the shorter period. Their conclusion is that wage inflation was largely the result of successful union wage bargaining, prompted by the failure of net real wages to grow at the desired rate.

The various estimates and the theory underlying them are very controversial, and they have been criticised by a number of authors both within and without the cost-push school. As a theory of union wage policy it echoes the view of Samuel Gompers, the early American trade union leader, who, when asked what were the aims of American trade unions, replied 'more'; but, as Rees (1962) notes, this does not satisfy the economist who wants to know how much more. The failure in the empirical work to find evidence of an important unemployment effect on wages in recent years can be used to support the view that unions now pay little attention to unemployment; but alternatively it may reflect the fact that recorded unemployment became a poor measure of excess labour supply after the mid-1960s, and that inflationary expectations also changed. The theory's institutional roots seem less secure than those of the relativities approach. It has been seen that there is much evidence of unions citing movements in relative pay to justify their own wage demands, but no such evidence is referred to in discussions of the target theory. In fact the theory's expositors make little if any reference to the literature on union wage policy.

The failure to explain what determines union wage targets has prompted Wood (1978) to argue that the theory is 'quite hollow', as there is always some assumption about real wage targets which, given what has actually happened to real wages, is consistent with the observed behaviour of money wages. Sceptics would suggest that this is what is assumed when the target is based on the trend in real wage growth. Scott (1980) finds it difficult to accept that the UK has avoided an explosive inflation just because the target rates happen to equal productivity growth rates. Jackman et al. (1981) observe that if it is claimed that target rates are determined exogenously by unions, then equal target and productivity growth rates could only be regarded as coincidental. The theory's weakness is also demonstrated by its failure to predict wage movements from 1975 to 1978. It could be argued that the large increase in unemployment that occurred in those years caused unions to reduce their targets and thus their money wage demands, or alternatively that it became more difficult to achieve them in the face of more resistant employers. One does not need to resort to target wage theory to explain a link between rising unemployment and a lower rate of increase of money wages however; standard economic theory is quite adequate.

Two further issues that the theory needs to address are the effects of the so-called 'social wage', and the international aspects of inflation. The studies cited have not included the social wage in their measurement of real wages, yet workers may consider that a better Health Service, for example, is some compensation for an increase in personal taxation. If so, this will moderate money wage demands arising from higher taxation. The studies also confine themselves to explaining UK inflation, yet other theories have recognised the need to come to terms with the similar inflationary experience of many countries, and it would seem important for the target theory to do likewise.

Another criticism is that the empirical results can be interpreted as supporting a competitive rather than a monopolistic theory of wages. Competitive theory predicts that the real wage will rise as the marginal product of labour increases if the supply of labour is less than perfectly elastic, and that in equilibrium, the real wage equals labour's marginal product. At a real wage below the equilibrium level, labour demand will exceed supply and money wages will rise to clear the market. If, therefore, real wages have lagged behind the trend increase in marginal productivity (Parkin 1978), the process of adjustment in the labour market may be the explanation of the catch-up variable described earlier, rather than it being regarded as compensation for failure to reach a real wage growth target. In fact Sargan (1971) acknowledges that while his results at the aggregate level can be used to support the target hypothesis, they can also be interpreted as supportive of a competitive wage determination model of the kind formulated by Kuh (1967).

In the light of these criticisms, a degree of scepticism is called for in treating real wage growth as a sound theory of union wage policy, let alone a theory of inflation. It is a relatively new approach to union wage policy, and in the absence of a generally acceptable theory it seems premature to use it to fill the void.

The development of the target theory in recent years means that there are now two rather distinct explanations of inflation in terms of union bargaining power. To some extent they are complementary, for as noted above, some writers believe that reductions in real wages intensify resentments about relativities; but it is also possible for them to conflict. Dissatisfaction with relative pay can presumably cause inflation even if real wages are growing at the target rate; failure to achieve the latter will do likewise, even if the wage structure is widely regarded as equitable. The policy implications of the theories may also differ. If wages are determined by real wage targets, policies to contain inflation must presumably focus on educating workers to accept feasible targets or on adopting measures aimed at generating economic growth. Artis (1981) suggests that incomes policies might have an educative effect, while the Cambridge Group advocate policies which they believe will generate higher real income growth and are sceptical about incomes policies. Alternatively, if competitive wage bargaining over relativities provides the inflationary impetus, the achievement of real wage targets would not be the whole solution to wage-push inflation, and policy must be concerned with wage differentials. Incomes policies might help for, according to Tobin (1972:13), 'The trick is to find a formula for mutual de-escalation which does not offend conceptions of relative equity.' One suggestion is that synchronised wage settlements would help to persuade workers that their position in the wage structure would not deteriorate if they moderated their wage demands in line with a policy norm (Llewellyn 1980). A feature common to both theories is that they now regard quite high levels of unemployment as insufficient to constrain union wage bargaining. Given that the early fears of wage-push inflation sprang from the apparent removal of the fear of unemployment, this is indeed a marked change in cost-push theorising.

In each theory dissatisfaction with wages causes unions to exert more pressure on employers to induce them to grant acceptable wage increases. More industrial action may be one result of this and economists have, therefore, looked for evidence of a union effect on inflation by examining the relationship between strikes and wages. Before examining this work it is worth noting that union pressure to raise wages need not involve industrial action. Thus in an environment of 'guaranteed full employment', government willingness to increase the supply of money in response to union wage push not only dilutes union fears about unemployment but also employers' fears about profits. In these circumstances wage increases would be conceded without industrial action, and strike activity becomes an unreliable guide to the inflationary impact of unions.

## STRIKES AND WAGES

A study by Godfrey (1971) used the number of strikes as a measure of union militancy. For the years 1956–69 he examined the relationship between the number of strikes beginning in each quarter and the rate of change of wage rates, with unemployment and price inflation as the other variables in the regression. He found that strikes were an important determinant of the rate of change of wage rates. Subsequent work by Godfrey and Taylor (1973), using earnings rather than wage rates and a measure of excess labour demand which included labour hoarding, also found the number of strikes to have a significant influence upon the rate of wage inflation for the years 1954–70. Contradictory results were reported, however, by Ward and Zis (1974) who examined wage inflation in the manufacturing industries of the UK, France, West Germany, Italy, Belgium and the Netherlands from 1956 to 1971, with the rate of increase in male hourly wage rates as the dependent variable. In addition to the number of strikes, working days lost because of strikes and the number of striking workers were also used as regressors, while the rate of unemployment was used to represent labour market conditions and a lagged price change variable to proxy price expectations. The results indicated that strikes did not affect wage inflation, with the possible exceptions of Italy and France. In a subsequent paper Zis (1977) re-estimated Godfrey's 1971 equation using annual rather than quarterly strike data, as there is evidence (Goodman 1967; Turner et al. 1967) that strikes have a seasonal pattern. The results showed strikes to have a negative effect upon wage inflation. In view of these conflicting findings, it would clearly be wrong to reach a firm conclusion about the relationship between strike activity and inflation. Even if a positive relationship were established, it would not necessarily provide evidence of a causal relationship showing wage inflation to be the result of union militancy, for changes in macroeconomic variables are themselves likely to influence strike activity.

Models of collective bargaining often predict that strikes occur because negotiators miscalculate each other's intentions (Zeuthen 1930; Nash 1950). Thus Rees (1952) argues that worker and employer expectations may diverge at the peak of the business cycle, when workers expect the prosperous times to continue while employers begin to see signs of a decline in activity. Strikes can occur, therefore, because unions overestimate the wage employers are willing to pay, and different expectations could be the reason for the cyclical pattern of American strike activity. Changes in the rate of inflation are also likely to increase uncertainty if employers and unions form different expectations about the future course of inflation and also, therefore, about the acceptable level of wage settlements. Inflation thus becomes a cause and not an effect of increased strike activity, and strike incidence becomes an unreliable indicator of union militancy. A number of statistical studies have in fact found that economic conditions are important in explaining strike frequency, including those of Pencavel (1970), Knight (1972), Shorey (1977), Davies (1979) and Smith (1980). Though the results are diverse, important variables are price inflation, the level of real profits, and changes in productivity, with incomes policies having a temporary influence.

These are not the only problems that arise when strikes are used as a proxy for union militancy. The number of strikes is not the sole measure of strike activity. Working days lost because of strikes and the number of workers involved in strikes in any period are two others and, as Purdy and Zis (1974) note, these variables might be a more appropriate measure of militancy. Do a large number of short strikes involving small numbers of workers represent more or less militancy than a few lengthy ones in which many workers are involved? There are also other forms of industrial action, such as work to rule, overtime bans and withdrawal of co-operation, which Clegg (1979) states are probably more common than strikes. An ideal index of industrial action would incorporate them, but in its absence strikes have become the focus of investigation. The studies cited above do, of course, recognise many of these problems, but their existence increases the need for caution in using variations in strike activity to indicate union militancy. This is particularly relevant to recent British experience where the annual average number of working days lost in stoppages rose approximately threefold in the years 1968–77 compared with 1958–67 (Smith 1980), at a time of much higher inflation. As Flemming (1976) notes, the increase in strike activity was unlikely to be independent of the previous experience of inflation.

## UNION MEMBERSHIP AND WAGES

An alternative method of judging union power is to use union membership figures on the assumption that, *cet. par.*, high membership signifies a powerful union and rising membership, increasing strength. It seems reasonable, therefore, to correlate changes in money wages with each of these variables, but in doing so one must be careful to note Friedman and Schwartz's (1963) warning not to confuse 'high' with 'rising'. It was mentioned earlier that conventional theory suggests that unions will aim at achieving an optimum wage for their members, which will change only if the constraints within which they operate alter. Thus a nation with a high union density such as the UK may have a higher wage level because of this, but not a rising one. Even increasing membership may not result in a union growing steadily more powerful as the relationship between membership and power is unlikely to be linear. If, for example, membership amounts to 90 per cent of a firm's employees another 10 per cent will make little difference; and similarly for a union with 15 per cent rather than 10 per cent of its potential membership. There are criticisms of conventional theory, however, and Chamberlain (1959) and Okun (1981) suggest that union monopoly power differs from that of firms in being essentially dynamic. Trade unionists, it is claimed, will not be satisfied with receiving the same relative wage advantage year after year and will press their leaders to do more for them. The same view of union behaviour is suggested by Brown (1979:3):

> Is there a mechanism capable of producing a stream of wage demands, at least some of which are at least partly satisfied? Of course there is: the stream of demands is sufficiently explained by the simple human desire for more — for more absolutely in general, and for more in relation to selected reference groups in particular; and by the urge of the officials of trade and professional unions to justify their existence and stave off competition by getting these desires satisfied.

A study by Thomas (1974) examined the relationship between wage inflation and union density for a number of industries in the years 1962–70. He found that the degree of unionisation increased the rate of wage inflation associated with a given rate of unemployment, i.e. it raised the position of the short-run Phillips curve. He also found that changes in unemployment, when unemployment was low, caused greater changes in wages in low unionisation industries than in high unionisation ones, and vice versa, i.e. it changed the slope of the Phillips curve. To explain the slow union response in tight labour markets he suggested the delays caused by lengthy collective bargaining procedures. These results were largely confirmed by a time-series study of aggregate data for the years 1893–1972 (Thomas 1977), but in this case there was no evidence that unions retarded wage change in low unemployment periods, perhaps because of the very small variation in total union density in the early post-war years of high employment. Some North American studies, such as those by Vanderkamp (1966) and Pierson (1968), also find that the Phillips curves for the strongly unionised sectors of the economy lie above those of their weaker brethren.

In the UK, however, most of the work on union membership and inflation has been concerned with changes in union density, and the most prominent studies have been those of Hines (1964, 1968, 1969, 1971). He proposed that such changes are an indicator of the militancy of unions, on the grounds that militant action to advance a wage claim will be accompanied by efforts to strengthen the union by increasing its membership. Not only will a larger membership reduce an employer's ability to substitute non-union for union labour, but it will also stiffen the resolve of the members during negotiations. More militancy accompanied by more trade unionists will result in higher wages, therefore, and union membership statistics provide a means of measuring union pressure on wages. Now while this is a plausible hypothesis about some union bargaining, no evidence is provided as to how extensive it is in the UK and, in any case, it cannot apply to all negotiations. There are unions with 100 per cent membership and, as noted earlier, even those with somewhat less may gain little from extra members. For these unions, increasing the strike fund may be a better way of impressing employers than expenditure on recruitment. Hines's hypothesis is not, therefore, a necessary condition for success in union bargaining.

Hines (1964) tested the hypothesis for the years 1893–1961, using the proportion of the labour force unionised as well as its change in the estimating equations, together with unemployment as a measure of excess labour demand, and the rate of change of prices lagged by 6 months. The results indicated that the rate of change of unionisation was an important explanatory variable for the whole period and for each of the three sub-periods. For the 1893–1912 period it accounted for almost half the variation in wage rates; between the wars over 90 per cent, and for 1949–61 almost two-thirds. After the Second World War increases in density were found to have a greater effect on wages than hitherto. Two possible explanations were suggested: at the relatively high level of post-war membership, union recruitment may have become more difficult and a given change in union density may represent more militancy than in the pre-war years of lower membership; alternatively, imitative wage behaviour may have become more pronounced, so that the effective link between membership and wages was confined to a few industries whose wage increases spread elsewhere independently of union membership change. Hines also found that the unemployment variable became insignificant in wage equations containing changes in both union density and the price level, a result suggesting the subordination of market to institutional forces in wage determination. Moreover, unemployment and other indices of excess demand did not explain the variance in union density apart from the 1893–1912 period, so that changes in union density could not be interpreted as representing changes in excess labour demand; although in a study of union growth between 1893 and 1970, Bain and Elsheikh (1976) found that unemployment had a negative and significant effect upon union growth. Hines's subsequent articles, including an inter-industry study for 1948–62 (Hines 1969) and a macro one for 1949–69 (Hines 1971), confirm his earlier conclusion that money wage inflation is significantly associated with his measure of union militancy.

Both the statistical results and their interpretation have been subjected to much critical scrutiny. Thomas and Stoney (1970) showed that the three-equation model used by Hines in the original article was dynamically unstable, but they also showed that by redefining the price variable the model became stable. Purdy and Zis (1974) re-estimated Hines's equations after making various adjustments to his data. The self-employed and armed forces were excluded from the labour force in measuring union density, on the grounds that they would not be candidates for union membership. The gross domestic product price deflator used by Hines for much of the period was replaced by the index of retail prices, and an annual index of wage rates was used rather than one based on end of December wage rates. With these and other revisions, Purdy and Zis found that variations in union density were still a significant variable in explaining wage change, but that they were much less important than suggested by Hines's work. As noted by Parkin (1978) Hines's result for 1949–69 indicates that a 1 per cent proportionate change in density causes an 8 per cent increase in wages, while according to Purdy and Zis it produces a rise of only 0.5 per cent.

Having found a much smaller union wage effect while working with Hines's hypothesis, Purdy and Zis go on to a more substantive criticism. They point out that a changing distribution of the labour force between heavily and lightly unionised industries, and variations in the number of workers covered by the closed shop, will cause changes in union density unconnected with intensified union recruitment campaigns. They proceed to estimate an index of change in union density which corrects for such developments. Regressing the rate of change of wages on this 'pure militancy index' for the inter-war years showed a significant but very small effect, while for the years 1949–61 the result was insignificant and the militancy variable had the wrong sign. Purdy and Zis conclude that there are substantial grounds for doubting the adequacy of Hines's measure of union militancy. In a subsequent exchange (Dogas and Hines 1975; Purdy and Zis 1976), the respective authors have reaffirmed their basic positions. However, the latter's conclusions are broadly confirmed by Henry et al. (1976) in their study of wage inflation for 1949–74. For the sub-period to 1966, which includes Hines's post-war estimating period, and for the whole period studied, they did not find that changes in union density affected money wage inflation. Wilkinson and Burkitt (1973), after respecifying Hines's wage and unionisation data so that they were both measured at the mid-point of the year, also found that the relationship between the union density variables and changes in wages was very weak in a study of twelve industries in the years 1949–62. In two further studies a different data source of union membership was employed in estimates for the inter-war years (Burkitt 1974) and for the years 1949–67 (Burkitt and Bowers 1976). The first study did find a significant positive relationship between the rate of change of earnings and the rate of change of unionisation, but the latter results for thirty industries showed a predominantly insignificant association. Different specifications of the relevant variables can therefore, considerably alter the results.

There are other points which need to be considered in evaluating Hines's work. If the union effect on relative wages is a positive one then, as noted by Mulvey and Gregory (1977), a rise in union density for reasons other than a rise in union militancy will inevitably cause the general wage level to rise. Moreover, Purdy and Zis suggest that simultaneous increases in union membership and wages may be due to workers joining trade unions during pay negotiations in order to claim entitlement to union strike benefit if negotiations break down; an increase in union density could then be regarded as an indicator of workers' estimates of employer intransigence rather than their own militancy. In sum, therefore, it is clear that there are many criticisms of Hines's results and, as with the strike variable, changes in union density in the period covered by the studies have not been generally accepted as providing convincing proof of the cost-push hypothesis.

The problems associated with using membership as an indicator of union power can also be illustrated by more recent experience. In the years 1968–76 union density rose by about 20 per cent and, as this coincided with both increased strike activity and inflation, it is not surprising that it has been cited as evidence that increased militancy caused the serious inflation of those years. But, as with the strike variable, it can be argued that the growth in membership was itself the result of inflation. Thus Price and Bain (1976), using the union growth model of Bain and Elsheikh (1976), found that the rates of both price and wage inflation had been significant determinants of union membership growth in the post-war years to 1974. Possible reasons for this are that substantial increases in money wages stimulate union membership because workers, rightly or wrongly, credit unions with these gains, and that higher inflation, by threatening employee living standards, encourages union membership. Another point, suggested by Smith (1980), is that unanticipated inflation adds to worker uncertainty about the appropriate size of wage increases and increases employee demand for unions as specialised information gatherers. Moreover, much of this growth in union membership and in strikes occurred among public sector workers, and it has been argued that both were the response of these workers to incomes policies which they felt discriminated against them (Elliott and Fallick 1981).

Noting the difficulties in using either membership or strike data to represent union power does not, of course, disprove the thesis. Increased union militancy can result in more strikes and greater membership and, even if these developments are initially the product of inflation, they can in turn add to it. Many economists remain persuaded that union militancy has been a cause of inflation. Thus, while Williamson and Wood (1976) believe that excess demand was responsible for UK inflation up to the mid-1960s, and that excessive monetary expansion caused it to accelerate in 1974—75, they consider that increased militancy is the most plausible explanation of the 1969—70 wage explosion. Meade (1971) and Perry (1975) also suggest that this experience was the result of increased union pressure. Nevertheless, the evidence can be explained within the framework of an excess demand cum expectations theory of inflation.

## 4.   Conclusion

The controversy about the inflationary role of trade unions shows little sign of being resolved, despite its longevity. It persists largely because of the lack of a well-established model of union behaviour; neither of the cost-push theories discussed constitutes such a model. The strength of the relativities approach lies in the evidence, from many studies, that wage comparisons have an important effect upon wages, but this interaction has not been developed into a model which could produce testable hypotheses about the future course of inflation. In contrast, the target theory is not short of empirical testing, but it is deficient in explaining how the supposed targets are determined. Nevertheless, despite these weaknesses, the evidence has persuaded many economists that unions have been an important cause of inflation. Wiles (1973:391) confesses: 'I have indeed no model. If "model" means an enclosed self-actuating working model of a human society subject to cost inflation, I am not clever enough. I am only clever enough to observe that all the existing models, which exclude cost inflation, are quite false. ...'

Historically, cost-push theorising has evolved from a concern with the inflationary potential of a 'full employment guarantee' to the question of how to explain the juxtaposition of high unemployment and inflation. The explanation of inflation in the high employment years had a persuasive logic behind it in that it is based on the removal of the unemployment constraint on union behaviour and, in this respect, is an application of orthodox economic theory. Subsequent inflationary experience has been explained by referring to the greater use of union power prompted by the increased militancy of trade unionists, but the difficulties of verifying this thesis directly have been noted.

The alternative explanation of post-war inflation is that it is largely the result of increases in the supply of money and the development of inflationary expectations. Wage inflation increases when the excess demand for labour rises or when workers expect price inflation to accelerate; wage relativities and wage targets have no place in this approach. In some monetarist expositions, such as those of Johnson (1972) and Parkin (1974), the wage-push argument is seen as a resort to amateur and undergraduate sociology with no credence attached to it. But, despite their rather *ad hoc* treatment in the literature, the features of the UK labour market examined in this survey are believed by many economists to be crucially relevant to an understanding of inflation.

## References

**Artis, M. J.** (1981) Incomes policies: some rationales, in Fallick, J. L. and Elliott, R. F. (eds), *Incomes Policies, Inflation and Relative Pay,* Allen & Unwin: London.

**Ashenfelter, O.** (1976) Union relative wage effects: new evidence and a survey of their implications for wage inflation, Princeton University, mimeo.

**Ashenfelter, O. and Johnson, G. E.** (1972) Unionism, relative wages, and labour quality in US manufacturing industry, *International Economic Review,* 13, 488–508.

**Azariadis, C.** (1975) Implicit contracts and underemployment equilibria, *Journal of Political Economy,* 83, 1183–202.

**Bain, G. S.** (1970) *The Growth of White Collar Trade Unionism,* Oxford University Press.

**Bain, G. S. and Elsheikh, F.** (1976) *Union Growth and the Business Cycle,* Blackwell: Oxford. ·

**Baxter, J. L.** (1973) Inflation in the context of relative deprivation and social justice, *Scottish Journal of Political Economy,* 20, 262–82.

**Becker, G. S.** (1964) *Human Capital: A Theoretical and Empirical Analysis with Special Reference to Education,* National Bureau of Economic Research: New York.

**Behrend, H.** (1973) *Incomes Policy, Equity and Pay Increase Differentials,* Scottish Academic Press: Edinburgh.

**Beveridge, W. H.** (1944) *Full Employment in a Free Society,* Allen & Unwin: London.

**Blackburn, R. M.** (1967) *Union Character and Social Class,* Batsford: London.

**Bowers, J. K.** (1979) The theory of cost inflation, in Bowers, J. K. (ed.), *Inflation, Development and Integration,* Leeds University Press.

**Brechling, F. P. R.** (1973) Wage inflation and the structure of regional unemployment, *Journal of Money, Credit and Banking,* 5, 355–79.

**Brown, A. J.** (1979) Inflation and the British sickness, *Economic Journal,* 89, 1–12.

**Brown, W. A.** (1980) The structure of pay bargaining in Britain, in Blackaby, F. T. (ed.), *The Future of Pay Bargaining,* Heinemann: London.

**Brown, W. A. and Sissons, K.** (1975) The use of comparisons in workplace wage determination, *British Journal of Industrial Relations,* 13, 23–53.

**Burkitt, B.** (1974) The relationship between earnings and unionisation in the inter-war years, *Applied Economics,* **6,** 83–93.

**Burkitt, B. and Bowers, D.** (1976) Wage inflation and union power in the United Kingdom, *Applied Economics,* **8,** 289–300.

**Burton, J. and Addison, J. T.** (1977) The institutional analysis of wage inflation: a critical appraisal, in Ehrenberg, R. G. (ed.), *Research in Labour Economics,* Vol. 1, JAI Press: Connecticut.

**Chamberlain, E. H.** (1959) Labour union power and the public interest, in Bradley, P. D. (ed.), *The Public Stake in Union Power,* University of Virginia Press: Charlottesville.

**Clegg, H. A.** (1971) *How to Run an Incomes Policy,* Heinemann Educational Books: London.

**Clegg, H. A.** (1979) *The Changing System of Industrial Relations in Great Britain,* Blackwell: Oxford.

**Clegg, H. A., Fox, A. and Thompson, A. F.** (1964) *A History of British Trade Unions since 1889,* Oxford University Press.

**Copeland, L. S.** (1977) Wage inflation, productivity and wage-leadership, *Manchester School,* **45,** 258–69.

**Coutts, K. Tarling, R. and Wilkinson, F.** (1976) Wage bargaining and the inflation process, *Cambridge Economic Policy Review,* **2,** 20–7.

**Cowling, K. and Metcalf, D.** (1967) Wage – unemployment relationships: a regional analysis for the UK 1960–1965, *Bulletin of the Oxford University Institute of Economics and Statistics,* **29,** 31–9.

**Creedy, J.** (1979) A note on the analysis of trade unions and relative wages, *Bulletin of the Oxford University Institute of Economics and Statistics,* **40,** 39–46.

**Cripps, F. and Godley, W.** (1976) A formal analysis of the Cambridge economic policy group model, *Economica,* **43,** 335–48.

**Daniel, W. W.** (1977) *The Next Stage of Incomes Policy,* Political and Economic Planning Report 568, London.

**Davies, R. J.** (1979) Economic activity, incomes policy and strikes: a quantitative analysis, *British Journal of Industrial Relations,* **17,** 205–23.

**Demery, D. and McNabb, R.** (1978) The effects of demand on the union relative wage effect in the United Kingdom, *British Journal of Industrial Relations,* **16,** 303–8.

**Dogas, D. and Hines, A. G.** (1975) Trade unions and wage inflation in the UK: a critique of Purdy and Zis, *Applied Economics,* **7,** 195–211.

**Dunlop, J. T.** (1950) *Wage Determination under Trade Unions,* Basil Blackwell: Oxford.

**Dunlop, J. T.** (1957) The task of contemporary wage theory, in Taylor, G. T. and Pierson, F. C. (eds), *New Concepts in Wage Determination,* McGraw-Hill: New York and London.

**Eatwell, J., Llewellyn, J. and Tarling, R.** (1974) Money wage inflation in industrial countries, *Review of Economic Studies,* **41,** 515–23.

**Edgren, G., Faxén, K. O. and Odhner, C. E.** (1969) Wages, growth and the distribution of income, *Swedish Journal of Economics,* **71,** 133–60.

**Elliott, R. F.** (1976) The national wage round in the United Kingdom: a sceptical view, *Bulletin of the Oxford University Institute of Economics and Statistics,* **38,** 179–201.

**Elliott, R. F. and Fallick, J. L.** (1981) *Pay in the Public Sector,* Macmillan: London.

**Fellner, W.** (1959) Demand inflation, cost inflation, and collective bargaining, in Bradley, P. D. (ed.), *The Public Stake in Union Power,* University of Virginia Press: Charlottesville.

**Flanders, A.** (1967) *Collective Bargaining: Prescription for Change,* Faber & Faber: London.

**Flanders, A.** (1970) *Management and Unions,* Faber & Faber: London.

**Flemming, J. S.** (1976) *Inflation,* Oxford University Press.

**Freeman, R. B.** (1976) Individual mobility and union voice in the labour market, *American Economic Review Proceedings,* **66**, 361–8.

**Friedman, M.** (1976) *Price Theory,* Aldine: Chicago (2nd edn).

**Friedman, M. and Schwartz, A. J.** (1963) *A Monetary History of the United States, 1867–1960,* Princeton University Press.

**Godfrey, L.** (1971) The Phillips curve: incomes policy and trade union effects, in Johnson, H. G. and Nobay, A. R. (eds), *The Current Inflation,* Macmillan: London.

**Godfrey, L. and Taylor, J.** (1973) Earnings changes in the UK, 1954–70: excess labour supply, expected inflation and union influence, *Bulletin of the Oxford University Institute of Economics and Statistics,* **35**, 197–216.

**Goodman, J. F. B.** (1967) Strikes in the United Kingdom, *International Labour Review,* **95**, 465–81.

**Hahn, F.** (1982) *Money and Inflation,* Basil Blackwell: Oxford.

**Haberler, G.** (1959) Wage policy and inflation, in Bradley, P. D. (ed.), *The Public Stake in Union Power,* University of Virginia Press: Charlottesville.

**Hart, R. A. and Mackay, D. I.** (1977) Wage inflation, regional policy and the regional earnings structure, *Economica,* **44**, 267–81.

**Hayek, F. A.** (1959) Unions, inflation and profits, in Bradley, P. D. (ed.), *The Public Stake in Union Power,* University of Virginia Press: Charlottesville.

**Henry, S. G. B. and Ormerod, P. A.** (1978) Incomes policies and wage inflation: empirical evidence for the UK 1961–1977, *National Institute Economic Review,* **85**, 31–9.

**Henry, S. G. B., Sawyer, M. C. and Smith, P.** (1976) Models of inflation in the United Kingdom: an evaluation, *National Institute Economic Review,* **77**, 60–71.

**Hicks, J. R.** (1955) The economic foundations of wage policy, *Economic Journal,* **66**, 389–404.

**Hicks, J. R.** (1974) *The Crisis in Keynesian Economics,* Blackwell: Oxford.

**Hicks, J. R.** (1975) What is wrong with monetarism?, *Lloyds Bank Review,* **118**, 1–13.

**Hicks, J. R.** (1976) Must stimulating demand stimulate inflation?, *Economic Record,* **52**, 409–22.

**Hines, A. G.** (1964) Trade unions and wage inflation in the United Kingdom, 1893–1961, *Review of Economic Studies,* **31**, 221–52.

**Hines, A. G.** (1968) Unemployment and the rate of change of money wage rates in the United Kingdom 1862–1963: a reappraisal, *Review of Economics and Statistics,* **50**, 60–7.

**Hines, A. G.** (1969) Wage inflation in the United Kingdom 1948–1962: a disaggregated study, *Economic Journal,* **79**, 66–89.

**Hines, A. G.** (1971) The determinants of the rate of change of money wage rates and the effectiveness of incomes policy, in Johnson, H. G. and Nobay, A. R. (eds), *The Current Inflation,* Macmillan: London.

**Holt, C. C.** (1970) Job search, Phillips' wage relation, and union influence: theory and evidence, in Phelps, E. S. *et al., Microeconomic Foundations of Employment and Inflation Theory,* Macmillan: London.

**Hyman, R. and Brough, I.** (1975) *Social Values and Industrial Relations,* Blackwell: Oxford.

**Jackman, R., Mulvey, C. and Trevithick, J.** (1981) *The Economics of Inflation,* Martin Robertson: Oxford.

**Jackson, D. and Turner, H. A.** (1972) Inflation, strato-inflation and social conflict, in Jackson, D., Turner, H. A. and Wilkinson, F., *Do Trade Unions Cause Inflation?*, University of Cambridge, Department of Applied Economics, Occasional Paper 36.

**Johnson, G. E.** (1975) Economic analysis of trade unionism, *American Economic Review, Papers and Proceedings*, **65**, 23–8.

**Johnson, H. G.** (1972) Panel discussion: world inflation, in Claassen, E. and Salin, P. (eds), *Stabilisation Policies in Interdependent Economies*, North-Holland Publishing: Amsterdam and London.

**Johnson, H. G. and Mieszkowski, P.** (1970) The effects of unionisation on the distribution of income: a general equilibrium approach, *Quarterly Journal of Economics*, **84**, 539–61.

**Johnston, J.** (1972) A model of wage determination under bilateral monopoly, *The Economic Journal*, **82**, 837–52.

**Johnston, J. and Timbrell, M.** (1974) Empirical tests of a bargaining theory of wage rate determination, in Laidler, D. and Purdy, D. (eds), *Inflation and Labour Markets*, Manchester University Press.

**Kalecki, M.** (1944) Three ways to full employment, in Oxford University Institute of Statistics, *The Economics of Full Employment*, Blackwell: Oxford.

**Keynes, J. M.** (1936) *The General Theory of Employment, Interest and Money*, Macmillan: London.

**Knight, J. B. and Mabro, R.** (1972) On the determination of the general wage level: a comment, *Economic Journal*, **82**, 677–86.

**Knight, K. G.** (1972) Strikes and wage inflation in British manufacturing industry, 1950–68, *Bulletin of the Oxford University Institute of Economics and Statistics*, **34**, 281–94.

**Knowles, K. G. J. C.** (1962) Wages and productivity, in Worswick, G. D. N. and Ady, P. H., *The British Economy in the Nineteenth Fifties*, Oxford University Press.

**Knowles, K. G. J. C. and Robinson, D.** (1962) Wage rounds and wage policy, *Bulletin of the Oxford University Institute of Economics and Statistics*, **24**, 269–329.

**Kuh, E.** (1967) A productivity theory of wage levels – an alternative to the Phillips curve, *Review of Economic Studies*, **34**, 333–60.

**Laidler, D. E. W. and Parkin, J. M.** (1975) Inflation – a survey, *Economic Journal*, **85**, 741–809.

**Layard, R., Metcalf, D. and Nickell, S.** (1978) The effect of collective bargaining on relative and absolute wages, *British Journal of Industrial Relations*, **16**, 287–302.

**Lerner, S. W., Cable, J. R. and Gupta, S.** (1969) *Workshop Wage Determination*, Pergamon Press: Oxford.

**Lerner, S. W. and Marquand, J.** (1963) Regional variations in earnings, demand for labour and shop steward combine committees in the British engineering industry, *Manchester School*, **31**, 261–96.

**Lewis, H. G.** (1963) *Unionism and Relative Wages in the United States*, University of Chicago Press.

**Lindbeck, A.** (1977) *The Political Economy of the New Left*, Harper and Row: New York.

**Lipsey, R. G.** (1979) World inflation, *Economic Record*, **55**, 283–96.

**Llewellyn, D. T.** (1980) Can monetary targets influence wage bargaining?, *The Banker*, **130**, 49–53.

**Lockwood, D.** (1958) *The Blackcoated Worker*, Allen & Unwin: London.

**Lydall, H. F.** (1958) Inflation and the earnings gap, *Bulletin of the Oxford University*

*Institute of Economics and Statistics*, **20**, 285–304.

**Machlup, F.** (1960) Another view of cost-push and demand-pull inflation, *Review of Economics and Statistics*, **42**, 125–39.

**Mackay, D. I., Boddy, D., Brack, J., Diack, J. A. and Jones, N.** (1971) *Labour Markets under Different Employment Conditions*, Allen & Unwin: London.

**Mayhew, K.** (1981) Incomes policies and the private sector, in Fallick, J. L. and Elliott, R. F. (eds), *Incomes Policies, Inflation and Relative Pay*, Allen & Unwin: London.

**Meade, J. E.** (1971) *Wages and Prices in a Mixed Economy*, Institute of Economic Affairs: London.

**Metcalf, D.** (1977) Unions, incomes policy and relative wages in Britain, *British Journal of Industrial Relations*, **15**, 157–75.

**Metcalf, D., Nickell, S. and Richardson, R.** (1976) The structure of hours and earnings in British manufacturing industry, *Oxford Economic Papers*, **28**, 284–303.

**Minford, P. and Peel, D.** (1981) Is the government's economic strategy on course?, *Lloyds Bank Review*, **April**, 1–19.

**Mitchell, D. J. B.** (1980) Unions, wages and inflation, *The Brookings Institution*, Washington, DC.

**Mulvey, C.** (1976) Collective agreements and relative earnings in UK manufacturing in 1973, *Economica*, **43**, 419–27.

**Mulvey, C. and Abowd, J. M.** (1980) Estimating the union/non-union wage differential: a statistical issue, *Economica*, **47**, 73–9.

**Mulvey, C. and Foster, J. I.** (1976) Occupational earnings in the UK and the effects of collective agreements, *Manchester School*, **44**, 258–75.

**Mulvey, C. and Gregory, M.** (1977) The Hines wage inflation model, *Manchester School*, **45**, 29–40.

**Nash, J. F.** (1950) The bargaining problem, *Econometrica*, **18**, 155–62.

**National Board for Prices and Incomes** (1966) *General Report, no. 19, April 1965–July 1966*, HMSO: London.

**Nickell, S. J.** (1977) Trade unions and the position of women in the industrial wage structure, *British Journal of Industrial Relations*, **15**, 192–210.

**OEEC** (1961) *The Problem of Rising Prices*, Organisation for European Economic Cooperation: Paris.

**Okun, A. M.** (1981) *Prices and Quantities: A Macroeconomic Analysis*, Blackwell: Oxford.

**Parkin, J. M.** (1974) United Kingdom inflation: the policy alternatives, *National Westminster Bank Quarterly Review*, **May**, 32–47.

**Parkin, M.** (1978) Alternative explanations of the United Kingdom inflation: a survey, in Parkin, M. and Sumner, M. T. (eds), *Inflation in the United Kingdom*, Manchester University Press.

**Parsley, C. J.** (1980) Labour union effects on wage gains: a survey of recent literature, *Journal of Economic Literature*, **18**, 1–31.

**Pencavel, J. H.** (1970) An investigation into industrial strike activity in Britain, *Economica*, **37**, 239–65.

**Pencavel, J. H.** (1974) Relative wages and trade unions in the United Kingdom, *Economica*, **41**, 194–210.

**Perry, G. L.** (1975) Determinants of wage inflation around the world, *Brookings Papers on Economic Activity*, **1975:2**, 403–35.

**Phelps Brown, E. H.** (1966) The influence of trade unions and collective bargaining on pay levels and pay structure, *Minutes of Evidence 38, Royal Commission on Trade Unions and Employers' Associations*, HMSO: London.

**Phelps Brown, E. H.** (1971) The analysis of wage movements under full employment, *Scottish Journal of Political Economy,* **18,** 233–43.

**Phelps Brown, E. H.** (1975) A non-monetarist view of the pay explosion, *Three Banks Review,* **105,** 3–24.

**Pierson, G.** (1968) The effect of union strength on the US Phillips curve, *American Economic Review,* **58,** 456–67.

**Price, R. and Bain, G. S.** (1976) Union growth revisited: 1948–74 in perspective, *British Journal of Industrial Relations,* **14,** 339–55.

**Purdy, D. L. and Zis, G.** (1974) On the concept and measurement of union militancy, in Laidler, D. E. W. and Purdy, D. L. (eds), *Inflation and Labour Markets,* Manchester University Press.

**Purdy, D. L. and Zis, G.** (1976) Trade unions and wage inflation in the UK: a reply to Dogas and Hines, *Applied Economics,* **8,** 249–65.

**Reder, M. W.** (1948) The theoretical problems of a national wage – price policy, *Canadian Journal of Economics and Political Science,* **14,** 46–61.

**Reder, M. W.** (1962) Wage structure theory and measurement, in National Bureau of Economic Research, *Aspects of Labour Economics,* Princeton University Press.

**Reder, M.** (1965) Unions and wages: the problem of measurement, *Journal of Political Economy,* **73,** 188–96.

**Rees, A.** (1952) Industrial conflict and business fluctuations, *Journal of Political Economy,* **60,** 371–82.

**Rees, A.** (1962) *The Economics of Trade Unions,* Cambridge University Press.

**Rees, A.** (1963) The effects of unions on resource allocation, *Journal of Law and Economics,* **6,** 69–78.

**Rees, A.** (1979) *The Economics of Work and Pay,* Harper and Row: New York (2nd ed).

**Richardson, R. and Catlin, S.** (1979) Trade union density and collective agreement patterns in Britain, *British Journal of Industrial Relations,* **17,** 376–85.

**Robinson, D.** (1970) External and internal labour markets, in Robinson, D. (ed.), *Local Labour Markets and Wage Structures,* Gower Press: London.

**Robinson, J.** (1937) *Essays in the Theory of Employment,* Macmillan: London.

**Ross, A. M.** (1948) *Trade Union Wage Policy,* University of California Press.

**Ross, A. M.** (1957) The external wage structure, in Taylor, G. W. and Pierson, F. C. (eds), *New Concepts in Wage Determination,* McGraw-Hill: New York.

**Royal Commission on Trade Unions and Employers' Association** (1968) HMSO: London.

**Runciman, W. G.** (1966) *Relative Deprivation and Social Justice: a Study of Attitudes to Social Equality in Twentieth Century England,* Routledge: London.

**Sargan, J. D.** (1964) Wages and prices in the UK, in Hart, P. E., Mills, G. and Whittaker, J. K. (eds), *Econometric Analysis for Economic Planning,* Butterworth: London.

**Sargan, J. D.** (1971) A study of wages and prices in the UK 1949–1968, in Johnson, H. G. and Nobay, A. R. (eds), *The Current Inflation,* Macmillan: London.

**Schmidt, P. and Strauss, R.** (1976) The effect of unions on earnings and earnings on unions: a mixed logit approach, *International Economic Review,* **17,** 204–12.

**Scott, M. F. G.** (1980) The need for radical reform, in Blackaby, F. (ed.), *The Future of Pay Bargaining,* Heinemann: London.

**Shorey, J.** (1977) Time series analysis of strike frequency, *British Journal of Industrial Relations,* **15,** 63–75.

**Smith, D. C.** (1980) Trade union growth and industrial disputes, in Caves, R. E. and Krause, L. B. (eds), *Britain's Economic Performance,* Brookings Institution: Washington, DC.

**Stafford, F. P. and Duncan, G. J.** (1980) Do union members receive compensating wage differentials?, *American Economic Review,* **70,** 355–71.

**Stewart, M.** (1976) Determinants of earnings: estimates from the General Household Survey, Centre for the Economics of Education, London School of Economics, mimeo.

**Stigler, G. J.** (1947) The kinky oligopoly demand curve and rigid prices, *Journal of Political Economy,* **55,** 432–49.

**Stigler, G. J.** (1966) *The Theory of Price,* Macmillan: London (3rd edn).

**Stigler, G. J.** (1978) The literature of economics: the case of the kinked oligopoly demand curve, *Economic Inquiry,* **16,** 185–204.

**Streeten, P.** (1962) Wages and productivity, *Kyklos,* **15,** 723–31.

**Thomas, R. L.** (1974) Wage inflation in the UK: a multi-market approach, in Laidler, D. E. W. and Purdy, D. L. (eds), *Inflation and Labour Markets,* Manchester University Press.

**Thomas, R. L.** (1977) Unionisation and the Phillips curve, *Applied Economics,* **9,** 33–49.

**Thomas, R. L. and Stoney, P. J. M.** (1970) A note on the dynamic properties of the Hines inflation model, *Review of Economic Studies,* **37,** 286–94.

**Thomas, R. L. and Stoney, P. J. M.** (1971) Unemployment dispersion as a determinant of wage inflation in the United Kingdom 1925–1966, *Manchester School,* **39,** 83–116.

**Thomson, A. W. J., Mulvey, C. and Farbman, M.** (1977) Bargaining structure and relative earnings in Great Britain, *British Journal of Industrial Relations,* **15,** 176–91.

**Tobin, J.** (1972) Inflation and unemployment, *American Economic Review,* **62,** 1–18.

**Turner, H. A.** (1957) Inflation and wage differentials in Great Britain, in Dunlop, J. T. (ed.), *The Theory of Wage Determination,* Macmillan: London.

**Turner, H. A.** (1959) Employment fluctuations, labour supply and bargaining power, *Manchester School,* **27,** 175–202.

**Turner, H. A.** (1970) Collective bargaining and the eclipse of incomes policy, *British Journal of Industrial Relations,* **8,** 197–212.

**Turner, H. A., Clack, G. and Roberts, G.** (1967) *Labour Relations in the Motor Industry,* Allen & Unwin: London.

**Vanderkamp, J.** (1966) Wages and price level determination: an empirical model for Canada, *Economica,* **33,** 194–218.

**Wabe, S. and Leech, D.** (1978) Relative earnings in UK manufacturing: a reconsideration of the evidence, *Economic Journal,* **88,** 296–313.

**Ward, R. and Zis, G.** (1974) Trade union militancy as an explanation of inflation: an international comparison, *Manchester School,* **42,** 46–65.

**Wiles, P.** (1973) Cost inflation and the state of economic theory, *Economic Journal,* **83,** 377–98.

**Wilkinson, F. and Turner, H. A.** (1972) The wage-tax spiral and labour militancy, in Jackson, D., Turner, H. A. and Wilkinson, F., *Do Trade Unions Cause Inflation?,* Cambridge University Press.

**Wilkinson, R. K. and Burkitt, B.** (1973) Wage determination and trade unions, *Scottish Journal of Political Economy,* **20,** 107–22.

**Williamson, J. and Wood, G. E.** (1976) The British inflation: indigenous or imported?, *American Economic Review,* **66,** 520–31.

**Williamson, O. E., Wachter, M. L. and Harris, J. E.** (1975) Understanding the employment relation: the analysis of idiosyncratic exchange, *Bell Journal of Economics and Management Science,* **6,** 250–78.

**Wood, A.** (1978) *A Theory of Pay,* Cambridge University Press.

**Worswick, G. D. N.** (1944) The stability and flexibility of full employment, in Oxford University Institute of Statistics, *The Economics of Full Employment,* Blackwell: Oxford.

**Zeuthen, F.** (1930) *Problems of Monopoly and Economic Warfare,* Routledge and Kegan Paul: London.

**Zis, G.** (1977) On the role of strike variables in UK wage equations, *Scottish Journal of Political Economy,* **24,** 43–53.

# Author index

# Subject index

ability, 10-13, 30-5: of twins, 33-4;
  schooling and, 50
absenteeism, 108-10
affirmative action, 80, 140-1
aggregate demand, 138
aggregate wages: and excess demand,
  215, 225; and price expectations,
  214-15, 225; and unemployment
  benefit, 213
apprenticeship, 46

bargaining model, 112
baseball, 108

class, 80
cognitive dissonance, 110
collective bargaining: and employer
  attitudes, 197; and labour mobility,
  189; and labour quality, 198; national
  and local, 193, 195, 198
credentialism, 51, 58, 61: and educational
  discrimination, 58, 71n32
crowding hypothesis, 114-17

discontinuous labour force experience,
  131-4
discrimination: consumer, 104-5;
  definition of, 85-90; effects of
  legislation on, 139-41; employee,
  102-4; employer, 92-102;
  governmental, 103-6; and market
  structure, 99-102; measurement of,
  120-37; pre- and post-entry, 90-2;
  radical approach to, 111-12;
  statistical and erroneous, 106-10
dual labour markets, 63, 116-17

earnings: effect of children on, 131;
  foregone, 7, 8, 49; functions, 21, 42,
  49; inequality, 82; international
  differences, 84

education: determinants of schooling,
  48-50; external benefits of, 58;
  investment in, 90-1; quality of,
  38-9, 127-8; rate of return, see
  internal rate of return; subsidies, 8-9,
  13, 51
employment contracts, 159, 175
equal rights amendment, 118
expectations, 165, 166, 176, 178

federal employment, 82

human capital, 160, 173: basic model,
  6-8; capacity earnings and, 14;
  criticisms of, 61-3; depreciation of,
  14-15, 133; and earnings structure, 8;
  imperfections in market for, 12;
  measurement of, 11

immigrants, 80
incomes policy, 201-2, 218
injury rates, 116
inter-generational transmission of
  inequality, 5, 49, 63
internal labour markets, 116
internal rate of return, 7, 126-8:
  dispersion in, 39-41; comparison
  between human and physical capital,
  40, 63; empirical measures of, 29, 35;
  to experience, 128-30; and
  measurement error, 66-8; private and
  social, 54, 64
international trade theory, 92-4

job rationing hypothesis, 115
job search, 44, 118-20, 130-1: cost of,
  165, 171-2; fixed sample, 162-3;
  and human capital, 160; intensity,
  163, 168; and learning, 167;
  non-random, 165; sequential, 163;
  speed of, 159